MAINTAIN ME,

I'M YOURS

BY

GERRY AUBREY

DEDICATED TO MY WIFE

CAROL WHO MUST

BELIEVE IN A HERE

AFTER IF SHE DECIDED

TO SPEND HERE WITH

ME.

TABLE OF CONTENTS

FORWARD	6
FACT OR FICTION	8
A WALK AROUND YOUR HOME	13
REPAIRING CONCRETE	19
LADDER SAFETY	23
ASPHALT SHINGLES	27
FINDING LEAKS	31
GUTTERS	36
VINYL SIDING	46
BRICK WALLS	50
STUCCO, GOOD OR BAD?	55
ELECTRICAL SERVICE AND PANEL BOX	60
SWIMMING POOLS	66
FENCES	71
FRONT DOORS	75
A VISIT TO THE KITCHEN	79
COOKING FIRES	83
SMOKE DETECTORS AND CO DETECTORS	87
DISHWASHERS	92
APPLIANCES	95
STAINS	98
PAINTING DO'S	102
PAINTING DON'TS	106
LEAD PAINT	110
PULL DOWN STAIRS	114
WINTERIZING YOUR HOME	118
FREEZING PIPES	127
ATTIC VENTILATION	131
WOOD FLOORING	141
HAVING A DRY BASEMENT	144
RADON	151
MOLD	157
CHECKING YOUR FIREPLACE	163
HOW DOES MY HEATER WORK?	170

INSPECTING YOUR CHIMNEY	173
HEATING SYSTEM CHECK UP	178
HEAT PUMP, GOOD OR BAD?	182
HOW IS YOUR DUCT WORK?	189
RADIANT HEAT	194
GAS OR OIL?	197
HUMIDIFERS	201
ELECTRICAL INSPECTIONS	205
ARC FAULT INTERRUPTORS	209
A TRIP TO THE BATHROOM	213
TILE REPAIR	221
DRINKING WATER	225
WATER MAIN	230
CROSS CONNECTIONS	233
WATER HEATERS	237
TANKLESS WATER HEATERS	244
HOME REPAIRS	248
THE GARAGE	252
ICY WALKWAYS AND DRIVEWAYS	257
ANTS OR TERMITES	262
SELECTING A BUILDER	267
ENERGY AUDITS	272
ASBESTOS	277
PRICE RANGES ON ITEMS	282
LIFE EXPECTANCY OF ITEMS	287
HOUSEHOLD TIPS	289
WILL IT FALL DOWN?	294
IS IT HAIL OR DID THE SHINGLES FAIL?	306

FORWARD

Thank you for buying this book. The purpose of this manual is to acquaint you, the Home Owner, with many of the nuances of your home. A house is a big thing. (Big as a *house?)* A house is made with a wide variety of materials and has many diverse systems. They are all designed "in theory" to work in concert. In most cases they do. However, there are two things that wear a house down. The forces of Nature, and the forces of Man. Nature consists of water, (Water wins), sunlight, (Ultra violet rays or UV rays), temperature variation such as freeze thaw cycles and excessive heat. Wind also plays a role. There isn't much you can do about an F4 tornado, or a major hurricane, but the average home may encounter 30 to 50 mph winds in any year. There is also the not so occasional insect infestation such as termites. Man is the other culprit. Man walking puts pressure on homes. Man keeps things such as furniture, and a whole host of items from fine art to McDonald's plates from the early 1980's and everything in between. Man breathes, sweats, cooks, and does all the other things related to human life in a house. Man also tries to do things they can't do very well or that they just don't understand. This last item can really create problems. More homes are damaged by Home Owners "fixing" things than by Nature tearing them down.

This manual is a collection of articles that will help you, the Home Owner, get familiar with the systems and the materials used. It will help you deal with Nature and give you a few tools so you can fight back when Nature starts winning in its' battle with your home. (The length of the articles makes them perfect for reading in that one person "library" we all visit about once a day.) It also will help you understand how you are affecting your home in a negative way, just by living in it. Once you understand these effects, you are better equipped to take measures to protect your home. The articles are about 800 to 1500 words each. They are not tediously technical, but rather simplistic and somewhat homespun. You won't be able to build a home based on this book. But, you will have a plan of action on taking on a lot of Home Owner type chores, and you will have a pretty good grasp on a whole host of "maintenance type" issues that most Home Owners know nothing about. There are countless tips on making your home safer and working the way it was designed to work.

For a lot of these projects you will need some basic tools. Just about every project mentioned involves tools most Home Owners have. If you don't have some of them, in rare circumstances, you may need to rent them from a tool rental store. This book will give you a working knowledge of what's going on in the home. It will help you maintain it. It will also discuss jobs you are better off getting professional to address. One last thing, when you buy this book you get me. From the day you buy this book forward, if you have questions about your home, send an e-mail and we'll help you solve the problem. We stop answering questions when you stop asking them. There is no guarantee we will have every answer. One thing we absolutely know is what we don't know, and if we don't know the answer we will tell you that, and we will do my best to direct you to the answer.

Please Note: Companies all over the country buy this book for their clients. If your home Inspector/contractor gave you this book, it shows their commitment to you and their effort to provide you with helpful information in home ownership.

FACT OR FICTION

In dealing with the general public about their homes, it amazes me how little people actually know about their homes. They live in them every day and frequently people lack basic knowledge about the systems and how they work. There are a host of misconceptions and fallacies about how a home works and about how to maintain them. I'm not claiming to be the hosts of "Myth busters" but I would like to clear up a few things I hear on a very regular basis.

A basic electrical misconception is that a ground fault circuit interrupter or GFCI has to be grounded to work. It does not. It will provide life-saving protection even if it is not grounded. Many people think the breakers in the main panel box will keep the home from burning down in the event of an electrical malfunction. Not true. Ask any veteran fire fighter and they will tell you they have seen many house fires started on electrical circuits with code approved protection. The electrical industry has developed arc fault interrupters that do in fact provide far greater protection against fires than a typical circuit breaker. Quite frankly, a traditional circuit breaker is little more than an on/off switch for that line. Are circuit breakers safer than fuses? The truth is circuit breakers can stick. A fuse will always break the power connection to the line if it is overheated. Fuses, however, lend themselves to cheating by inserting a penny behind it. They are also more dangerous to replace than just resetting a breaker. You decide which is safer.

"Let's close off the vents in the attic in the winter to save heat," is a comment I still hear. You need ventilation in your attic more in the winter than you do in the summer. The warm air rising through the insulation into the attic contains large quantities of water vapor. This moisture condenses on cold surfaces, the underside of the roof, and can rot out the wood under the roof in a relatively short amount of time. Another fallacy is the belief that rust on the nails in the attic is caused by the roof leaking. False. It is caused by poor ventilation or excessive moisture in the home. The number one source of this excessive moisture I have seen is a heater mounted humidifier. That type of humidifier may actually do some good in some homes. In truth, I have seen them cause so much damage in 16 years of inspecting homes that I greatly discourage my clients from using them. "The more insulation in the attic, the better." Not so. Do not put insulation up against the underside of the roof unless there is a clear air passage behind it from the eave to the ridge. An attic needs lots of ventilation and the more insulation in the attic the more it needs ventilation. You want the attic to be very cold in the winter and within 20 degrees of the outside temperature in the summer.

"You only need to change the filter in your heater at the start of the heating season." False. Read the instructions on the filter. The best filters tell you they will last "Up to 90 days." The key words there are "up to." If you have pets or more than 4 people in the home, you may want to change it more often. The number one source of dust in a home is human skin. The more people in the home, the more dust you will have. The selection of the filter is also important. The inexpensive fiberglass filters that we see so often, we call boulder catchers. They only catch the big particles. Filters with a MERV rating of 8 or higher can provide as much as 5 times the filtering of the thinner fiberglass filters. A grade above this is an electrostatic filter which is considerably more expensive but is very effective. The advantage of an electrostatic filter is it does not reduce air flow as it filters. One superintendent for a local construction company told me that pleated filters with a high MERV rating will cut the life of your heater blower in half. I have researched this several times and found no supporting data for that claim. The facts are, change your filter at least every ninety days if it services both your heating and air conditioning system and get a filter system with at least a MERV rating of 8 or higher. (1000 ppm. rating also works well).

Mold. Does your house have mold? Yes. Molds exist everywhere on the planet including Antarctica. "Black mold is dangerous, run!" This is a very common misconception. Many houses have black mold present. Look at the grout in your bathroom tile. Many homes have black mold growing there. Should you clean it? Yes. Should you panic? No. There are hundreds of black, or dark green molds. Mold comes in a variety of shapes, colors and sizes. Everyone's immune system is different and we react differently to different molds. There are some that are more likely to result in an adverse reaction but the color is not going to tell you that. According to the EPA, "Scrub mold off hard surfaces with detergent and water, and dry completely." Do not use cleaners that contain phosphates. They are like steroids for molds. Do not mix cleaning products that contain chlorine bleach and ammonia. This will give off a very toxic gas. Should I use bleach to clean up mold? As per the EPA, "The use of a chemical or biocide that kills organisms such as mold, (chlorine bleach, for example) is not recommended as a routine practice during mold clean up." It may be recommended in some instances. For more information on mold, go to EPA.gov, keyword: mold, or call 1-800-438-4318. [1]

---

[1] www.epa.gov, key word "mold"

"We are buying a new home so we don't need to have it inspected." That statement makes the assumption that today's construction workers are prefect. The truth is there are many reputable builders building high quality homes that are inspected by diligent municipal inspectors. But let's be realistic. You may be paying in excess of a half million dollars for the home, far more if you factor in the interest on the loan. It just makes sense to spend about $500.00 for another opinion on how the house is constructed. I have found defects in every type of home, new or previously owned. "Our house doesn't have a basement, so we don't need to test for radon." False again. In order to have radon you need a strong radon source under the home and a means of entry such as a crack somewhere in the slab. The only way to know if your house has radon is to have a professional test it. Lung cancer is a very sad way to die. Radon is the leading cause of lung cancer in nonsmokers. Get your home tested. If not for you, then do it for your children. Radon causes accumulative damage, similar to sunburn. If you put sun screen on your children then you owe it to them to test your home for radon.

These are only a few of the most common misconceptions I hear on a regular basis. This is not the end of the list. There are many more "myths" floating around out there. If you are uncertain about something you have heard about your home, contact me. I don't have all the answers but I may help point you towards the answer. Don't let your home kill you.

Maintenance tips:
1. Test GFCI outlets monthly.
2. Change HVAC (That's Heating, Ventilation, Air Conditioning) filters every 90 days when in used. If the A/C is not part of heating system, only change in the cooling season and vice versa.
3. Get your home inspected. If you have been in your home for more than 10 years, you should get a

maintenance focused home inspection. You get a physical don't you? You get your car inspected, same thing.

4. Clean up immediately after water leaks or spills. Keep your house dry.

5. Get a radon test. I recommend getting it tested professionally.

A WALK AROUND YOUR HOME

It is a good idea to periodically take a leisurely stroll around your home and take a close look at it, top to bottom. Often people are surprised at the various conditions they observe. Nature is busy assaulting your home. It's a good idea to see who's winning once in a while, your home or Mother Nature. Let's start with the roof. If you are not comfortable on a ladder, don't get on one. Check it with binoculars. If you are losing shingles, it needs work. The shingles are supposed to be up on the roof, not down in the bushes. It may be just about worn out, or it may have had some defects when it was installed. These weaknesses may finally be succumbing to the ravages of Nature. Don't forget, Mother Nature sides with the small defect. Either way, your roof is crying for attention, whether it is a repair or a completely new roof. Shingles on the ground mean its time to call a roofer. Selecting a contractor is covered in another section of this book. Next, be sure your gutters are clean. Clogged gutters can damage the foundation, the basement, the sides of the home, and the gutters themselves. If you are not sure about the gutters, look at the ground directly below them.

Do you see a groove in the ground? The water overflowing the gutters often leaves a small trench in the soil that indicates the gutters have been overflowing. Also look for debris peeking out from over the gutters, or a stray leaf hanging on the edge. Stand back from the home. Does the gutter seem to have a smile in the middle? The low points in the gutters should be at the downspouts, not in the middle of the gutter. Be sure the splash blocks or extensions at the bottom of the downspouts are clear, angled away from the home, and drain at least three feet from the foundation, or far enough to take the water away.

Take a look at the outside air-conditioning unit. It should be level, and free of leaves and debris. One line coming from the house should be insulated. Check to be sure that the insulation is in good condition. DON'T START YOUR AIR CONDITIONER IN COLD WEATHER! Wait unit it is warmer. The overnight temperature should be above 65 degrees before you start  the unit. While most modern units have a crank case heater that keeps the oil thin in cold weather, it is best not to take a chance in very cold weather. Be sure to take any winter protection off the outside unit before you start it. If it's a heat pump, don't run it in the air conditioning cycle until it is above 65 degrees. You may damage the unit. Cut back shrubbery that is growing within about 24 inches of the sides, and about eight feet above it. While you are cutting back the bushes, cut back any bushes that block

 your ability to walk between the shrubbery and the house. There should always be a clear path between the house and the shrubbery. Look for openings at the foundation where water or unwanted guests may enter. They should be closed off with mortar. As a temporary measure, you might consider steel wool. Mice have a hard time getting through it.

Now it's time to test your outside and garage receptacles. They should all be wired through ground fault circuit interrupter protection. The outlet may be a GFCI or GFI, (they are the same), outlet in which case the test and reset

14

button is right there on the outlet. In many newer homes, they are wired to a GFCI breaker located in the main panel box. Another common location for the protection device is a GFI protected outlet right under the main panel box. To test them, get a tester at your local home center. Plug the tester in and push the test button. You will hear the circuit trip. If it is not on the outlet itself, it is somewhere in the home. Check the areas I just mentioned first. There is a test and reset button that will trip. Time to go and reset it. Then push the test button on the GFCI itself. Be sure that the power cuts off at the receptacle. These safety devices do fail. They last five to ten years. It is suggested that they be tested every month. Test them often. The more often they are tested, the longer they seem to last. While you are at it, test them in the bathrooms and kitchen. Often one will operate all the GFCI receptacles for the whole house. There is more on this in the electrical sections. If they get wet, they may not reset even after they are dry.

Next, take a look at the walkways and paved areas around the home. Large cracks in the concrete work should be filled. Hairline cracks are common and usually not repaired effectively. Small cracks between the home and walkways can sometimes be filled with a small amount of silicone caulk. Work it into the crack with your finger, and wipe the excess away. If the crack is large enough, you may have to fill it with a special mortar mix designed for masonry repairs. Great Stuff[2] spray foam works well also.

Asphalt repairs are usually best done in the fall. If you coat or patch asphalt in the spring, it may remain tacky through the summer and get tracked into the house on hot days. If you have a wood deck, it's a good idea to wash it down with a mild bleach, and TSP, (tri-sodium phosphate), solution. [3] There is "outdoor bleach". You'll find TSP at

---

[2] Trade name for a type of foam insulation
[3] Tri-sodium phosphate box

most larger garden and home centers. Follow the instructions on the box. You can wash it with a hand garden sprayer or a sponge mop and bucket. A high pressure spray is not recommended. It can drive water into the wood. This will kill any algae or fungus that may be growing on it. If you want to resurface the deck, use a linseed-based stain or preservative that soaks into the wood. MAB's semi- transparent stains had the best reviews in Consumer Reports magazine the last time I checked. Do not use a water proofing or water repellent material. Most of these materials will leave a very slippery surface when the deck is wet. Also, the trapped water in the deck can accelerate the deterioration of the wood under the repellent. If you paint a wood deck, it is doubtful it will hold up very well. You will probably be painting it much more frequently than you would other wood surfaces outside. This is due to the moisture entering the wood from other sides and then being drawn through the surface by the heat of the sun. This will crack the paint. It will also crack the next coat of paint. My advice, don't paint wood decks. While you are checking the deck, drive back any nails or screws that may have worked loose. You usually find them with bare feet while running out with a tray full of hot dogs and hamburgers on your way to the barbecue.

Next, crawl under the deck and check the way it is attached to the house. Look to see if it is pulling away or if any of the supports have cracked. If the deck is attached to the house with nails, add 3/8-inch lag bolts between each set of joists. Add the first 1/3 of the way down from the top of the joist and as close to the outside or band joist on  the deck as possible. The next should be installed in the next bay but as far from the first joist as possible and still in the bay. This bolt should be 1/3 of the way up from the bottom of the joist. You want them alternating between 1/3 of the distance from the top and 1/3 of the distance from the bottom. Generally they are installed about 24" apart. They don't have to be every 16" on center as the joists are. The nails will fail as they rust between the house and the deck. You also want to check for insect infestation. The most common culprits are bees. Be careful when you enter. Look for bee traffic to and from a nest. You don't want them living under an area where the family relaxes. If the wood appears to have mud tubes on it, or evidence of rot, check it with a screw driver. The mud tubes might be termites. If the tube leads to the ground, call a termite company. Some bees make mud tubes as well. The safest way to get rid of bees is also an exterminator. I personally get a spray you can use from a distance and spray them after dark. They are all in there at night and they have trouble flying in the dark. One thing I see under most decks I inspect is bird's nest. My personal feeling, leave them alone. Birds are good.

The best way to construct a deck is on its' own supports, free standing from the house. It also is a good idea to check the slope of the deck with a level each year. It should drain slightly away from the home. Any sudden movement or change in the slope is obviously a cause for alarm. Now if everything is in good working order, and you found no repairs needed, sit back, relax, and get yourself psyched for a nice season of mowing the lawn. Oh, did I mention there's a lot more things in and around the home to check? We are just getting started.

Maintenance tips:

1. At least twice a year, perform a slow cautious walk around the home. Take your time. Watch out for bees and critters and look for anything different such as new cracks, holes, or soil depressions.

2. Keep the shrubbery trimmed back so you can fit fairly comfortably between the house and the bushes.
3. Test your GFCI outlet protection monthly

REPAIRING CONCRETE

"Step on a crack, you break your mother's back," was an old saying that I remember from my childhood. Today, a crack in the sidewalk won't break your mother's back, but it can result in people twisting their ankle and possibly linking up with some salivating lawyer looking to collect from you and your insurance company. Because a cracked or uneven sidewalk is a safety concern and an unrepaired crack will get worse rather than better, it's a good idea to repair any cracks in the your sidewalks. Don't forget, you walk on that sidewalk more than anybody. You or a family member may turn an ankle on it. You cannot sue yourself.

There are a wide range of masonry materials available for these repairs. Some are specifically designed for repair of existing concrete surfaces. Any large home center should have a selection. Tell the clerk what you plan to do with the mortar. There are "Patchcrete"[4] and quick setting mortars that are exactly what you need. They also come in smaller bags so you don't end up buying a lifetime supply. To complete the repair you will need a chisel, screwdriver, hammer, trowel, a flat surface (such as an old quarter sheet of plywood), goggles, a small container of water, and a broom. Obviously, you will also need the masonry material.

---

[4] Brand name for a type of concrete

The first step is to be sure the crack is wide enough to accept the patch. Hairline cracks won't allow enough mortar to enter. Put on the goggles and chisel the opening until it is at least ½" to an inch wide. Dig out below it with a screw driver or other probe. You want a fairly deep opening to receive as much mortar as possible. Sweep the area clean.

Now is the exciting part. Mix the water on the flat surface. You may also use a bucket to hold the mix. When you start mixing, it doesn't take as much water as you think it does. It is very easy to put in too much water. You don't want to make soup. If you do, you add more mortar and suddenly you have more mortar than you need. So be sparing. Now for the next tip, MOVE QUICKLY! The mortar sets up extremely fast. You will suddenly find yourself cutting through the rapidly hardening mortar with your trowel.

Did I mention you have to work fast? Using the trowel, pack the mortar into the crack. Pack it down as deeply as possible and keep moving the trowel over the finished area to clean it off. It will be a different color than the old concrete. That's unavoidable. If you are trying to build up between two blocks because one was heaved, break apart the edge of the lower block first so you have an area for the new mortar to grab. Rough up the surface of the lower block with the chisel. This will also help the new mortar get a hold. Keep scraping off the excess mortar as you go. One other tool I forgot to mention is knee pads or a cushion. That concrete sidewalk gets pretty hard after sitting or kneeling on it for a relatively short amount of time. You don't want to hurt your knees over a cracked sidewalk.

Keep moving across the crack, filling it as deeply as possible. Smooth with the trowel as best you can. Once you have finished, clean all of your tools of mortar. If you mixed the mortar in a bucket, clean it out completely. This mortar sets up about 10 times faster than regular mortar.

Let the job sit for about a half hour. Then sweep it off going horizontally across the crack. Concrete is often finished with what is called a broom finish. A mason will drag a broom across new concrete surfaces to give it a slightly rough edge so it's not too slippery. Your repair should have a similar finish. In repairing cracks, be sure to clean out the crack at least a couple of inches down so the mortar has sufficient mass to hold. If you are tapering the mortar to smooth out an uneven rise between two slabs, taper the new mortar at the rate of about 3" per half inch rise. So, if the distance between the two slabs is about 1½", a significant tripping hazard, you would taper the concrete out about 9 inches.

My concrete repair is holding up very well. It is over eight years old as of this writing. I do have a confession to make. I did the repair in Florida where the paved areas aren't subjected to freeze/thaw cycles. The temperature extremes wreak havoc on masonry surfaces. The masonry absorbs moisture. Anything that absorbs moisture, and then freezes, can be damaged by the expansion and contraction that occurs. The more rigid the material, the more  vulnerable it is to damage. My advice is to make the repairs; it will make you home a little safer for you, your family, and that unsuspecting stranger who's tuned out with their iPod on as they jog over your sidewalk.

There is a company that will grind down your sidewalk to a safe level. They have a patented process that is designed to also save the side walk. Obviously if the block is heaved too much it won't work. They will grind away too much masonry material. They can be reached at www.alwaysafesidewalks.com

Maintenance tip:
1. Check all paved area around the home annually.
2. Weed your sidewalk. Pull out weeds growing up between the cracks or through any cracks in the driveway. The bigger they get the more damage they do.
3. Coat your driveway every fall. Use a squeegee or roller rather than a brush, they are easier to use.
4. If you have steps up to your home, be sure railings are firm and don't move when you grab them.
5. Check the height of your steps. They should be uniform and about 9" in height. Uneven steps are hazardous, particularly when carrying packages.

LADDER SAFETY

At some point in home ownership, the Home Owner is confronted with the dilemma of working with a ladder. This is a big decision and should not be taken lightly. If you have made the decision not to venture into this world and want to skip this article, fine, you have made a wise decision. A huge number of household accidents involve a Home Owner and a ladder. If you have chosen to continue and a ladder is in your plans, let's start with the purchase.

Most homes need more than one ladder. There is the small step ladder for changing light bulbs in ceiling fixtures, painting the edges in a room and general home maintenance. First rule in buying a ladder, get one bigger than you think you need. Picture yourself on a step ladder. The degree to which you have additional ladder in front of you as you elevate is the degree to which you feel secure and are less likely to fall. Overextending yourself on the higher rungs of a ladder is where people get in the most trouble. Never, ever, use the top of the ladder or the tray on the opposite side as a step. The ladder people aren't kidding when they write that warning. That tray won't hold you, period, end of discussion. Next consideration is the ladder's composition. The options are normally fiberglass, wood, or metal. All work well. Here are some pros and cons of the different materials. Aluminum is light weight. Some aluminum step ladders I would never buy. They are very tight to set up. I often pinch my fingers closing them and they feel unstable when I'm on them. Other than that, I guess they are okay. I cringe when I am with a client and they say, "Use my ladder" and it's a cheap aluminum step ladder. In the roofing industry we used to call poorly designed or worn out ladders "widow makers." There's a reason. Wood and fiberglass ladders are much heavier and safer. They don't conduct electricity, so if you accidentally come in contact with an electric current, they reduce your chances of becoming a conductor. They are also normally very stable. As a rule, don't buy cheap ladders. You may need it only once or twice a year, but your safety is worth the extra money. I have a four section folding aluminum ladder I purchased at Sears Hardware that I call the "vegamatic"[5] of ladders. It is both a step ladder and an extension ladder and can also be used as a platform or scaffolding. It took a little practice to get the opening and closing down but I find it extremely handy. If you live in a ranch house or have no intentions of going up on the 2nd floor roof, this might be the only ladder you need. It has wide stabilizers at the base which keeps it very steady. The only downside of it is with stabilizers at both ends, you can't get one end into tight areas very well. A good example of this is the attic scuttles. There is no narrow end to extend through the opening when you need to go up there. A traditional step ladder also works well. My preference in those is wood or fiberglass. Next we have the full extension ladder. A 28' medium weight aluminum extension ladder should do the trick. Werner makes a very good one. When it comes to extension ladders, my preference is just the opposite of step ladders. I prefer aluminum ladders. The others are too heavy. I am usually alone when I set up my ladder, and I don't have someone to foot it. With a heavier ladder, or when someone who does not work with ladders regularly sets it up, you need someone to foot it. Lay the ladder on the ground. One person puts their full foot on the one end of the ladder. Put all your weight on that foot and don't let up. The other person walks the ladder straight up starting at the opposite end. That being said, STOP! Before you start walking it up, look overhead and be sure there are no wires. Every wire is live! Once you have the ladder vertical, generally one reasonably strong adult can move it around. Be sure to consider the wind. Ladders can be extremely difficult to control in mild breezes, trust me. Use the rope to extend it. When I worked with roofers, many of them cut the rope off

---

[5] Kitchen tool sold in infomercials.

a new ladder as soon as they get it. They said it gets in the way of their feet when they climb it. As a Home Owner, trust me, you are better off using the rope to pull up the ladder. When you set up the ladder, be sure the footing is level. Even the slightest unevenness at the base will cause the ladder to slide if you put weight on it. Always extend the ladder 3 rungs above the gutter line. This will give you a nice firm area to hold onto if you are getting on and off the roof. (You want some of the ladder in front of you).

When you go up on the roof, take a bungee cord up with you. Hook the cord on the gutter and w Hook the cord on the gutter and wrap it around the ladder, then hook it on the other side. This won't hold the ladder if you slide down the roof. It will keep it from sliding if wind picks up. Every time I set up a ladder, there is a gust of wind waiting around the corner to challenge me and move the ladder. When you are stepping off the roof, be sure to know where the bungee cord is. You don't want to trip on it.

Here are a couple other simple reminders about ladder safety. Don't try and force the ladder through trees. If you force it through branches, the branches will win. If you set it up next to bushes down low, the branches will kick the base out as the weight falls forward. These may seem like common sense, but you would be surprised how scarce common sense can sometime be. When you are climbing the ladder, don't hold on to the rungs as you climb. Every time you take your hand off a rung, you have less of a grip on the ladder. Put your hands on the side rails and slide them up as you climb. If you are working off the ladder, keep your belly button between the rails of the ladder. This will keep your center of gravity on the ladder. Don't carry things with one hand as you go up the ladder. If you need tools up there, get a tool belt and wear them up. Belts are cheaper than funerals. If you have heavy things like roofing shingles, let the professionals get them up there. Many companies do roof top deliveries. You don't want to "hump" shingles as we used to call it. It's too dangerous.

Maintenance tips:
1. Check your ladder for stability before getting on it. Look for rot in wood ladders.
2. Lubricate the moving parts in a step ladder. They get corroded.
3. Check the base. The rubber feet sometimes tear and come off.
4. Replace the rope on an extension ladder when it gets frayed.

ASPHALT SHINGLES

It's been said that nuclear power plants are designed by geniuses to be run by idiots. Homer Simpson may argue that the plants were not designed by geniuses, but agree with the rest of the statement. I recently had a tour of a testing laboratory for an asphalt shingle manufacturer. While I would never be critical of the roofing mechanics who install asphalt shingles, I must say that the people who manufacture asphalt shingles might slip into the genius category. Roofing is difficult work performed in dangerous conditions. The installers are exposed to the extremes of nature. The product is designed to survive even worse conditions for 20, 30, 40 years or more. The design, manufacture, and installation all require huge amounts of skill. The Homer Simpsons of the world need not get involved. Asphalt shingles were first developed as a spin off from the rolled roofing industry. Rolled roofing was invented by accident. There was a fire in a pitch plant in Massachusetts and the pitch melted into the hemp warehouse next door. The pitch coated the hemp creating what seemed like an indestructible mat. Lloyd Fry, who owned the warehouse, then worked with the product, eventually developing it into a material sold to cover flat roof areas. Through trial and error the weaknesses in the product were refined. It was found that ultra violet rays degraded the materials and soon slate and mica granules coated the product to protect it. Slope roofing material used before World War II was almost universally hard roofing. It consisted of slate, wood, terra cotta and asbestos tile. Flat roofing was evolving, but the basic recipe changed little in the first half of the twentieth century. Flat roofing today is the product of laboratory development with little chance for trial and error.

An asphalt shingle is also a highly refined scientifically developed building product. A shingle must first resist wind. Sustained winds of 60 and 70 miles per hour are rare in most climates, but short gusts in thunderstorms greatly exceed that and are common throughout the U. S. The shingle must hold. The hemp mat has evolved into a tear resistant fiberglass mat that first appeared on the market in the mid 70's. The first mats were linear strands and cracked easily. Today's mat is spun, woven, and constantly tested for tear resistance. The industry has adopted a minimum tear resistance standard that is finally working its way into national standards. Shingles that have been on roofs over 10 years are still being tested to check the mat's durability. If they fail, the manufacturers want to know why and how they can extend the shingle's life. The pitch has evolved into asphalt. Pitch was a little too carcinogenic. Pure asphalt was found to be ineffective when exposed to temperature extremes. The asphalt is now refined with many oils worked out of the raw product. Fillers are then added. The best fillers are limestone although a variety of products have been tried. The limestone powder must be a certain size and consistency. The refined asphalt is worked with the limestone to create a homogenous mixture that is the right consistency to adhere to the fiberglass, provide waterproof protection, and retain flexibility in weather extremes. The roof's surface temperature may drop 100 degrees in a few minutes at the start of a thunderstorm. The material must also resist freeze thaw cycles. Water turning to ice cracks engine blocks. If it cracks the shingles, that's not acceptable. The quality and blend of the asphalt is constantly being monitored for consistency.

Asphalt shingle manufacturers are in the fashion business. The roofing material must be the perfect compromise of form and function. A roof may be more that 50% of the visible area of a home. It must look good and work better. The old slate and mica granules once used have evolved. They are still stone particles. They are ground, dyed and coated to preserve the color. They can lose color to the UV rays, or the asphalt can bleed into the product from below. Because of this, the right combination of dyes and transparent silica coating is constantly being researched. The roof must look the same ten and twenty years after it is installed. The shingles must also match each other. At one time, dye lot numbers were critical to match existing shingles if a home were to be repaired or an addition added. Today, the stone particles are blended onto the shingle with computer precision. The color must be a perfect blend, repetitively constructed, with the look of random variety. The goal of the shingle is still to replicate the varied natural hues of slate and wood. The finished product is constantly being tested. Pieces of the shingles are put in weather chambers. They are constantly cycled through heat, cold, and rapid temperature extremes. In 50 days they can experience years of stress. (It might be compared to raising a teenager.) A shingle must first protect the home. It must be attractive to the Home Owner, and the next home buyer. It must survive the worst nature has to offer, never change in color, and perform these tasks for a quarter of a century or longer. Can you name another product that can stand up to those demands? Asphalt shingles work, and they keep working better.

Does your roof have black or dark green streaks down it? If it doesn't, your roof is the exception. The streaks are caused by algae. You can treat them with tri-sodium phosphate, bleach and water. You can try reducing the streaking the natural way. Z-stop[6] zinc strips can be installed at the ridge area of the roof. Z-Stop can be contacted at 1-800-845-5863 or **www.zstop.com.** The rolls are 50' long, last 20 years and cost about $15.00 per roll. I've heard they are less effective down the roof because as you get further from the strips, the cuprous oxide is diluted and therefore doesn't work. I've read they are effective for about 3'. I would consider that ineffective, but that's just my opinion. If you treat the roof with chemicals, count on going back up there in a few years and doing it again. Also, don't

---

[6] Brand name for zinc metal strips

expect the lines from the streaks to completely go away. One more thought: BE CAREFUL! The solution makes surfaces very slippery. My suggestion? Get AR rated shingles, or algae resistant shingles. I have read Certainteed patented system and it makes the most sense of any system I have seen. The older AR shingles were far less effective. None of them have what I would consider a legitimate warranty on the algae resistant part of the product. If you hire a contractor to clean the roof, verify that they are using environmentally friendly products. If you use your own TSP and bleach try and capture the run off and dispose of it in the household sewer. Don't let it enter the ground water. To repair a damaged or torn shingle, use a prybar to loosen the nails in the shingle above the damaged shingle. Gently pull the nails, don't tear the shingle. Next, pull the nails out. Now remove the nails from the remaining piece of the damaged shingle. Install the new shingle with four nails, slightly below the seal tab strip and offset from the old nails. Seal the new shingle down with a quarter size dab of roof cement. Apply the cement with a caulking gun, it's easier use. Then seal the shingle above it to the new shingle. Seal any other lifting shingles the same way. Don't tear them. Perform the repair in mid-morning, after the dew is gone and before the roof gets too hot.

FINDING LEAKS

My roof is leaking. HELP! It has been raining for a few days and you go into your son's room, (scary thought). You notice he has the trash can out in the middle of the room, and you hear dripping into it. "At least he put the trash can under it," you say to yourself. "When did the roof start leaking," you ask? "About six months ago, but it only leaked once and this is the first time it leaked since then," he replies. You do the math, and six months ago was last fall. It is now April. "Did it leak when the snow melted." you probe? "No, I told you it leaked about six months ago, and only once, so I didn't think it was that important," he retorts. "That doesn't make any sense, if it's leaking, it's leaking," she fires back. Actually, he just gave you very valuable information to find out the source of the leak. Now, let's play my favorite game, "Leak Detective."

You have water entering your home damaging your ceilings and possessions and you want to stop it. You are afraid to call a roofer because you feel they will just try and sell you a roof. After all, they are in the roofing business and have to make a living. Let's start with a basic fact. Roofs leak in three places, where they start, where they stop and where they change directions. If you get a leak in the middle of the roof, your roof is completely shot and you need a new roof, an individual shingle blew off, or something damaged the roof like a tree. All three of those scenarios are pretty straight forward and easy to diagnose.

The next basic premise is a roof gets wet every time it rains. Sounds simple enough, but the truth is, if your roof is leaking, it will leak in every rain of any duration. It will also leak with melting snow. If it leaks every six months, as in the example above, it is not the roof that's leaking. If you get a leak in wind driven rain, it is a wall or something other than the roof leaking. So, a leak appears. It has never leaked before. Is it windy out? If so, get a compass and note which side of the home the rain is hitting. Thunderstorms generally blow rain against the north to northwest side of the home. Occasionally, they will come up from the south but that's rare. If it leaks in what we call, Nor'easters, wind driven rain from the northeast, then there is a wall on that side of the home that is leaking. Once you have determined the side of the home that's getting wet, and after the rain has stopped, check out the wall above that side. The most common place for leaks to originate in walls is around windows or where dissimilar materials meet, such as a vinyl sided wall meeting a chimney. In many cases, these leaks can be repaired with silicone caulking. Clean and dry the openings before repairing them. I was in a home this week and the lady says, "Caulk, that's all they put there?" Yes, that is all they put there in many situations. And caulk is not forever. It is a maintenance item that needs to be redone every 3 to 5 years. They will put on the tube of caulk that it lasts 20 years. I have been chasing leaks around for 35 years and I have never seen caulk last 20 years. It might happen, but I haven't seen it.

This is a slight digression but it's a good idea to start a leak log. What to put in the log? Let's start with the date. Next, how long after it was raining did the leak appear? How long after the rain stopped did the leaks continue? What were the weather conditions? Putting down it was raining is not that helpful. Listing wind direction, duration of the rain and intensity of the rain is much more helpful. If it leaks with melting snow, put that down. Does it leak after the third shower of the day in the same bathroom? This often indicates problems with the grouting or caulk in the shower.

There are also seasonal leaks that appear. "It only leaks in the summer" I have heard on more than one occasion. One such home had a leak from a window unit air conditioner. The sill below the unit was very deteriorated. The rain would land on it as it ran off the air conditioner, as well as wind driven rain landing on the sill. The water then migrated into the home. The sill area on the home is not waterproof. A very similar condition exists with storm windows. We open the storm window, and put in a screen. Wind driven rain blows right through the screen. There are two weep holes in the bottom rail of storm window frames. They clog easily with debris as well as caulk. Keep them open to allow water to run out. Clogged gutters can cause leaks as well. The gutter overflows and saturates a wall or a windows area that doesn't normally get wet and you have a "roof" leak. Again, this comes down to maintenance. A clogged drain on a flat roof can not only cause a leak, it can collapse the building! If you have a flat roof, be sure someone gets up there and cleans the drains a couple times a year. Leaks caused by ice dams are covered extensively in another section of this book.

Now for a commercial announcement:

If your roof is wearing out, if you are not sure if you need a roof, or if you have decided you are buying a roof but don't know what to believe, I have several roof related videos. There is a video on both shingle roofs and flat roofs. The videos will help you get a handle on how bad your roof is.

And it will give you solid information on how a roof should be installed. Also, if you have a leak you can't find and have had a roofer back to fix it more than twice, I have a video on analyzing and finding hard to find leaks. They are almost two hours long each. It is too much to cover in this publication. Call me at 1-888-336-2355 or e-mail me at gerryaubrey47@gmail.com and I will give you more details on each of these videos.

What to do with the water? If you have water dripping through the drywall in the ceiling, make a hole in the ceiling so the water can run out. You want the water to come out, not spread over the drywall. Now you have this drip, drip, dripping all night. Get an old sheet. Cut a strip out of it so you have a long skinny strip. Now, tack it up in the hole. The sheet will act like a wick and draw the water to it. Next, put the end of the sheet in a bucket. You won't hear the dripping. If the roof is leaking along a rafter in the attic and it is dripping off the rafter in several places, tack up a sheet at the point of entry. You may need to add a few more if that doesn't get it. Another condition is an insidious leak that you can't seem to find, and you are not sure if it's still leaking. You never get any water running, but you keep finding white dust or power on the floor below it. This type of stain is often the result of moisture being absorbed into a porous material, migrating past the flashings and leaching out on the inside wall. This is very common with chimneys. The white materials left behind are salt deposits. This is called efflorescence.

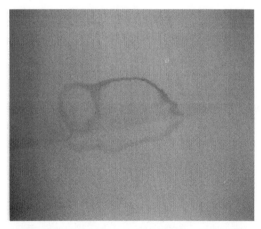

A good way to monitor this leak is to draw a pencil line around the stain and see if the water spreads past the line. This is sometimes done with bandages bleeding through on a patient. This technique often takes months of monitoring. If this is the only visible sign of a leak, it is just about always the chimney or masonry wall leaking and not the roof. The basic rules about leaks I stated earlier ALWAYS apply. Another axiom of Murphy's Law applies to stains as well. If you think a leak has stopped leaking, paint inside. The next heavy rain it is bound to return. Some leaks are tricky. I have been tracking them for over 35 years and I don't find them all. There is another type of leaking I occasionally see is a wall that seems to get wet near grade. The Home Owner scrapes and cleans the wall, seals everything outside, and the peeling paint comes back. This type of stain is cause by rising damp. Moisture is drawn from the ground up into the wall and it migrates through the wall. The solution for this is often reframing with a good vapor retardant between the drywall and the moisture source. (Use pressure treated wood.) Insulating the new wall also helps considerably. Once the wall is rebuilt, paint it with an exterior grade primer and paint. This can greatly "reduce" the potential for the stain reoccurring. Don't forget, "Water wins."

GVTTERS

Some Home Owners have told me how they can simplify their lives just by removing the gutters from their homes and throwing them away. If only life were that easy. I have a friend who is a very skilled mechanic. He doesn't do it professionally, but he has great mechanical skills. He has fixed my cars, my bikes and my computers. When he is done working on them, there is always a small pile of parts sitting there. I always say to him, "What about these parts?" And he always answers the same way, "You don't need them." And we both laugh. Now let's look at your home. I don't care what system of the home we are discussing, the heating, the electrical, and especially the structure, when you look at all those parts, YOU NEED THEM! There are no spare parts. The gutters are the same way. If you didn't need them, Builders across the country would have eliminated them, charged you the same amount for your new house, and picked up a nice new sofa for their home. If they built a development, the money they save could buy them a new power boat. Don't start taking parts out of your home, because you don't think it needs them.

Your home needs the gutters. They are an integral part of its' defense system. Your home is constantly under attack from the elements. The sun, heat, water, wind and cold, are always working to level your house. Their job is to break down the things they meet. They are very good at it. Gutters protect your home from water, a major damaging exterior force. The most basic rule I have about water is: Water wins. Period. (I know I just said that in the last chapter but I feel it needs repeating). It may not win against your home in your lifetime, but it wins. When they find remnants of civilizations past, they call them "ruins." There's a reason, water ruined them. Now that we have established their necessity, let's deal with maintaining them.

First, look at the exterior walls of your home. If your home is brick or stucco, water can directly erode these masonry materials. They are very porous. Any material that absorbs water is broken down by water, particularly when water combines with its friend, freezing temperatures. Ice is water on steroids when it comes to breaking things down. Water freezing expands with enough force to crack an engine block. Think about how freezing water is impacting your masonry surfaces. These walls get wet often. Without gutters they would get soaked. This soaking can erode pointing and stucco, and enter the interior walls. It is then absorbed by wood and insulation and it rots the structural members. It can also create a fertile habitat for molds and fungi, which can be unhealthy. Let's not forget what mold does. Molds are tiny living things that break down materials, such as wood. But, like all living things, they can't live without water. So, indirectly, the water is responsible for the mold that breaks down the wood. Do you see a pattern here?

If your home is covered with synthetic siding material such as vinyl or aluminum, these materials are not nailed snugly on your home. They are really hung in place. They expand and contract with temperature changes, and therefore cannot be tight. Wind or rain penetrates them. Flooding them with the run off from the roof is an invitation to similar problems that exist with saturating masonry materials. The siding material itself is more durable, but the water gets behind the siding just the same. All siding leaks, and without gutters, the siding leaks a lot more. Don't forget the wood areas of your home. They are very susceptible to damage by water. Wood is always expanding and contracting depending on temperature and humidity. Also, the aging process of wood causes it to change size and shape. The principle change that occurs in wood as it ages is it loses moisture. This loss of moisture causes the cells to shrink for the most part. (We are back to water). Because of this, we are painting and caulking wood on a regular basis. Running torrents of water against the wood on a regular basis will wear down the paint, break loose the caulk, and cause the wood to fail. The seals on insulated windows also break down faster when exposed to water on a regular basis.

Now think about your shrubbery. The rain coming off the roof and bombarding those bushes will kill them. Next, we go to the basement. The leading cause for water entry into the basement is improperly working gutters. If you eliminate the gutters, you are inviting the rainwater into your home. Poured concrete foundations are very durable and rarely have cracks resulting in structural failure. However, if a crack exists, and water enters through it, you now have water in the basement. The second concern is water expands the opening through which it is traveling. The best example of this is the Grand Canyon. Continued water entry can result in structural failure of any foundation. If you have cinder block walls the problem gets worse. The ground gets saturated in the first three or four feet below grade. It then freezes. The ground expands and snaps the block wall in one of its mortar joints. A long horizontal crack appears. This creates a "hinge" effect in the wall, and eventually the wall collapses. This is a serious structural concern. In many cases, thousands of dollars of structural repairs are needed because of dirty or improperly working gutters. Removing the gutters will accelerate the problem.

How about gutter screens? There is no system of gutter screening that I have seen that I whole heartedly endorse. I ran a roofing company for eighteen years, and have been inspecting homes since 1994. I have not seen a system that works perfectly yet. The first problem is many of them deflect water over the gutters, and can reduce the water entry into the gutter by more than fifty percent. Debris then gets under the covering, and the gutters still need to be cleaned. If you had gutter screens on them, when you take the screens out, you cut your hands, and then the screens won't go back in the way they came out. But didn't you buy the screens so you didn't have to clean the gutters? I was at a Trade Show in Baltimore and they had displays of the newest and latest systems to keep leaves out of the gutters. They had a Velcro like material with a hose running on it. The lady said, "Isn't it great?" I said, "What about pine needles?" And she said you have to clean those out by hand. So they still need to be cleaned. I have seen other convex type protection systems where the company comes out, and replaces your gutters with their own gutter system and then installs their gutter protection system over them. Some of these are very effective. I have still seen very fine debris in them. I have also seen saplings growing out of the most sophisticated gutter protection systems. Some also state emphatically that if you put a ladder against them, you void the warranty. There are many reasons to put a ladder on the side of your home besides cleaning the gutters. The system should be strong enough to handle this.

How do you clean the gutters? My recommendation is don't get off the ladder. Wear rubber gloves. And when you reach to remove debris, always keep your belt buckle between the side rails of the ladder. This will keep your center of gravity on the ladder. I recommend you have someone foot or hold the ladder at grade. You may also flush the gutters from the high end to the downspout with a garden hose. If you do this, put a loop of the hose over the top of the ladder and position it so the hose is hanging on the ladder and you aren't holding it the whole time. It is much easier to work if you are not dealing with the dead weight of a hose full of water. If you decide to venture on to the roof, be careful. I don't recommend this for the average Home Owner. Do this only if you have a very low slope roof. Read the section on ladder safety before attempting this. Once on the roof, sit down at the edge of the roof and scoop out the leaves. If you lean near the edge, follow these rules: Put one foot at the edge of the roof and stand straight up with your legs spread comfortably, and the other foot a couple feet back onto the roof. You should only look in a straight line with the gutters. If you lean down, always have your belly button over the roof. This is easily accomplished by the stance I just described. Your belly button won't go out past the foot that is at the edge of the roof. Some people take a trash bag up onto the roof and ladder and put the leaves and debris directly into it. I don't recommend this either. It is a matter of safety. Carrying a bag keeps a hand busy that can be holding on keeping you safe. The wind can also flip the bag around into the rungs of the ladder and create problems. You can inadvertently think holding onto the bag is more important than holding onto the ladder. My advice is throw the debris on the ground; you can clean it up when safely standing on the ground. The picture on the last page shows debris that got into the gutter despite the top rated gutter protection system properly installed. The picture above

shows screens that have fallen into the gutter. They still need maintenance.

Let's look at the types of gutters. Gutters have a history. Early American gutter systems and even gutters today can be broken down into two basic types, built in gutters and hanging gutters. Hanging gutters were formed by taking conventional plumbing pipes and cutting them in half. They were then hung on the edge of the roof. This was done to catch the water for convenience so you didn't get soaked when you walked out the front door. These were called half round gutters because they were half of a round pipe. Bigger, more expensive homes had built in gutters that were actually part of the roofing system. Some merely had a large board nailed on the roof called a pole gutter. This also protected the Home Owner against snow sliding off the roof. The picture below shows a home with half round gutters on it.

Aluminum half round gutters are very light weight and are often installed with flimsy hangers. If you are in love with half round gutters, bite the bullet and get copper gutters with brass shanks and circles to secure them. They cost close to three times the cost of a good seamless aluminum K style gutter. If you have K style gutters there are a variety of hanger systems to secure them to the house. The most common fastener is a spike and feral. This consists of a long spike driven in like a nail and a tube that sits in the gutter sot it keeps its' shape and gives it rigidity. Ideally, these spikes are driven through the fascia and into the rafters. Therefore they should be installed every 16". The next time I see them every 16" will be the first. These spikes pull out regularly due to snow and debris loads in the gutters. Once you drive them back in a few times, the hole gets stripped. I am not a fan of this type of system. There are fasteners that sit in the top of the gutter. They snap up under the lip in the front and fit over the back of the gutter. They are then screwed in with two self- tapping aluminum screws. Get at least 1½" screws with a hexagon head on it for a ratchet set. You may need an extension on the ratchet to fit under the shingles. Another nice feature of these hangers is they aren't visible from the ground. With spikes, you see the head of the spikes every 16" and if you are like me, you will miss at least once driving them home and dent the gutter. There are also roof mounted gutter hangers called OG13's in the business. I have no idea why they are called that. You may need them if your home doesn't have a flat fascia to attach the gutter. If you are hanging a full gutter, remember, the downspout is at the LOW end, and use a level. Gutters should be sloped. If you have no idea what type of hanger you need, don't be surprised. There is a huge variety. Take a detailed picture of the conditions on your home and take it to the supply house and ask them what you need. I would suggest going to a roofing supply or aluminum supply store. Don't count on the major home centers to have much of a variety in hangers.

Does your gutter leak? Murphy's Law says the Contractor put the seam in the gutter directly over the front door. If you are replacing your gutters, only replace them with seamless gutters. It makes no sense to install gutters with seams today. Supply house will often do what is called a detail and deliver on your gutters. That means the delivery person will measure your home, cut the gutters to fit, and leave you the right number and type of hangers, the right number of miters, outlets and related products. Those being said, check everything before you start working. They won't take back a gutter with on outlet hole cut in it that you just discovered was 4" short. Believe me, that is the amount they are usually short, they are never off by feet. I digress once again. My experience is that sealing seams in gutters isn't very effective. They have silver solder as we used to call it which was a caulk that came in a squeeze tube specifically designed for gutters. The problem with repairing old seams is the sealant doesn't work on dirt. They have tape to repair the gutters. There is also metal faced peel and stick roofing material that is sometimes effective. Cut it so it overlaps the seam by several inches on each side. Clean the gutter very well. Then prime the gutter with an asphalt primer before adhering the membrane. If the gutter is very secure, this can be fairly effective. The problem is if the gutter moves, the repair can split open. This type of material is reasonably effective at repairing built in gutters, box, or Yankee gutters. The gutters are lined with metal, often copper, which erodes and gets pinholes where the water runs off the roofing material. Peel and stick repairs can sometimes buy you time with these gutters but don't expect more than a few years of protection. Once the built in gutters fail, the can severely damage the roof deck, the soffit, and the decretive wood molding often found on the older homes that have this type of gutter. My experience has been that you eventually have to replace the lining in the gutter. This can be a rather expensive installation due to it being so labor intensive.

The downspouts should be tight to the house. Downspouts come in two basic sizes, 2" x 3", and 3" x 4". As a rule of thumb, the smaller downspout will drain 800 square feet of roofing and the larger 1200 square feet. As to how many you need, that can get complicated, based on your area. Most downspouts have corrugation in them so they expand and contract with ice. When downspouts fail, the seams in the back of them pop. If this happens, replace the downspout. There is also a variety of fasteners for downspouts. The most common fastener system is a rack, key, and drive. The drive is hammered into the wall, and the rack attached to the downspout. The key then locks them together. When doing repairs or re-securing an old downspout, your best bet is a downspout strap. The downside of them is they are visible on the face of the downspout. There is a variety of downspout fasteners as well. See what the supply house has and pick the fastener you prefer. Be sure the downspouts drain away from the home. The home should be the highest point within at least 10' in any direction. That being said, I have seen homes with that kind of clearance but they are sitting in the middle of a basin and will always be vulnerable to run off problems. The downspouts should drain far enough away that the water runs away from the home rather than back to the home.

One last point I hear as a reason to get rid of the gutters is they cause ice dams and leaking in winter. Gutters have nothing to do with ice dams. Gutters require maintenance, but they are your home's best friends against the attacks of nature. Embrace them.

Maintenance tips:
1. Be sure the downspouts are connected to the underground system.
2. If there is no underground system, be sure the splash blocks to drain the water away from the home are in place. Believe me. These things grow legs. You put them in place and come back 6 months later and they have moved.
3. Clean the gutters three times a year, at least. Memorial Day weekend, Labor Day weekend, and Halloween in very northern climates. For the rest of the country, Thanksgiving weekend for the final cleaning. You want to get the spring buds, the early leaf fall and the final leaf fall. Don't put if off past the time when your gutters freeze, whenever that is in your area.

4.   Wipe them down with a mild mixture of TSP and outdoor bleach every other year. Follow the instructions on the TSP for the quantity. You will be amazed at how dirty gutters get in a few years.
5.   Drive any spikes back in that work loose over the winter. If the hole gets stripped from years of loosening, pull out the spike. Now get toothpicks and cover them with carpenter's glue and stick them in the spike hole. Put in as many as you can. Now drive the spike in the same hole. The toothpicks and glue should hold the spikes for more than a season or two.

VINYL SIDING

Does your home need a face lift? Does it suffer from the ravages of wind, rain, ice and snow? A home can be completely changed by replacing the exterior siding with vinyl siding. There are still a huge number of homes with asbestos siding that was considered the better quality siding of the post-World War II construction boom. Asbestos exterior wall and roofing materials actually had its roots in the 1920's when it was considered a durable alternative to slate. Aluminum siding was also used extensively in the post war construction boom and was pushed extensively as a covering for frame houses. The selling feature was it eliminated painting on the outside of the home. It was guaranteed not to chip, crack, flake, or peel. The lovely gentlemen who "encouraged" you to buy this material were immortalized in the movie "Tin Men."[7] Rodney Dangerfield actually sold siding as well as painting prior to his comedic career. Steel siding also made a brief run as a more dent resistant material.

Today, vinyl has all but replaced the other materials. It is dent resistant, light weight and the problems initially occurring in installation have been solved. Vinyl is not nailed tightly on the home as other materials are. It has a very high rate of expansion and contraction. The slots for attaching it are long to allow for movement. When installed it should be overlapped to allow for the movement. While most Home Owners hire a contractor to side their home, a Home Owner with good carpentry skills can take on the project. Home supply centers have good manuals that detail the steps of the installation. You will need basic carpentry tools as well as a break. This is a large aluminum tool that is used to bend aluminum coil stock to form it over the existing trim. This is probably the most difficult part of

---

[7] Movie directed by Barry Levinson, 1987

the job for a handyman to complete. A twelve foot break can be rented from most rental centers.

Let's start at the beginning. The first step is wall preparation. If you have old, tired, dented aluminum siding you have to remove it. You can get about $.40 to $.50 a pound for it. (Price was determined during the spring of 2007.) A four bedroom home may yield close to $1,000 in scrap metal which greatly reduces the cost. If you think you are removing asbestos siding, call the Consumer Product Safety Commission for advice. Their number is 1-800-490-9198. That is also a good agency to contact about recalls of products. If you are unsure about asbestos removal in your area, call the local Building Inspector. The regulations can vary greatly from town to town. In Pennsylvania, it is not regulated on residences with less than five units at this time. Many times the walls of the home require some form of preparation once the existing siding is removed. This could be shims or possibly 1" x 3" nailers. The goal is to provide a clean tight surface for the siding. Most vinyl siding today is installed over some form of wall covering. The most common is Tyvek[8] House Wrap. I have heard contractors say it's a waste of money and you really only need to tape the seams in the plywood or wall board to reduce air infiltration. The truth is, siding leaks. All siding leaks. The wall covering provides a layer of protection to keep moisture off the exterior wall material. The tape on the seams reduces air leaks. When you tape around windows, tape the seam below the window first, then the two sides and top so that you overlap as you go up. The first piece of siding is held in place with a starter strip. You can also use J channel. This is a material that is higher in the back than front so when water enters the track, it overflows outside away from the home. The seams in the siding are staggered, and the siding should be laid out with the siding going on in the least visible area first and overlap

---

[8] Dupont Brand name

usually towards the front. That way in the area where people view the home, the seams disappear into the siding. The obvious critical area is the first course being level. Where the siding meets windows and walls a J channel should be installed. Do not just cut the material and butt it against openings. This is particularly important on dormers that meet shingle roofs. The overhangs on a home are covered with soffit panels. They should always be vented, and the best job is to rip off the old wood in the overhang so the venting actually works. The manuals will fill in the details for cutting, and fitting the siding. As a rule, don't nail it too tight, it will buckle.

Once the job is done, there are a few things to note. In time, mildew or moss will grow on the shady areas. This can be cleaned with a solution made up of water, bleach, and TSP A.K.A. Tri-sodium phosphate. (Yes, the same solution we talked about in the roofing section).You can wash down these areas, but do not use a pressure spray as they will drive water behind the siding, (remember, siding leaks). Some of these solutions can also be damaging to plants. Be sure to protect you plants. There is

 another section in this book with more details on the cleaning process. The photo on the left shows before and after of cleaning siding with TSP and bleach. The results are striking. Another quirk of vinyl siding is on new construction homes with solid second floor joists, the siding panel that lines up with the floor joist pops off when the home is five to ten years old. The floor joist shrinks, and the pressure pops the panel off. It is easily repaired. One last note, vinyl siding will melt. It is vulnerable to heat damage. Many Home Owners melt their siding with their barbecue grill. Set the grill up at least

ten feet away from the home. I have also seen vinyl siding melt from the neighbor's windows. I know that sound bizarre but what happens is the light form the window concentrates into a single beam. This is similar to starting a fire with a magnifying glass. The light heats up as it is focused and causes the siding to melt. You may see a panel right in the middle of an otherwise undamaged wall with a few panels that are warped. You get this in town homes, or as I like to call them Suburban row homes. You don't want your home crying like the wicked witch, "I'm melting!"

Maintenance tips:
1.   Look for loose or damaged panels at least once a year. Repairs or replacement of vinyl panels can be difficult. You may need a handy man.
2.   Look particularly close to the ground. Weed whackers and stones from the mower can often damage siding.
3.   Check the caulk around windows, door frames, etc. Caulk doesn't last forever, and more is not always better. If caulking, be neat. Use your finger to gently push it in place. One slow continuous motion can give it a nice finish.
4.   Hail can damage aluminum siding far more easily than it damages vinyl siding. If you have suspected hail damage, check the trim on the windows and rake boards as well as the top of the gutters.

BRICK WALLS

We all know the story of the three pigs and how the brick house was the strongest house. Brick, stone, or masonry houses all have a nice solid secure exterior surface. But these walls are not without their complications. It is true that the big bad wolf couldn't blow down the brick house, but water running against it will eventually destroy it.

There are many options for brick or solid masonry surfaces. The walls themselves are made of individual masonry units. They can be brick, stone, or some form of manufactured concrete block work. The courses are laid in straight lines with the brick and block work, the stone is more of a random pattern. All should be vertically straight. The concern with all of these building materials is their permeability. Anything that absorbs water will be broken down by water. Water wins, behold the Grand Canyon. Let's focus on red brick walls first.

Water breaks down brick walls in a variety of ways. First the flow of water over the surface causes a gradual deterioration. This is the same force that carved the valleys of Pennsylvania. The second force water exerts is freeze thaw cycles. The freezing water causes cracking and a network of passages for the flowing water to attack. As these passages expand, the water flow increases, accelerating the deterioration. The third damaging effect of water is the impurities contained in the water. The rain water in the eastern half of the United States is very acidic. This acid adds to the deterioration. Brick walls will get cracking within the brick. The older original mortar used in the joints was porous. It allowed moisture to exit the bricks. As the pointing breaks down, newer mortar is installed that is often less porous. The pointing is the mortar that holds the bricks together. The bricks then retain the moisture as it can't bleed out on the bottom edge of the bricks. This trapped moisture causes the bricks to spall, or break down.

They look like someone hit them with a chisel. Repointing is good, but be sure it is done by someone familiar with working with older brick. Repointing is not a job most Home Owners can tackle. Do not seal the joints with silicone caulk. This will trap dirt and moisture. It will discolor and break down the bricks and you will have an ugly brick wall. Other than that, it's not a bad idea. (Just kidding). Don't do it. The picture below shows a chimney where the pointing on the left was flush with the outside edge of the brick and did not leak. The pointing on the right was recessed into the chimney and the edge provided a shelf for the water and resulted in leaking.

So how do we protect our homes against such formidable odds? The first step in protecting your walls is keeping the gutters and downspouts in good working order. Next, examine your walls. Brick walls should have small openings at or near the bottom course. These weep holes should be present every few feet around the perimeter of the home. They allow the water that enters the bricks to leave. All brick walls absorb water. You want the water to have a means of departure once it enters. These weep holes tend to fill up in time. Mortar may break down in the joint above it and clog it. The most common debris in them is atmospheric dirt and tree debris. I have seen bees find these little cracks and form nests behind the bricks. Next check all of the openings in the walls, such as doors and windows. They should be caulked every three or four years. Caulk is not forever. A good silicone caulk works best and will have less bleed out of the color than latex caulks. I know I just said not to caulk the mortar joints and now I'm telling you to caulk the doors and windows. There is a big difference. Caulk is a form of flashing. It is a pliable material that seals, allowing for the junction of dissimilar materials to remained sealed despite the differential in their coefficients of expansion and contraction. Translated, both materials move. This seals the opening that expands and contracts depending on temperature, humidity and wind. The tops of all windows and doors should have metal flashing sometimes referred to as a water table to kick the water out from behind the brick. Some newer windows are designed with a built in flashing system that eliminates the need for this detail. If you have a newer home, the window specifications may cover this.

Now let's look at the style of pointing on the home. Take a look at your mortar, and think like a rain drop. Is there a nice fat ledge protruding on the top of the brickwork where you could sit? Is the mortar recessed into the wall? The tops of the bricks may look level and in most cases are relatively flat. Flat or angled inward mortar will transfer water into the brick. A very slight angle outward and downward will discourage the water from accumulating on the brick and wicking into the mortar. To ask a mason to be sure every brick has a hairline slope downward and outward is beyond his pay scale. It's not going to happen and you can't blame them if it doesn't. This type of mortar is specified by Architects, loved by home buyers, and designed to fail. This mortar requires regular examination and frequent reconstruction. Mortar that is flush with the brick tends to hold up well. The best pointing for long term performance is slightly recessed, and has a slight smooth curve to it. The pointing should be convex rather than concave. Pointing, like painting is best done sooner rather than later. The longer the pointing is allowed to deteriorate, the more the brick itself is eroded. The more the brick is eroded, the weaker the wall becomes. There are other mortar patterns where the mortar extends out past the brick, acts as a wick and can cause leaks.

A common problem in old row homes is that the front and back walls essentially develop pot bellies. The walls bow in the middle. The wall is usually not properly fastened to the interior framing. This bowing can be quite pronounced and can result in interior cracking. If the wall is out more than about an inch in an eight foot elevation the wall should be checked by a structural specialist, such as a licensed structural engineer. Left unchecked, the wall could collapse. The remedy is the insertion of star bolts through the front wall. They are run deep into the structure through the second floor joists. The bolts are then fastened to the joists and bolts are visible on the front wall. This is a legitimate repair if done properly and the metal stars can be attractive. Any kind of bowing in any wall is a major concern and is best checked by a professional. Any horizontal cracking is also a concern. A horizontal crack weakens the wall and creates a hinge effect in the wall. When examining your wall and you find cracks, view them collectively. A series of 1/8" cracks, about the thickness of a dime, should be viewed collectively and may amount to ½" crack or more. A crack of that size will definitely require professional examination.

Keeping the bricks clean can go a long way towards extending their life. Algae and moss can grow on brick walls, usually on the North side of the building. Ivy, while poetic and sometimes perceived as emblematic of academic wisdom, destroys the walls. Cut it off at the roots and once it has died, remove it. Now, here are a couple of do's and don'ts with brick walls. Don't sand blast them. You can do a generation's worth of deterioration in a day's work by sand blasting them. Don't seal them with any of these silicone based water proofing liquids. They don't completely waterproof the wall and they inhibit the natural evaporation of moisture from the bricks. Remember, there are gallons of water produced in a home that has to go somewhere. If it begins flowing through the brick, let it keep going. Stopping it at the outside surface will destroy the bricks prematurely. If your brick walls are severely stained, hire a professional. Some materials such as muriatic acid can leave the bricks blotchy weeks later. For brick cleaning materials, Google brick cleaning products. A whole host of products came up including TSP which is mentioned elsewhere in this book. Boric acid is also a good cleaner. That can be rather labor intensive as you scrub the whole wall. The age of the brick, and the type of stains you are removing, can be factors in selecting the right cleaning chemicals. For this reason, a Google search for the products makes sense. This book can't possibly cover all the cleaning conditions you may encounter. Brick walls are good strong walls, the third little piggy was right. But, like everything else in life, they require frequent examinations. Repair of the little problems is always better done before they become big problems.

Maintenance tips:

1. Check your brick walls for stains, and clean as needed. In most cases this will be every few years.
2. Check the mortar joints and stay after them. Wire brush out the loose mortar and repair any small damage yourself, (Remember-recessed joint). Don't repair the mortar with silicone caulk. It doesn't work and it will discolor in time and scar the wall.
3. Be sure the weep homes are open. Probe them with a screw driver once a year. They do clog with debris in time.
4. Don't sand blast them or use muriatic acid. There are better cleaners.

STUCCO, GOOD OR BAD?

Recently I performed a property inspection for a couple  buying a home with stucco siding. The wife was terrified. She had heard many horror stories about stucco and was concerned that she might be buying a home with hidden problems that would develop into catastrophes down the road. The truth is all siding leaks. You can have problems with moisture trapped behind any exterior wall cladding. Problems inside exterior walls are very difficult to find during a routine home inspection, and often require a specific stucco inspection.

There are two basic types of stucco installations. There is the traditional hard coat stucco that has been on homes for centuries. The newer stucco installations, for the sake of brevity, contain some form of insulation built into the wall to improve the overall insulation quality of the wall system. The insulation is not porous. Moisture hits it and either stops its migration or slows its movement to the point that problems develop. A basic rule of nature is that water wins. (Not again, I know, I keep saying it). Water made the Grand Canyon. Steam drives locomotives. The moisture comes from two sources. The moisture we create by living in our home, and moisture from external sources. An average family with 2.3 children, (I still haven't seen the .3 child they talk about), puts about 2½ gallons of water per day into the air in their home. The outside sources are the soil and atmospheric moisture. Wind driven rain and moisture in the soil are huge sources of moisture effecting homes.

Any stucco material should not extend below grade on the exterior walls. The stucco should stop 6" above the soil. A condition known as rising damp can allow the wall cladding to wick moisture up out of the soil. Through capillary action, the water runs up hill. The water comes in contact with the wood framing and the back of the drywall. The resulting condition is you now have a dark warm wet spot where mold loves to grow. The mold lives on the food source, the wood, and "mushrooms" into rot. Repairing this damage can be extremely expensive.

"The devil is in the details" is often said about legal agreements. This expression translates into construction quite well and I refer to it as "Mother Nature sides with the hidden flaw," the fifth axiom of Murphy's Law. Anywhere that the walls start, stop, or change direction, there is the potential for water entry. Windows are just such a location.

The junction of the sills and the rails on the sides of the windows will leak. The Home Owner can be the problem in many of these cases. Many believe caulk is forever. These areas should be examined often for peeling paint or evidence of wood failure. It is far better to paint these wood areas a year or two early than a year or two late. Examine the junction of the stucco and the side rails of the windows. A raised bridge joint should be installed to create a buffer between the stucco and the wood. You don't want the stucco run directly into the wood areas. The top of the window should also be flashed. There are windows that contain a self-flashing system that serves as the flashing. I prefer to see a metal flashing installed that is secured behind the wall. There are about 30 window manufacturers in the area with a wide range of windows. It's not humanly possible to know every window that contains a working weeping system to properly transfer water to the exterior.

Doorways require the same attention to detail. I was recently involved in a home with moisture issues where water had entered around a sliding glass door that entered onto a deck. This area contains a variety of special conditions. The threshold can leak. The side rails on the doorway may leak. The fasteners for the band joist for the deck are all openings that, if not done right, can provide channels for water entry. There are other complications in this area that exacerbate the problem. Wood expands and contracts based on moisture and temperature. This movement allows water entry. As the caulk hardens in time, the constant percussion of the door opening and closing creates a drum beat for water entry. The big problem with the synthetic stucco systems is their reduced permeability. This concept, developed as an asset, is unforgiving when these minor defects allow water penetration and afford it no means of egress.

Now let's take a look up a little higher on the home. Contractors often have the gutters installed on the home, followed by the stucco. This recesses the gutters into the stucco wall. If the gutters back up for any number of reasons, the water is now funneled into the stucco wall with disastrous results. The home on the right was less than

 one year old and the Home Owner had taken several steps to keep the water out. The gutter ran right into the stucco wall. Stucco walls are sealed with pieces of metal referred to as step flashings. They carry the water down the roof and prevent water entry where the roof and wall meet. At the base of the wall, the roof often

terminates into the stucco wall. This detail again creates a channel for water to run behind the stucco. A kick out flashing should be present here. It is an L shaped piece of metal, and sits above the gutter deflecting the water into the gutter and away from the stucco. This detail didn't exist in roofing 20 years ago. Now it's practically a necessity on stucco installations. Retrofitting the kick out into a stucco wall is a labor intensified proposition. Even with the diluted wages being paid by contractors today to skilled workers, this can be a costly retrofit.

Hairline cracks in this stucco clad chimney resulted in leaking for days after the rain had stopped. All those little cracks added up to a larger crack that allowed water entry.

There are a host of other passageways for moisture entry into a perfectly installed stucco application. Exterior light fixtures need to be sealed to prevent water entry. The screws for the downspout straps need to water tight. Any interruption in the wall needs attention. Hose bibs coming though the wall, supports for attaching cellar well covers can be a source of leaking. Many homes with decks and patios have canvas retractable awnings that can pull and open with time. The problem with many of the repairs done to these homes is the contractor runs down to a home center and buys whatever caulk they have or that might be on sale. There is a wide range of caulks on today's market. They are chemically formulated for specific applications. One size does not fit all.

While the newer synthetic stucco installations have received the bulk of the notoriety on these moisture issues, traditional stucco has many of these problems. A complete stucco specific inspection takes time, is costly, and requires tools specific to the task such as moisture detectors and is sometime intrusive into wall cavities. It can't be done in a pre-purchase real estate transaction. If you decide to have your stucco inspected, be sure you have an inspector who is familiar with the product on your home, and is properly equipped to do a complete inspection. Mold sampling may then follow if moisture issues are discovered.

Maintenance tips:
1.   Keep the stucco clean. Don't seal stucco walls with clear silicone or any kind of waterproofing paint.
2.   Stucco cracks. If you have a good three coat stucco installation you can hope for 10 years or so before significant cracking occurs. The thinner coats may crack in less than 12 months. Hairline cracking s normal. If the stucco starts pulling off, or the rain catches in the crack and begins to cause streaks, call a mason for repairs. Many cracks are repairable and a few cracks are not a reason to spend thousands of dollars and re-stucco the house.
3.   If the dampness from the stucco is creating mold behind it, then you may be looking at very extensive repairs. Musty smells in closets on walls with stucco are a source of concern. Get mold testing done by a professional. If mold is growing behind the stucco, it is unhealthy and can result in serious structural damage to the home.

ELECTRICAL SERVICE AND PANEL BOX

Electrical systems are an extremely safe, dependable network that we use every day. With a little bit of care, they can continue to be safe. An annual examination of the system can protect you and your family from many of the concerns and dangerous aspects of electricity.

Let's start with the service coming into the home. Check for trees and shrubbery growing around the wires. A trees or branch loaded with ice adds hundreds of pounds of weight to your service. If an ice storm takes down your wires, chances are you're a low priority to the electric company since many major lines servicing thousands of people are also down. The electric company will trim the trees and shrubs that are touching the wires at no charge. Don't trim them yourself. The insulation may be worn, and they can be very dangerous. Leave trimming around them to professionals. Always assume that all wires connecting to your home are live, carrying lots of electricity, and are poorly insulated. Better to be pleasantly surprised that they are insulated or carrying low electrical current, than horribly surprised that they are carrying very high electrical loads and aren't properly insulated.

Once the service is attached to your home, it becomes your responsibility. The thickness of the service varies depending on the material used, and the amperage of the system. A gauge is needed to determine the age. The insulation on the wire should be intact. No strands or fibers from the mesh under the rubber jacket should be showing. The rubber should not be painted when the house is painted. Look up at the top of the wire. The wire should form a loop at the top. This area of the wire wears out first. Any area of the service wire that is facing up, wears out first. There are two reasons for this. The first is the UV rays of the sun dry it out. The second is rain and snow hit it directly. On the side walls they don't get the direct wear of water and snow landing on them. Look for any frayed material hanging off it. The best place to examine this is on the roof. Do not get on the roof unless you are comfortable up there and the roof is clearly walkable. Don't set the ladder up next to the wires and then try and peek over the top of them. The ladder may slip and you may come in contact with the wires. Set the ladder up a safe distance away, and look off the roof onto the wires. If the wire is worn, have it replaced. Some people wrap them with electrical tape, but I recommend a licensed electrician replace them. If the strands are showing, it may not electrocute you, but it will allow water to enter the system, and create rust in the meter box or in the main panel box. I inspected my mother in law's house. My brother in law and I thought it would be a good idea to inspect it for safety. My father in law had died several years ago and she was in the house by herself. We were concerned that she may not be staying on top of things with regards to maintenance. When I opened the electrical panel, the entire right side was loaded with rust. The water had entered through the failed electrical service on the exterior and was rusting out the box. There was the potential to burn the house down. If you have an older relative that has been in their home for many years, the best act of love you can give them is buy them a home inspection. Houses deteriorate quietly. People living in homes a long time tend to think that problems will be dramatic and sudden when they present themselves. It's better to find out about a deteriorating condition before it's a failed condition.

Now look at the meter box. The meter is contained in a round glass globe with several dials that point to various numbers. The meter should be firmly attached to the wall.

Check the bottom of the box for rust. Rust is often present with poor wire insulation or the absence of the loop at the top. Severe rusting on the box is reason to have it replaced. While you are at the electric meter box, feel the box with the back of your right had while your left hand is not touching anything. If it is warm, call an electrician. Mine was 100 degrees when I checked it with an infrared camera. The one lug had worked itself loose with time creating heat. The lights in part of the home were flickering.

If your service comes in underground, the PVC conduit that contains the wires should have all the sections connected. There should be no openings in it. On some homes, there is a ground wire in the area of the meter. This is a solid bare copper wire that is attached to a rod in the ground. The wire should be bolted to the grounding rod. Pull on it. It should be tight. This wire is designed to take lightning to the earth. The grounding system can vary from home to home. The best system and one required if you are building a home today, calls for a rod submerged eight feet into the earth, and a wire from the main panel box inside to the cold water plumbing in the home. Many older homes have one system or the other. All wires coming into the home should be connected to a ground. The phone and cable wires should also be connected to a rod in the earth. Take a look at how the electric enters the home. In many cases it runs from the back of the meter box directly into the home. In others, there is an additional service drop type cable that runs in the wall. I have seen the service leave the meter and run long distances on the outside wall before finally entering the home. Check the condition of this wire also. It should be secured tightly to the wall. It should also not be frayed. When the wire enters the home there is often a gap around the wire. Bees love these kinds of openings. Seal it off with caulk or Great Stuff[9]. Great Stuff is a foam insulation that expands in the opening, seals it

---

[9] Trade name for foam insulation product

off, and is very sticky when touched. Once it dries, it hardens. Shave it with a utility knife.

The main electrical panel should be on the inside wall near the outside service. (The picture is on next page. Microsoft Word did weird things when I tried to put the picture on this page). If the wire runs more than six feet inside the home, there should be a disconnect or shut off on the wire. Now that you are inside the home, let's look at your main panel. It should not be rusted. If the box contains fuses, there are usually two large black boxes inside the box, with metal handles on them. If you pull these boxes, you will shut off the power. Frequently, I see additional sub panels or smaller boxes around the fuse box. These are additions to the system. They are often done for particular appliances, such as a water heater or air conditioning system.

We have a saying in the inspection business: If it doesn't look right, it probably isn't. Professional electricians tend to be neat. Electricians get points for neatness, but not for originality. If the wires are going all over the place, with several boxes added onto each other, you might want to have an electrician take a look at it. You can add boxes, but there is a right way and a wrong way. If the brother-in-law did it when he replaced the water heater, you might want to have it checked. Fuse box  systems can be safe. If you have fuses, be sure there is a fuse in every opening. If you find yourself replacing fuses, call an electrician. A breaker system consists of a row or two of black switches contained in a gray or black box. The rows are called buses. These switches are as safe to throw as the wall switch in your living room. There should be no openings in the box. If there is no breaker in a slot, a blank should cover the slot. Put tape over the opening until you can have it properly covered. Don't use duct tape. This is not a duct. It is an electrical box. Duct tape can conduct electricity. Use electrical tape, hence the name. Children are curious, and sticking a finger or a metal object in the opening can be fatal. If you find the breakers are tripping, call an electrician. Don't replace it with a larger breaker. The breakers are sized for the wiring. An oversized breaker on small wiring can cause a fire. Faulty amateur electrical work may jeopardize your fire insurance. It's not worth the risk. Now turn on most of the major appliances in the home. You can't run the air conditioning in the winter, but you can turn on the electrical range, and run the hot water for about five minutes. Run the back of your right hand down the row of breakers. If they get hot, or you hear a humming sound, have an electrician check the box. Checking these items is a good place to start on checking the electrical system. Most Home Owners are shocked when they finally notice them.

There is one more item to check in the main box. The main shut off switch should have a number on it, from 100 to 200. The box should also have a label on it. The rating on the box should be the same as the main breaker. If they are different, the number on the main disconnect should be smaller. Testing and inspecting the branch circuits is a little more time consuming, and requires some special tools. That is covered in another section of the book.

Maintenance tip:
1.   Check your electrical service annually.
2.   Check for trees overhanging or coming in contact with the service.
3.   Trip your GFCI protection monthly as it says on the device.

4. Label your electrical panel. Use a loud radio and listen for the circuit to shut off. Never believe the labeling already in the house.
5. Turn each breaker off and back on individually once a year
6. If your lights dim when the A/C, dryer or electric range goes on, call an electrician. This can be a symptom of a serious problem.

SWIMMING POOLS

Nothing seems to fascinate Man more than water. Beach front property will often hold its value longer than the house next door that is off the beach. Lake front properties are not far behind, and nothing soothes like the gentle babble of mountain stream. But what do the rest of the poor land locked souls do who don't own this prime real estate and still want to enjoy the ambiance of a body of water. We can buy it. And it comes in many shapes and sizes. Invest in a backyard swimming pool. (I know it's a poor investment from a return standpoint). A pool changes the dynamics of summer living. We have had a pool for over twenty two years and we refer to our back yard as our summer home. The cheapest way to buy a pool is to buy a house with one. A pool will limit the market for your home at the time of resale, but I believe the rewards of pool ownership far outweigh the liabilities.

The first concern I often hear is people don't want the added maintenance. The amount of maintenance required with a pool is directly proportional to the size and number of trees near the pool. Our back yard has border shrubbery for privacy but few high trees creating leaves, and the related work. The trees have been doing what trees do, they are growing. It is almost time to take something off the top. The other thing that trimming the trees down will do is allow late afternoon sun to hit our pool. A warm pool on a warm day is nice, but it is surprising how much difference shade makes in your comfort when in the pool. We open the pool ourselves, and pay to have it closed. Opening the pool can be an all-day affair.

Closing the pool properly in the fall can greatly reduce the work when opening the pool. We vacuum the pool just before we put on the cover. We then add five gallons of liquid chlorine, which we will talk about later. We then put the cover on immediately. We use water bags as ballast to hold the cover in place. These bags break over the winter and we replace about a third of them every year. The amazing thing about the chlorine is that when we pull off the cover in spring, you can still smell the chlorine in the water. Opening it starts with getting the water off the cover. It is a good idea to pump water off the cover all winter. An interesting phenomenon about a pool is you can cover it with a "waterproof" cover. In reality, the cover has some permeability. If you leave the water on the cover, it pushes the cover down into the pool and when you pump the water off the cover, you are actually pumping water out of the pool. This increases the cost of startup and wastes water. One winter we just couldn't keep water off the cover as our area had over 80" of snow and weeks of subfreezing temperatures. You can't pump ice.

A small submersible pump left on the cover for a few days will do the trick. Last, get as much water off the cover as possible. Water is heavy. A cubic yard of water weighs 1,600 lb. Once you are near the end of the water, use a bucket to scoop out the last few drops. There are often leaves that can clog the pump. The better quality covers drain the water into the poll while keeping the dirt and debris out. Many also have an anchoring system that keeps the cover taut. They say the system works so well they say you can walk across the cover. One company shows an elephant standing on the pool cover. My personal experience totally contradicts this picture. And I had the soaking wet pants to prove it.

Now it is time to start the filter. There are a variety of filter systems, some working on sand, others on white powdered earth. The filter removes the particles from the water. Cleaning the parts of the filter and re-assembling it takes an hour or so. It doesn't require a huge level of mechanical aptitude. With the filter up and running, it's time to vacuum the bottom of the pool. No matter how well you cover it, some debris settles in the bottom. The next step is to chemically treat the water. The pool can be treated with bromine or chlorine. If you are using chlorine, the pool should be shocked with liquid chlorine. Protect your eyes with goggles. I keep mine closed as well as wearing eyewear. Wear old white clothes when you add it. It is a very powerful chemical. Chlorine is like roof cement. A little goes a long way and gets on everything, and once it's there, both tend to leave their mark forever. Chlorine will burn a hole in denim jeans. A five gallon container will sanitize most pools.

The pool is now vacuumed, cleaned and chemically treated. Unfortunately, it is usually pretty cold at this point. The water temperature to start the season is usually in the low 60's. There are solar covers that will raise the temperature as much as 15 degrees with three or four days of sunshine. A gas or propane fired heater will also heat it nicely, but it can cost several hundred dollars for a warm pool. The opening of the pool changes the mood of the household. Instead of a black body of water with an occasional confused pair of mallards floating on it, you now have a glistening crystal clear aqua blue mirror reflecting twinkling highlights into the living room.

Once it is up and running it requires an hour or two a week to check the chemicals, skim the leaves and occasionally vacuuming the bottom. Heating a pool can extend the swimming season by a few months adding the months of May and September to your pool season. Last year we replaced the liner. Our pool has steel sides, a sand bottom, and a vinyl liner. The old liner was over twenty years old, and the replacement liner cost less than $3,000.00. If you have a vinyl liner and are considering replacing it, hire somebody. Removing the water from a pool leaves the structure's sides weakened while the pool is dry. Also, a large vacuum device pulls air from under the cover as it fills with water to ensure a snug fit. It's a job for a professional. The water for refilling the pool spiked our water bill upward about $100.00. A concrete pool will require cleaning down the sides and repainting far more often, thus increasing the cost and maintenance of the pool. There are other options on the pool structure such as fiberglass, and tile. They have pools to fit every yard and every pocketbook.

It may sound like a lot of work at the start, but once it's up and running, the maintenance is surprisingly low. You can pay a pool service to open it, pay them to come and maintain it, and pay them to come and close it. My feeling is most of this work we can do. When you are cleaning the bottom, it doesn't feel like work, as you are in a bathing suit, and can dive in if you get a little warm. The upside? On those hot summer days, I float on a huge inflatable raft, drifting into the gentle world of semi-conscious dreaming. Unfortunately, my world is often shattered by the chilling spray of the garden hose from my adult children who still seem to find humor in disturbing my tranquility. The pool is a great source of family bonding. Did I mention how much the grandchildren like it?

Maintenance tips:
1. Keep the pool clean of leaves and debris. The more often you clean it, the happier it is.
2. SWIM IN IT! This may sound basic but the interesting thing about a swimming pool is the more it is used, the easier it is to maintain. If the water remains stagnant the quicker algae grows in the pool. The agitation of the swimming cuts down on algae growth.
3. Test it weekly. Get a small test kit at a pool supply store and test it weekly. You want to monitor the PH. If the PH is good, the chemicals for cleaning it work much better. Rain makes the pool more acidic. Once or twice a season we have to add baking soda to neutralize the acid. Several 5 lb. boxes usually do the trick.

4. Clean out the skimmer box every few days. If your pool is a chlorine purified pool, you may need to add tablets to the skimmer box. Many newer pools have automatic systems to add chlorine or bromine.
5. Vacuum the bottom as needed. The more often you skim leaves off the top, the less you have to vacuum.
6. Back wash the filter as needed. Ask at the pool supply store about this and have the make and model of the filter with you. We back wash our filter usually twice, once at the end of the season, and once around the middle of July.
7. I guess pools are a little bit of work. These are the most tips of any section in the book, but, in the middle of all this maintenance, you can just jump in and take a break.
8. A pool can result in a new pet. We looked in the scupper box one day and found a cute little red eared slider turtle. We got an aquarium for him and he has been with us for over a year now. We named him Tank.

FENCES

Have you taken a look at the fences around your property lately? Fences loosen, fall, get pushed down, and for any number of reasons fall into disrepair. Want a small example of how fragile a fence can be. See how well it holds up against a tree encroaching on it. I have seen trees knock down fences. I have also seen trees grow around a metal fence and completely encapsulate it. Fixing a fence requires only a few tools, and a little physical work.

There are basically three types of fences: metal fences, such as cyclone or chain link. They are installed with metal poles. In the business they call all metal fencing chicken wire fencing. Split rail fences have wood posts and consist of two or three rails. The last: stockade fences,

(picture on left); provide a wall of fencing that gives the owner the most privacy. Stockade fencing comes in a variety of forms as well. Replacing broken or rotted posts, or attaching the fencing to the posts, are the most common repairs. When reinstalling a metal fence, the post should be set in concrete. Wood posts should not be set in concrete as it will rot the wood. The one exception is the gate. The swinging of the gate puts additional stress on the post so reinforcing it with concrete makes sense.

When repairing a fence, the first order of business is removing the old post from the ground. If it's a metal post, it probably has fallen down, and you have the post in hand. A wood post is a little more difficult to remove. Wood posts rot from a combination of water and exposure to the air. The post will rot at ground level, and stay whole several inches below the ground. In order to remove the solid piece underground, you have to dig it out. A wrecking bar and post hole digger are the best tools for this. A post hole digger looks like two shovels joined together. These tools can be rented, if you don't have them. Digging out the old post is a little like root canal work on a large scale. Dig around the post on all sides. Work it loose moving it back and forth with the wrecking bar. Now measure the hole. Often fence posts are not installed to the proper depth. Posts for a four foot fence should be installed at least eighteen inches deep, over four foot, twenty four inches, and over eight foot, thirty six inches. Dig the hole to the right depth, plus a few inches. When you start, put a piece of tape on the post hole digger at the depth you want. This measures the hole as you dig it. Now take a couple of those rocks that you cursed as you dug them out and place them in the bottom of the hole. This helps water drain around the base of the post. Be sure you still have the required depth in the hole after you place the rocks.

Run a string from the two posts that are still standing so you keep the post in the same line with the existing fence. Now you are ready to set the post. If it's a metal post, knock the old concrete off the old post. You may be able to reuse the post. If this post kept falling down, it may not have been set deep enough. Chances are the post is too short now that the hole is the proper depth. Insert the post in the hole, and, using a two foot level, check to see if it's plumb. Stabilize it on the sides with a few rocks, but do not back fill around it. If it's a metal post, mix a small batch of concrete to install in the hole. When mixing it, make it a little on the dry side rather than wet. If it's too wet, you may have trouble getting the post to stay straight. Once the post is level, and in line with the string, and you have set the concrete, go inside and get caught up on the game as the concrete sets. You don't want to touch it and knock it out of plumb. Once concrete has hardened, attach the fence to the post. Use galvanized nails at least 2 ½" long on a stockade fence. Use finishing nails on a split rail fence to keep the rails from twisting in the future, and use wiring secured at a fence supply store for the metal fence. Check again to see that your fence is level, and your post is plumb. Back fill around the fence with dirt, and you have fixed the fence. The job is done.

If you are running a new fence, set you first post, and run your string to where the fence will end. Use a one hundred foot tape to measure for each post. I prefer a fiberglass tape because it doesn't rust, and is easier to rewind. Measure for your holes, and dig them. I secure the posts after I have connected each section of fence, just as you did when doing a repair. This makes it easier to make minor adjustments as you secure the sections. The Pros set all the posts and put up the fence last. There's an old expression that good fences make good neighbors.[10] So keep your fences in good repair, and you may get along better with your neighbors.

Maintenance tips.
1.   Walk the fence route once a year and check the posts for stability. They can rot and you may have to replace some every few years.
2.   Cut back trees or shrubbery that is in contact with the fence. I have seen trees literally grow around and entrap metal fences.
3.   Check the sections during this walk around. They can work their way loose from the posts.

---

[10] From a poem by Robert Frost

4. If the fence is to keep in a pet, check at grade level. Dogs sometimes dig holes under the fence and soon you will be dog gone. Other animals can dig the holes as well, and your dog may find the holes and think exploring is a good idea.
5. Fences don't work on groundhogs. They build a network of tunnels no fence can stop.

FRONT DOORS

Knock, knock. Who's there? Oh you. Oh you "who?" Oh you have a new front door! Looking for a way to improve the outside of your home and the inside, at the same time? Get a new front door. The front door is center stage on the front of the home. It occupies only about 5% of the surface area, yet it dominates the statement a house makes. Change your front door and you change the entire front of the home, relatively inexpensively. You will also totally change the mood of the room or hall on the inside of the home.

There are a wide variety of doors made today. You can choose from plain panel doors with no windows, to doors with arched or oval windows highlighted with a variety of cut glass laid in a brass caning. If you are going to change the opening size, from a single door opening, to a new entrance way with sidelights and a transom, my suggestion is you hire a professional. This will involve removing structural members, interior wall work, and a well thought out plan of attack. If you are going to merely replace the front door in the existing opening, it may be a project you can handle.

Start by measuring the opening. Take four measurements: opening width at the bottom and the top, and top to bottom on each side, and write them down. The opening may not be even in an older home. Now check the opening with a four-foot level on the sides and a hand held level on the top. Is everything plumb? I didn't think so. We'll address that later. Now select the door. If your opening is off by more than ¼" you may have trouble getting the door to fit. Wood doors can be shaved with a plane once in the opening, plastic or fiberglass doors cannot. Wood doors are significantly more expensive, and will require far more maintenance in the future.

If you buy a blank door with no holes or hinges, you can use the existing hinge and lock locations. When you get the door home put the door in the opening. Be sure it fits. It should be snug, but it should fit. If you buy a pre-hung door, remember it wasn't pre-hung in your house. You can save some time by having the hinges already installed on the door, and the lock holes pre-cut, but they usually don't match up with the existing hinges and lock holes in you doorway. My feeling is it's easier to make more holes in the doorjamb than it is to drill openings in a solid core door. Use a piece of wood the same height as the door to mark the hinge locations on the door. Then hold the wood inside the frame, and mark for you new hinge openings. Draw the hinge line and chisel out the wood to recess your hinges. Get help holding the door when you screw in the hinges. Once in place, check your clearance on all side. Chances are your old threshold won't work. Pre-hung doors come with a threshold in the frame. You may find yourself buying a new threshold that fits. We did.

If the door is too tight to the other side, you may have to chisel more wood away. If the door swings and it is uneven, you can pack out the hinges with strips of firm cardboard or even business cards wedged in between the hinge and door jamb. It may take some adjusting until it's even. If you install the screws for the new hinges and they seem loose, the holes may be too big for them or you may have stripped the opening. Either way, the door will not swing cleanly and can hit on the other side or the floor. Pull out the loose screws and get toothpicks. Coat the toothpicks with wood glue and pack them into the hole. Then re-screw the hole. If you have to do this to more than one screw hole, I would not keep opening and closing the door. Allow the glue time to set, at least an hour or so. If the door is level, (Hopefully), and it is hitting at the top, you may need to shave the header with a plane. Sometimes sandpaper works if it's merely rubbing and not completely blocking the door from closing. Now you can install the lock set. You may be able to save the old lock. With a pre-hung door, the holes in the door line up very well with a variety of latch/dead bolt sets that really dress up the opening. The chances the new locks will fit into the existing openings in the doorjamb are also slim. You may find yourself drilling, cutting and, again chiseling to get the right fit. There is filler you can buy to close off the openings for the old lock. Pack the opening with some of the wood you just chiseled out for the hinges and the new lock holes. Then fill the opening with the plastic wood material. It may crack, and require a couple of applications to get a nice finish. It can be sanded and painted once it hardens.

If you go from a door with a few small windows at the top, to an oval window with several types of cut glass, a brass setting, and an attractive wood finish on the door, the change on both the outside and inside can be dramatic. Stand out at the curb and admire your work. It's a full day's project, and then some. You will need chisels, levels, drill, assorted bits, assorted screwdrivers or a screw gun, and a fair amount of patience. Once the door is installed, you may find yourself awakened at night by the sound of the front door laughing at that old beat up screen door that remains. It didn't look so bad before, but now with the new front door, it's time for a change. The pointing is the mortar that holds the bricks together.

Maintenance tips:
1. Hit the lock with lock-ez or some other lubricant. Graphite works but it can be messy.
2. Check the weather stripping around the door. This tends to pull off and I find myself re-attaching or replacing ours almost every year.
3. Keep the front door and doorway painted. (The first impression of the house is a lasting impression).

4. Keep the hinges tight. Don't over turn them or you can strip the homes.
5. Check the top and bottom of the door so it closes easily. Doors that don't close all the way are not safe, and they cost you money with energy loss.

A VISIT TO THE KITCHEN

When I told my wife I was going to write about kitchen appliances she was curious about what I would say since she has never seen me operate one. I explained that I am a theorist and understand them conceptually. She proposed I gain some practical experience and make dinner. Let's start with the range. Gas is often the preferred fuel for heating. If you have an electric range, try using very flat copper pans for cooking. They will heat more rapidly and evenly than other pans. Electric ranges often draw more current than the breaker in the main panel box will permit to run through it. It's best to not heat all the burners and the oven at the same time. Using several burners and the oven simultaneously usually doesn't over load the breaker, but all at once may. There are a variety of types of electric ranges and burner surfaces. The better ranges have a light that lets you know if the burner area is still hot. Many are single surfaces with a hot area that glows red. These surfaces are much easier to clean than the old electric coil-type burners. If you have a gas oven, check the color of the flame on the burners and in the oven. They should always be blue. If the flame is yellow, it may be dirty and giving off carbon monoxide. It's a good idea to have a carbon monoxide detector in the kitchen with a gas range. On days when you are doing a lot of cooking with a gas range, such as Thanksgiving, leave the kitchen window open a couple of inches for ventilation.

Refrigerators use about 8 percent of all electricity used in the US. Older refrigerators are very inefficient and expensive to run. Air moving over the coils under the refrigerator cools them and displaces the heat removed from inside the refrigerator. A simple way to check the air flow over the coils is to hold a tissue in front of it on the right side and then move it over to the left side. The one side should pull in, and the other should blow out with about the same amount of force. If there is little air movement, there is a blockage. The reduction in airflow can put strain on the compressor and damage the unit. Clean the coils and the entire area around the motor with a vacuum cleaner at least twice a year. You will be amazed at how many of the cat's toys end up under there. Don't use the sides of the refrigerator as a storage area. If you put paper bags or other items there, they restrict air flow. Pull them out. Are they hot? If they are, they are blocking air flow around the unit. Leave a few inches of space around the unit. To check the seal on the magnetic strip around the door, put a dollar in the door. It should hold it in place. The temperature of the refrigerator should be about 36 to 38 degrees. The freezer should be zero to five degrees. If you move a refrigerator, always keep it vertical, particularly older models. If turned on their side, the oil runs out of the compressor and into the coils. The compressor will seize when you start it. Refrigerators and freezers should not be plugged into GFCI protected outlets. These are also two appliances that MUST be grounded.

Garbage disposals have gone from novelty to necessity. Do not use a garbage disposal if you have a private septic system. It will ruin the system. Garbage disposals occasionally jam. There is a small wrench that comes with the appliance to free them when this happens. They should be cleaned periodically as grease builds up in them. To clean them, dump the baking soda from the refrigerator, into the disposal. Now pour in about a pint of vinegar and let it sit until the foaming stops. Throw some ice into the disposal and run it. Then add cold water. The baking soda and vinegar frees the grease, and the ice coagulates it before it can reattach to the disposal. The ice also sharpens the blades. I have a hand held mixer with the same blades. I use it to mix smoothies. It is about seven years old and the blades are as sharp as the day I got it. Must be those ice cubes in the smoothies. My sampling of one says it works. Look at it this way, the ice cubes don't hurt it. Always run cold water in your disposal. The water cools the motor and prolongs the life of the unit. Hot water heats it and puts stress on the motor, resulting in premature failure. Disposals have the shortest life of any kitchen appliance, and may last a maximum of five to seven years.

One last item, all the receptacles above the kitchen counter should be on ground fault circuit interrupters, known as GFI"s of GFCI's. This is a safety device that is built into the receptacle. It cuts off the electricity in the circuit if you, water and electricity get together. They can be installed on ungrounded or two wire electrical systems, common in older homes. They save lives. If you don't have them, get them installed. It is suggested you test them monthly by pushing in the test bottom with an electrical device plugged into them. The more often you test them, the happier they are. When you test them, the power should stop. Then press the reset to start them. Never have a refrigerator or freezer plugged into them. The surge of the motor or even thunderstorms can cause them to trip, ruining a lot of food. If the power ever goes out, turn the refrigerator off. Newer refrigerators have an overload device that trips if there is a surge in power. It protects the appliance from being damaged by the electricity coming back on with too much voltage. Newer refrigerators have circuit boards that can get cooked by the power. Once the power comes back on, turn it back on manually and you should be fine. If the returning power knocks out the overload protection, it's about a $150 bill. They also will probably be coming a week from Thursday because everybody else had the same problem. You would think they would put a reset button on the built in "surge protection." You might realize, most computers have to be turned on manually after the power goes out. Now you know the reason. Too much voltage will singe their circuit boards.

Maintenance tips.

1. Test your GFCI outlet in the kitchen monthly.
2. Clean the garbage disposal every six months.
3. Clean the refrigerator coil area every six months.
4. Clean the oven as needed. Once a year is good.
5. Check under the sink twice a year. Small leaks can open up.
6. Allow access to the shut off valves in the event of an emergency. It's amazing how much stuff people store under sinks. They store plastic bags form the supermarket like they are gold.
7. Looking for dishwasher tips? They have their own section. Page 92.

COOKING FIRES

There is a commercial I saw on television that shows the remnants of a home after a fire and the conversation deals with putting a frozen turkey into a deep fryer. There is nothing funny about a house fire. There is also nothing funny about the dangers involved in using a deep fryer. According to the National Fire Protection Association, (NFPA), the number one cause of home fires is cooking fires. Also, the number one day for such fires is Thanksgiving Day which makes sense since that day probably has the most people cooking at home. Safety when cooking is of paramount importance. Sipping the cooking sherry periodically while cooking, is not a good idea. Holidays often involve drinking as well as cooking and the combination can be deadly.

Many cooking fires involve simple basic precautions that we sometimes overlook. Don't wear clothing with loose sleeves, or draw strings that can come in contact with the flame. Keep all flammable materials such as food packaging and pot holders away from burner areas. Keep small children, and adults that act like children, (you know that uncle that celebrates too much), away from the cooking area. Most people with small children know to use the back burners so children are less likely to grab the pot accidentally. Never leave the burner on if you are frying food and must leave the kitchen. If you are using a deep fryer, read the manual and follow the safety tips. Water and oil do not mix when hot. When grease or fat are ignited, they don't mix with water either. Not only do they not mix, they basically explode when you put them together. There are a few basic principles that take place when you throw water on an oil fire. First, oil is lighter than water. We have all seen the pretty rainbow from spilled oil around a gas station when it rains. That's the oil floating on the water. So the water goes to the bottom of the pan. Cooking oil is very hot. It is much hotter than the 212 degrees needed to boil water. The water hits this extremely hot area and immediately flashes to steam. Steam is powerful. It drives locomotives. A pound of water turning to steam has more explosive capacity than a pound of dynamite. The steam then throws the burning oil everywhere. You now get hit with a wall of burning oil and so does everything in the kitchen. This is a disaster. It is not a funny commercial. If you are frying, keep a lid nearby that fits on the pan you are using for cooking. Put the lid over the ignited grease or oil. Don't try to move the pan. Often moving the pan is hurried, clumsy, and ends in a spill, an injury, and a house fire. It is best not to fight the fire. Just get out of the house, and be sure everyone else knows there is a problem and leaves. Call 911. Thankfully, there are people who devote their lives to protecting us from fires. Let them handle it. That being said, keeping a fire extinguisher or baking soda next to the range can help you deal with small flare ups. Use sound judgment. Don't try and be a hero. When using a deep fryer, be sure to leave enough room for the food so the oil does not overflow. Fires often start by putting the food in when the oil is hot and the fryer overflows. Oil will bubble and froth when it is getting too hot. The frothing can sometimes overflow the pan. If you are cooking with oil in a dish, be sure the container is designed for the type of cooking you are doing. Corning wear and other similar serving dishes may not be designed to stand the excessive heat created by boiling oil. If you have a flare up in an oven, leave the oven door closed. The fire will run out of oxygen and have a difficult time sustaining itself. With any kitchen fire, turn off the heat source. This may sound basic but often in a panic we forget this.

Microwave ovens can also be a source of injury. Most adults know not to put metal in them. There are some metal trays that are safe, but metal saucepans or spoons in them are a danger and will destroy them. Never run a microwave without something in it such as water or food. When I test them during an inspection I put a wet paper towel in them. I run it for 10 seconds and the towel should come out hot. Running them with nothing in it will destroy the oven also. How do I know this? My daughter's friend used ours as a timer to go pick up a pizza. (No blonde jokes here, please). The most likely cause of injury with a microwave involves scalds or hand burns. The food and the pan are often very hot and we tend to be less careful when removing a dish from the microwave than we would from a regular oven.

I have never had turkey cooked in a deep fryer but I have heard many people rave about how tasty it is. That being said, according to the NFPA there is not a safe deep fryer for turkey. They use as much as 5 gallons of cooking oil. Many of them are unstable. The propane fryers are designed for outdoor use. In this climate, Thanksgiving and Christmas are too cold for outdoor cooking. This encourages people to cheat and use it in the garage or porch area. A fire here often spreads to the house quickly. Also, people set them up and then rain or snow starts so they try and move a hot cooker. Once again, this is a very dangerous idea. Rain or snow hitting the oil can cause it to spit out of the pot and result in burns. They do make an outdoor cooker that is oil free. The NFPA suggests you use that device. For more tips on safe cooking, go to the NFPA website, www.NFPA.org. The holidays should be a source of fun, family and friendship, not fire.

Maintenance tips:

Keep a working fire extinguisher that can be used on grease fires in the kitchen.

1. Use pot holders. Move slowly and cautiously. Most kitchen accidents happen due to hurrying with a hot

item. Short or tight sleeves. (Gloria in the Soprano's[11] had her robe catch on fire, remember?)
2. Keep the kids out of the kitchen.
3. Deep frying food? If you don't do it often set the deep fryer up outside.

---

[11] HBO series

SMOKE DETECTORS AND CO DETECTORS

Did you know your home is six times more likely to burn down in the Unites States than it is in Europe?[12] One very popular theory on it is that Europe has 220-240 volt electricity in their homes. That is twice as powerful as we have here. You may be wondering if the electricity is more powerful there, why are there more fires here? One word is the suspected culprit: Amateurs. In Europe, there is far less DIY electrical work being done. Therefore, the homes are wired better. The leading cause of damage to residences in the United States is not termites or fires; it is poor workmanship by Home Owners. But the focus of this article is protection and saving your life once the fire starts. Every residence in the United States should have working fire and smoke detectors, period. Well, we covered that issue. Actually there is a lot more to the subject. My Dad, while being a world class worrier, was way ahead of his time in some areas. I remember him getting a brand new 1957 Ford and going with him to Pep Boys to get seat belts installed. The mechanic joked with him about using the car for racing, but Dad failed to see the humor in it. I also remember him getting a job selling "smoke detectors" in 1960. They weren't smoke detectors as we know them. They were home fire alarms. They contained a bi-metallic element that, when heated, sprung a piece of metal. This completed a circuit and sounded a very loud alarm. I remember him demonstrating it to us with a match. That principle, a spring loaded bi-metallic element, is the basic operating mechanism in many fire sprinklers today. We'll talk about that later.

Back to the smoke detectors. There are two types of sensing devices contained in smoke detectors. There is an

---

[12] Homexam, Larry Reavis

ionization sensing device and a photoelectric sensing device.[13] The first uses radio activity to sense smoke. The second has some type of light crossing a field. If the light is dispersed by smoke, the sensor goes off. They also make smoke detectors that have both forms of sensing devices. The ionization sensor is cheaper but will not detect smoldering fires with very little smoke as quickly as the photoelectric sensor. They are also cheaper. All three are available as battery powered devices and hard wired protection. Hard wired means they are connected to regular electrical system of the building. Hard wired systems also have a battery back-up in them in the event of a power failure. They all chirp when the battery is low to provide a warning to change the battery. They should be installed by a licensed electrician. Smoke detection protection is usually part of a home security system. These systems should be monitored if at all possible. The cost of monitoring the system in our vacation home is about $20.00 a month. The life expectancy of smoke detectors varies. The radio activity in the ionization type has a half-life of about 400 years. That seems like enough for most of us. That being said, the recommended replacement cycle on smoke detectors is about 10 years. The recommended time for replacing the batteries is every year. October is National Fire Prevention Month. This makes sense because this is the time of year we crank up our heating systems after letting them sit all summer. They recommend replacing the batteries in October. My suggestion is don't wait for the battery to start chirping before you replace it.

Many municipalities require smoke detectors be present in the property prior to conveyance. In Pennsylvania, this ordinance varies greatly between municipalities. In existing structures, this is often a battery operated smoke detector. Multiple family units often have hard wired smoke detectors installed by an electrician. This may be required as a

---

[13] Wikipedia website

retrofit installation. They may also be connected to the local fire department. Many smoke detectors have sensors so if one goes off, they all go off. A hard wired interconnected system is required on all new construction homes by the International Building Code since 2003[14]. How can I tell if the smoke detectors are hard wired? There is a little red light in the unit you can see from below. Another easy way to tell if it is your home is hard wired is to take the cover off. There will be two screws that the unit locks onto coming through the unit. Look for a wire coming through the ceiling into the unit. As a home inspector, I don't inspect smoke detectors. There are a variety of reasons. I don't take the covers off. They are plastic and the older plastic can be brittle and the clips that hold the cover in place may break off in older smoke detectors. Another reason I don't inspect them is smoke detectors are battery operated. Home Owners have been known to take the batteries with them when they move. The buyer saw me test it and now thinks it works, when the people took the batteries with them. I tell buyers to check them when they move in. How do you test them? The correct way to test a smoke detector is to blow smoke on it. The test button will tell you if the battery works, if the test button works, and if the sounding device works. It won't tell you if the sensor that detects smoke works. You need smoke to do this. I don't smoke and I don't want to create smoke and leave soot in someone's home. Another reason I don't inspect them is they are inexpensive. As a matter of fact, in some cases they are free. Local fire companies will have drives where they give away smoke detectors. My best advice for a homebuyer is to go through the home and test every smoke detector in the home before they spend a night in the house. It would not be the first time that a fire occurs on the first night the new owner spends in the house. Things get disturbed, wires can get broken, etc. during the moving out by the previous owner and the moving in by the new owner.

---

[14] International Residential Code, 2003

Now that we have discussed smoke detectors, remember, smoke detectors protect the bank slightly more than they protect you. The safety device that protects you the best in a fire is a carbon monoxide, (CO), sensor. The conventional wisdom is a carbon monoxide sensor should be present in all homes with fossil fuel burning devices and/or fireplaces. That is true, but I would like to expand it to include all homes. The carbon monoxide from a fire can cause problems before the smoke detector goes off. Carbon monoxide is a byproduct of an improperly burning fossil fuel. Smoldering fireplaces can produce significant amounts of carbon monoxide. Improperly burning gas appliances can as well. A famous tennis player was killed by carbon monoxide coming off an improperly burning gas fired heater. Walt Disney's mother was also killed by problems from a gas fired heater.[15] The scary thought about both of these sources is that there is little or no smoke that accompanies them. Therefore, the smoke detector calmly sits there and doesn't go off. Another source of carbon monoxide in the home is running a gas fired motor in a confined space. The most common occurrence of this is the car idling in the garage. Never run the car in the garage. Also, once you bring the car into the garage, leave the garage door open for ten minutes or so to allow it to air out. This reduces the potential for CO to enter the home. You will also hear about people running gas fired generators in a garage or basement, and killing the whole family. Your neighbor's stupidity can also kill you. There have been instances of people living in row homes and the carbon monoxide spreading from home to home. This can sicken people in several homes. It happens often with cars running in the garage of one home and the CO moving down the block. CO detectors operate on quantity and longevity. You need an elevated level of carbon monoxide being sustained for a specific period of time. A

---

[15] Justdisney.com, Walt Disney Biography

puff of cigarette smoke contains carbon monoxide. I could go off on a rant here about cigarette smoking. I'll keep it short. If you smoke cigarettes you should get a tattoo across your forehead that says "I am stupid". That being said, cigarette smoke will not normally set off the device. There are several types and models. The CO detector I recommend on all inspections is one that has an LED screen that gives you the quantity of CO present. The other merely sounds an alarm once the levels are dangerous. I prefer to see if the levels are rising so I can take action to protect myself rather than waiting for an alarm. If you are in a home and the CO detector goes off, open all the windows immediately. Then get out of the home. Call the fire department. If you know what is causing the CO, TURN IT OFF! AND, get out of the house. That might seem rather obvious, but it still should be stated. The fire department will come out with huge fans to air out the home as well as sensing devices to track down the source. Don't be timid about this; it is literally life and death. Remember, the source may be a neighbor's home and by calling the fire department you may be saving their lives. There is no way to test a CO detector other than the test button on them. So, test them annually as you do the smoke detector. CO detectors should be replaced every three years.

Maintenance tips:
1. Install smoke detectors AND CO detectors in your home. (Follow instructions with devices).
2. Replace the batteries in these devices every year.
3. Test these devices annually.
4. Replace CO detectors every 3 years, and smoke detectors every 10.
5. Have a fire escape route planned. Get those chain ladders you hook on the windows for bedrooms that don't have a window onto a roof.

DISHWASHERS

My daughter was living out of state in our vacation home. She called me once at 8:00 AM so I knew there was a problem. Money calls are usually later in the day. She said she walked into the kitchen and the floor was covered with water. She checked under the sink and there were no leaks. She had run the dishwasher the night before so she concluded it was leaking. It didn't surprise me. The dishwasher is a beautiful shade of avocado so you can guess its age. They normally last about 15 years so I knew it was due. My daughter said, "What should I do?" I said, "Wash the dishes by hand like I did as a kid!" There was silence on the line.

Dishwashers leak in two places. The seal fails where the motor under the unit attaches to the mechanism. This can leak slowly and create a wet spot under the unit that can sometimes breed mold. If you have a basement, you can check under it for wetness. If you have a home built on a slab, you won't discover this leak until the water flows out onto the floor. This seal was the culprit on our dishwasher. The repair involves pulling the unit out, removing the pump and replacing the seal. The repair costs a few hundred dollars. The second way they leak is the gasket on the door. This can also be replaced and the cost is, you guessed it, a few hundred dollars. Either way, a dishwasher leaking is going to cost you a few hundred dollars. If a dishwasher is not run for six months or more, these seals may dry out and leak. If this happens, clean up the mess, and run it again. The seals can sometimes swell and stop leaking. It's worth running it a second time to save the money.

If it leaks the second time, you now have to make a decision. Do I repair or replace? If the dishwasher is over 10 years old, my suggestion is replace it unless it was a very expensive model when new. If the seal at the pump fails this year, the seal in the door may fail next year. The next decision is buying a new unit. What do I get and why? My suggestion on any appliance that uses a significant amount of energy is to include the efficiency of the appliance heavily in your selection. I don't see anything getting cheaper to run in the foreseeable future. There are units that have a setting so you wash only the bottom shelf of dishes. This might be handy for a single person that rarely fills a dishwasher to capacity.

Are you one of those people that wash their dishes BEFORE you put them in the dishwasher? With newer dishwashers that's not a good idea. Most of the newer models have a sensor that monitors the dirt in the water. If the water is clean, it shortens the cycle, and stops washing. If you rinse the dishes off too thoroughly, the sensor will think the dishes are clean and not run a full cycle. You will then look at your dishes that may still be soiled and think your dishwasher is malfunctioning. So, the best bet is to put the dirty dishes in the dishwasher. The next matter to consider is noise. The cheaper the dishwasher, the louder it will be. The very inexpensive models have the motor and controls in the front with very little insulation. These tend to be very noisy creating decibel levels in the high 50's. The rock group the Who used to perform at about 110 decibels so it's not quite deafening, but it will interfere with normal conversation in the kitchen. The higher end models produce sound levels in the low 40's. Some are so quiet they put a light in the front that indicates the unit is running. This might be very important if you have a small living area such as a condominium. The better units have a timer that allows you to run it when you are gone or in the middle of the night.

We run ours when we go to bed, but that might not be the best system. If the unit leaks during the night, you might end up with flood. The better units have a sensor that detects leaking and will shut the unit off if it starts leaking.

The interior of the better units are stainless steel. The more expensive models also have stainless steel cabinets which are the current trend. What ever happened to avocado? If you have a model with a plastic lining, it tends to yellow in time. This is due to the water being basic rather than acidic. If you run the dishwasher through a cycle with Tang in the soap trays rather than soap, the ascorbic acid in the Tang will help reduce the yellowing. Lemon juice also works.

There are a wide range of options and choices available in dishwashers. The life expectancy on the new models is still about 15 years according to the sales people we met. This may vary with usage. A dishwasher is one of those things that was once a luxury, but has become a necessity. At least, that's what my daughter has told me. I still haven't figured out how the appliances know when I get caught up with my bills, and they then decide to fail, thus keeping me from getting ahead.

Maintenance tips:

1. Feel the gasket around the outside. It should be soft to touch. If it is hard, it may soon be leaking.
2. Don't worry about the little bit of water that sits in the bottom of the dishwasher. That keeps the seal wet and is normal.
3. If you have a plastic lined dishwasher, run Tang or some other mild acid source through it every six months to reduce the yellowing that occurs from the PH in the water.
4. Check the connection between the dishwasher and the drain. The pressure of the pump from the dishwasher can sometimes cause small leaks in this connection.
5. Run the dishwasher with Tang or a couple of Vitamin C tablets in the soap holder if the insides get yellow. It whitens them.

APPLIANCES

The clothes washer is an appliance that just keeps working. Check the hoses that supply water to the appliance. These hoses are rubber in most cases. They dry out, crack and will burst and they know when you are away. Nothing can ruin the return from a relaxing vacation like finding that the washer hoses broke on the first day you were away. These hoses can be replaced with metal braided flexible hoses. If you have rubber hoses, and they are old, replace them with metal. Check the hoses. If they are swelling or cracked, replace them. The hoses fail at the metal fittings where they connect to the wall. They can also be put on a single shut off lever that is easy to operate and easy to check. The safest system is to shut off the hoses when the washer is not in use. Another problem with washers is they can get out of balance from uneven loads. Most washers will level by lifting the back and setting it down gently. The back legs are designed to automatically level.

The drain for the washer should also be kept at about the same height as the washer. In some basements, the waste water line is elevated and drains into a line that may be several feet above the washer. This can put additional strain on the washer pump and lead to premature failure. The long-term solution is to drain the washer into a laundry tub that has an ejector pump, designed to pump the water higher. This is a much stronger pump that is built for the job. If you drain the washer into a laundry tub, get a lint sock for the drain. This will catch the lint that can eventually clog the laundry tub drain. Where do I get a lint sock? You know that stray sock that you keep finding in the laundry and can never seem to find a pair for it. That's it! It now has a purpose. You can attach it to the hose with a rubber band.

While in the laundry room, let's take a look at the dryer. Look behind the dryer. Is there a lot of lint there? Dryers can and do cause fires in homes if not maintained. Clothes dryers are the number one source of fires residentially in the U.S. Clean the vent hose for the dryer at least once a year. If four or more people live in the house, clean it at least twice a year. It disconnects rather easily with a large O ring holding it to the dryer. Check the outside vent. Is lint on the ground? Clean it out. A screwdriver works well at cleaning out around the little door on it. That flapping door should swing open when the dryer is on, and close when it is off. Metal is greatly preferred as the material for the dryer hose. The hose should not extend more than 6 feet in the home. Dryer vents should never vent into attics. The moisture can seriously damage the property. Also dryer vents laying on attic floors and run to the overhangs will fill up with water in the low spots, blocking the airflow and creating an unhealthy condition. If the dryer vents into an attic, use a metal hose. Be sure it runs to an outside vent, and is angled downward towards it.

Nothing lasts forever. Everything we use that's mechanical requires some kind of periodic maintenance. The consequences of not maintaining your appliances can be as simple as the unit failing. This can cost you hundreds of dollars years before you may have paid it, had you maintained it. The more complicated result can be fire, destruction of your home, and possible loss of life. A little attention can go a long way. Dirty vents cause fires. Your vent should never look like this.

Maintenance tips:

1. Clean the lint catcher for the dryer after every load of wash. (Shown on left).
2. Turn the water off to the washer whenever the

washer is not in use. You can do this. I trained our children from the time they were ten to do this.

3. If you use cloth fabric softeners, run water on the lint catcher every six months. The water should run right through it. If the holes are blocked, scrub it with an old toothbrush. Some fabric softeners have been  known to clog these holes, trapping heat and causing fires.

4. Clean the vent and the vent hose for the dryer once per year per person doing laundry there. (The college student that brings their wash home every weekend counts as living there.)

5. Replace the plastic vent hose with a metal vent hose.

6. Use metal braided hoses for the washer.

STAINS

Could the walls in your house be the back drop for a movie? Would it be a scary movie? Have you noticed faint shadowy lines creeping up the walls and across the ceilings that you swear weren't there last fall? Do you have what looks like coffee stains on your ceiling? Do you have a stain that looks bigger or seems to change shape, but you are really not sure? Are the walls or ceilings beginning to shed a white powdery substance that flutters mysteriously to the floor when no one is in the room? Your house probably isn't haunted. There are probably not coffee drinking gremlins dancing on the ceilings when no one is home. There is a logical explanation for just about every pattern of staining that appears on your walls. The obvious stains shown below appear to be from running water. The problem was caused by CONDENSATION, not a roof leak.

Let's start with the coffee stains from those gremlins. When a roof or the plumbing leaks, it picks up dirt in its travels. The water will run to the lowest point. That lowest point may be a crack or opening in the drywall, or a separation in the ceiling tiles. The water drips from there. The water will leave tiny rings with a speck of dirt in the middle that look like coffee stains. Years ago I participated in the shooting of a video for a roofing company and to "make" the stains we brewed a pot of coffee and splashed it on the ceiling.

They are usually the result of a significant leak in the roof or plumbing. This winter, 2009-10, many homes experienced "ice dam" leaking from the snow melting on the roof. You may think your home was spared. Look at the top of the window frames on the north side of your home. You may find evidence of leaking you overlooked. Having a roof leak and not fixing it can be a scary proposition.

Now let's look at the mysterious white powder. Usually this will appear over the fireplace or where some other penetration joins the ceiling. This can be a tough one to completely remove. The chimney is made of porous masonry material that absorbs water. This water then migrates past the roof flashing. The flashing material generally penetrates the masonry wall about 1½". A light wind can drive moisture through an 18" stone wall in about 8 hours. The wind drives the water, soaking into the chimney. It then migrates down into the heated area. The water, in its travels, picks up salts and calcium. The heat inside the house evaporates the water and residual deposits remain, creating the white powder you see. Vibrations in the house from trucks on the street to your child's subwoofer can cause the powder to mysteriously fall when no one is in the room. Waterproofing the masonry areas with elastomeric paint or silicone helps reduce this, but this leak can be insidious.

You have dark shadows appearing as faint lines on the ceiling, often on cathedral ceiling. You tell your husband and he looks at you funny, and mumbles something about an optometrist. These lines are real. It's not your imagination. When they insulate a ceiling, the insulation is rarely installed uniformly. This creates warm and cold spots side by side on the same wall in relatively straight lines. Dirt accumulates on the cold spots. Warm air moves faster on the warm areas keeping the dirt particles suspended. They then settle on the colder adjoining spots. Another phenomenon occurs on these cold areas. Moisture accumulates on them. Moisture is attracted to cold surfaces. The dirt then clings to the cold surface. This dirt combines with the moisture to provide a perfect habitat for mold spores to germinate and create a colony. These stains get worse in the winter. When inspecting homes, I use a laser thermometer that has read as little as a 2 degree temperature difference between these two areas which is just enough to create the lines.

When you are cleaning suspected mold areas, use a mild bleach and water solution. Obviously do not add ammonia to bleach, the gases can be fatal. Lastly, do not use cleaners with phosphates when cleaning suspected molds. Phosphates are like steroids to molds. If you are cleaning suspected mold areas, check www.epa.gov and follow the search to mold for detailed instructions on how to clean it. This stain requires periodic cleaning.

Every day you look at that stain, and you can't tell if it's getting bigger, smaller or changing shape. Take a pencil and outline the pattern of the stain. Then check it after several rains and see if it moves past the pencil line. Keep in mind that different conditions will cause different leaks. If the roof leaks in every rain or with melting snow, it is the roof. That problem is easy to diagnose. If it only leaks under certain conditions, it's not the roof. I have also found that if you haven't had the stain get bigger in six months, and you are sure the leak "went away," paint the ceiling. It's the surest way to have the leak come back with the next rain, and ruin your new paint job. Roofs do not heal themselves. And caulk and roof cement are not long term solutions to roof problems. If only Lady Macbeth had these tips, she may not have been crying "Out, out, damn spot!"

Maintenance tips:

1. Wipe down the walls with a good household cleaner about once a year. Don't use too much water. Wipe

them down with a second rag to dry them right after you wash them. Don't use phosphate cleaners on suspected mold. Its' like putting the mold on steroids.

2. Clean out the cob webs from the corners. A rag on a broom works well, but they do have cleaning tools made for this purpose.

3. Clean off the ceiling fan monthly in the winter. If you forget to clean it and then turn it on in the spring, you will be amazed at how much dust has accumulated. The dust doesn't accumulate in the summer when it's in use.

4. What's the difference between a spider web and a cob web? Spider webs are still occupied by spiders. Cob webs are vacant. Sort of like abandon homes for spiders.

PAINTING DO'S

Let's talk about what you should do when painting your home. This is a project many Home Owners will tackle. Start by getting a small quantity of the paint and do a test area in an inconspicuous spot and see if the color is like the brochure. There's a house in every neighborhood that you drive by and say "What were they thinking?" The color is so loud you can almost hear it. A small sample of a color a couple inches wide can look a lot different when you cover several hundred square feet with it. Most paint stores will not let you return custom colors, so if you buy a lot of one color, and after doing a wall, decide this isn't going to work, you may be stuck with it. Bright colors tend to get a lot brighter when they cover a larger area. My wife often sends me back upstairs to get changed when we are going out, so I'm not the best person at matching colors, but if you are doing the home in one color and the trim in another color, making the trim a lighter color seems to work better in most cases. If the windows for example are darker, the house can look like it has black eyes.

Always get a primer and paint made by the same company. Stick with one brand all the way through. If you have a problem with it, and end up calling the manufacturer, they won't listen to you if you used someone else's primer and their paint. Also, save your receipts and the name of the color used. You would be amazed at how many shades of white there are. You can get bad paint. When you open the can, if it smells like rotten eggs or sulfur, take it back. Also if it is not adhering well to the test area, go back to the retailer and find out why. The test area should be cleaned before painting. Any holes should be filled with exterior grade wood fillers such as wood putty. Allow the filler to dry, and then paint the area with your primer and one finished coat. Once the paint has dried, press adhesive tape onto the paint and pull it off quickly like you would pull off a band aid. If the paint comes off you may be doing something wrong. If the primer pulls off, the surface may be dirty or poorly prepared. If the finished coat pulls off the primer, they may not be compatible. Check back with the store to be sure you are matching the right paint and primer. Once you have started painting, be ready to keep on painting. By that I mean, put on the second coat within a few days of the first coat. Don't wait any longer to paint. The second coat takes much less time and much less paint than the first coat. The second coat is well worth the effort, particularly if it is an area exposed to the weather. A second coat of paint now takes much less time than starting over and repainting the whole house in a few years. We mentioned filling in any cracks or divots in the wood with filler. Be sure and caulk any openings around the wood trim or windows. Seal these areas with a caulk that is compatible with the paint. A particular concern is any electrical or plumbing openings in the wall. While you are at it, clean out the dryer vent. Did you know that the clothes dryer is the number one cause of residential fires? (I know I mentioned it before, but it is important). Keeping the vent and hose clean makes your house a lot safer.

So you want to paint your brick wall? Please don't. It's just me, but I love a beautiful brick wall. If you must paint it, be sure the surface is clean and free of sand and loose mortar. If there is extensive cracking, get the wall pointed and serviced before you paint it. Paint won't hold a brick wall together. Then paint it with acrylic latex finished paint. You won't need a primer for it. If you are painting vinyl shudders, tell the clerk at the paint store what you are painting and they can guide you to a compatible product. The operative word here is "paint store". Behr is a great paint and it is sold by a major chain. While you may get a clerk that is very knowledgeable, my experience has been that I got the best advice at a paint store. I was shopping for paint for my pool's sliding board and the clerk at a major home center sent me to a paint store. I really respected her and thanked her for that. She was looking out for my best interests. Vinyl moves a great deal. A ten foot section of vinyl may expand and contract as much as 1/2" between winter and summer. The paint may not want to move this much so it will lose its grip and peel off. Some people have had success painting vinyl siding. If you do paint it, clean the surface with rubbing alcohol, and paint with acrylic latex paint. Most paint companies will not guarantee paint on vinyl siding. If you are painting a metal roof, paint it with a light color. This past summer we checked the temperature on a metal roof with a laser thermometer and it was 162 degrees. The heat from the metal roof can radiate back into the house. I was doing an inspection under these exact conditions. The rooms under the metal roof were 9 degrees warmer than the rest of the 2nd floor. Hot air rises, but radiant heat can travel back into the attic. The roof surface also moves less if it is not as hot. Every time the roof moves, the fasteners can pull loose, and the metal around the fastener can tear causing a leak. If the air stayed seventy degrees year round, our houses would require a lot less maintenance.

And of course, dress right for the occasion. Wear eye protection when sanding, using cleaners that can damage the eyes, or painting overhead. Use dust masks if you are sanding and creating a lot of dust. If the house is older, pre-1978, there is always the possibility of lead paint being air born during the sanding. Call 1-800-LEAD-FYI for more information about lead.

Painting is work. The preparation is time consuming, but the rewards are great. It is often the least expensive home project you can do and, unless you have rather "unique" tastes in color, it adds to the property value and curb appeal. Don't be afraid to ask questions. Ask the people at the paint store. Often, they can be very helpful. One last tip is to be very careful if you are working on a ladder. Make sure the ladder is stable, on the proper angle off the wall. Watch out for electrical wires when you set it up, and always keep your belly button between the rails or sides of the ladder. If you keep your center of gravity on the ladder, you are less likely to fall. Be careful, it's a long way down.

PAINTING DON'TS

When last we spoke, we were talking about the "dos" of painting your home. Painting is one of those jobs that if you procrastinate, the wood can be damaged by water entry, making the job more work and more money. Quick test. The number one cause of damage to residential properties is: A) Termites, B) Fires, C) Vandalism, or 4) Poor workmanship by well-meaning Home Owners? If you guessed 4, you are correct. There are many home projects that are beyond the scope of the Home Owner, but because of Contractor's prices, they decide to do it themselves. One project that many home owners tackle with relatively high success is painting the home. Painting a room is a project that can often be knocked out in a weekend with relatively low risk of injury. Sure there's the sore neck and shoulders, but that's a small price to pay for the rewards of doing it yourself. The work in painting is in the preparation. The surface should be cleaned and in some cases sanded prior to the painting. Occasionally there is also some carpentry or drywall work that must be done as part of the preparation. Fall is a great time to paint because you can leave the windows open and the outside temperature is usually pleasant with low humidity. There are a lot of little tricks to painting that will greatly improve your results. Don't buy cheap paints. After all that work of painting, you want your finished product to look nice for a while. My son in law, who prides himself in his knowledge of home maintenance, swears by Behr Paints.[16] Paint that is 100% acrylic is best. Don't paint when it is above 90 degrees or below 50 degrees. Painting above 90 degrees is not a problem for me. I don't like to get more than about ten feet from our pool when it's that hot. Some oil based paints can be applied at lower temperatures. Check the instructions on the can. Cooler weather makes the paint thicker and it has a harder time grabbing the surface. Don't

---

[16] Available at Home Depot

paint in direct sun at any temperature. The sun causes the paint to dry too fast. Paint the sunny side early in the morning before the sun hits it, or later in the day after the direct sun has passed.

If applying a second coat, let the first coat dry. Latex paint on a very porous surface such as new drywall will dry very quickly and the second coat can often be applied a few hours after the first. However, if using oil based paint on exterior trim for example, allow one to three days for drying. Don't wait more than two weeks to apply the second coat under any conditions. If you wait too long, the second coat has trouble bonding to the first coat. More is not always better. If you are painting areas protected from the rain, such as the soffits, paint them every other time you paint the house. Don't paint the brush dry. It's nice to squeeze every last drop of paint off the brush, but this can leave unsightly brush marks. Use the inside of the can to remove excess paint from the brush after you dip it in the can. When you are painting, don't use the whole can as your paint source. Pour some in a smaller container such as a gallon milk jug with part of the top cut off. Slap the brush against the sides to remove the excess paint each time you dip. If you use the can and wipe the excess on the top of the can, you can damage the bristles and it can get messy. Don't use a sprayer system unless you have a professional who has used it before working with you. Airless systems work well, but be sure you have proper protection for your face and breathing. When doing larger areas, a good roller works well. Don't get cheap brushes or rollers. Nylon bristles are good, and Purdy makes good brushes. Good brushes feel soft. They are also flexible. If you have trouble bending the bristles in the store, you will feel it when you are panting. If you are using oil paints, get brushes with natural bristles. They will clean up easier. "China bristle brushes" are made from hogs in China and work well with oil, poorly with latex paint. A 3/4" nap on the roller is fine for most textured surfaces. A smaller nap is fine on most other surfaces. I don't know if there are any paints made in China on the market, but I would avoid them in light of their apparent propensity for adding lead to just about everything they paint. During your prep work, be careful if you use a high pressure spray to clean the wood. If the wood is damaged, you can force water into the wood that may take months to get out. If you paint over the wet surface, the paint may not adhere. It may cover well while painting, but the heat of the sun will pull the moisture out later, causing the paint to peel. You also don't want to force water between cracks between the boards or the gaps around windows. Again, the water may take forever to drain out, or it may not drain out at all, and cause a growth behind the wall. Don't use attachments for your electric drill or a wire brush to remove old paint. They can leave metal fibers in the wood that later will rust through. Use sand paper and good old fashioned "elbow grease." Also, don't use a torch to burn off old paint. The worst that can happen is you burn the house down. This happens more often than you think. If there is lead paint under the layers of paint, the lead vaporizes and you can inhale it causing lead paint poisoning. If you are not sure about what you are doing, Sears has a toll free hot line, 1-800-9- PAINTS. Also, don't be afraid to ask the clerk in the store. In some cases they can be very helpful. Another advantage of painting in the fall is that the lower humidity helps the wood surfaces to dry before you paint. A good professional painting contractor will check the moisture levels in the wood before they paint. Don't use "waiting until fall" as a reason not to paint. If she wants that bedroom painted, my advice it to get right on it.

So you want to use oil based paints? I mentioned earlier I painted the sliding board for the pool with oil based paint. I cleaned it with a good glass cleaner first; after all, fiberglass is glass. I then applied an oil based primer. The primer was white. I brushed it on, but I could have used a roller. I put on two coats of primer. The second went much faster than the first. The next weekend I applied the finished coat of paint. The results were excellent. It was the first time in years that I had used oil based paint. It covers very well. The smell is a little strong and I was glad I was working outside. The cleanup is a little slower and I recommend doing it outside, again due to the smell of the solvents. If you are painting something that is exposed to the elements year round such as metal lawn furniture or other exterior items, consider painting them with oil based paints. They cover very well, and so far, they hold up extremely well.

LEAD PAINT

If your home was built before 1978 there is a possibility that lead paint was used on your house. Lead was an additive put into paint to make it better. It was used in better quality paint and therefore was most often used on better quality homes. It was often added to exterior paint more than interior paint but it can be present in either areas. It was phased out of residential use in the 1960's along with asbestos, but it was not completely banned as a residential building product until 1978. Painters often had deteriorating mental conditions as they aged, and the principle reason was exposure to chemicals, most notably lead.

How does lead paint poisoning occur? One must ingest lead particles into the body. Lead can enter the body from breathing paint dust that contains lead particles. It can also occur by drinking water with elevated levels of lead. Small children often get it by putting objects in their mouth that contain lead paint or are coated with lead paint dust. Lead can enter the drinking water through lead water mains in older homes. If you have a lead water main the chances are pretty good that the water may not contain elevated levels due to the water running through the main and removing the contaminants in time. Before you spend thousands of dollars to replace the water line have the water tested. Lead can also enter through the solder that was used in homes prior to 1978. The water lines in the home were a solder mix that contained lead and again it can leach into the water. The solder mix was changed in the 1970's and lead was phased out. Homes built prior to the 1970's may have trace amounts of lead in the water. Again, in time, the amount diminishes. It was suggested at the time that you run water for a few minutes in the morning before you use the water for drinking. The first batch of water was suspected of containing the most lead as it accumulated in the still water in the lines.

Lead is heavy. The dust from lead is heavier than ordinary dust. (Ordinary dust is primarily dander from skin, most often human skin). Because the dust is heavy, it falls to the ground quickly. To get lead paint poisoning from the dust, the most common exposure is by scraping the old paint off woodwork, walls or window frames that were painted with lead. Another way that lead is freed from the paint and exposure is possible is the simple act of opening and closing windows and doorways that were painted with lead. The movement of the two surfaces causes lead dust to become airborne. By replacing older windows you greatly reduce the potential for exposure to lead paint. Once the lead enters the body, the body gets confused. Your blood stream thinks lead is calcium. So your body takes the lead and stores it in the bones. Small children are particularly vulnerable because their bones are growing and trying to grab as much calcium as possible. That being said, lead poisoning can occur at any age. The elderly are also more vulnerable. Once the lead is in the bones, it affects the body's ability to transport oxygen throughout the body. It affects the red blood cells that carry oxygen. With a reduced level of red blood cells, you now have a reduction in oxygen. This reduction in oxygen levels effects how the brain functions. The end result can be impaired brain activity. Lead paint poisoning also affects other function of the body. It can appear in a variety of symptoms from headaches, loss of appetite, abdominal problems, cramps, etc. If you suspect lead paint poisoning, seek medical advice. They can test the blood of those suspected of exposure. Eliminating exposure to lead can reduce the lead in the body and the body eventually reverses many of the symptoms in adults. Children have a far more difficult time reversing the conditions and may suffer long term effects from lead paint poisoning. If you live in an older home, it makes sense to have the home tested for the presence of lead in the paint and drinking water.

The best test for lead in the paint is rather sophisticated. The inspector uses an XRF gun and basically shoots x-rays into the wood and walls. If there is lead present in the area tested, the x-rays bounce back and the gun makes a reading. The inspector presents a detailed report that will show the lead levels in literally hundreds of locations throughout the house. The tests cost about $300 to $500 depending on your geographic area and the size of the job. If you are having this done, have the inspector test any old painted children's furniture as well. Lead paint was sometimes used on furniture and toys. There was a recent recall on toys made in China that contained elevated levels of lead. We can blame the Chinese for the lead but, in my humble opinion we have only ourselves to blame. We buy items based on price. We have a demand for cheap items. This demand has forced American manufacturers to close their doors. We are then at the mercy of whatever these foreign countries will ship over here. We killed our own industries, so we have no right to complain about the junk we buy when we demanded it. We did it to ourselves. Isn't globalization grand? Sorry, once again, I digress.

Maintenance Tips:

1.   Get a preliminary test for lead done on windows and areas of friction between two pieces of painted wood. Buy a home test kit.
2.   Get your drinking water tested. Get a filtration system for your water. Some of these small pitcher type filters claim to remove lead.
3.   DON'T buy bottled water in little serving size bottles.
4.   Get a reusable drinking water thermos that is rated to not give off any toxic chemicals. Lead is only one problem. Fill the bottle from a pitcher or have a home water filtrations system.
5.   The regulations on lead may vary from state to state. As of this writing, a contractor who is working on a home built before 1978 must have the home

tested for lead BEFORE work starts. He must then have the lead removed by a contractor certified to remove it. Many contractors are getting this certification. Check your contractor's credentials. To be completely safe, call your municipal building inspector. They will be completely current with regulations that apply to your home.

PULL DOWN STAIRS

Junk expands to the size of the container. Although some birds such as crows and eagles, have been known to take seemingly useless items back to their nest and keep them, no animal on earth can match man's affinity for accumulating useless belongings. In order to feed this idiosyncrasy we find places within the house to store them. Things we will never use again, such as a complete set of McDonald's plates or your daughter's Strawberry Shortcake collection, are viewed as family heirlooms and tucked away with the reverence attached to relics. Where do we put them? Let's look at the attic. How do we get there? That's the problem.

Attics in newer homes are designed so we won't use them for storage. The opening is small, usually not much more than two feet square. The Builder puts it in a narrow closet. It opens into an attic with insulation three to six inches above the ceiling joists, which makes navigation up there treacherous and storage impossible. Also truss support systems in attics are not designed to support loads. The solution? We buy pull down stairs, throw down flooring, and turn this vast wasteland into a vault to store our memories. Installing these stairs is a project many weekend warriors can tackle. The stairs come in a variety of shapes and sizes. Bessler is the most recognized manufacturer of these stairs, although there are others who make very nice units. Installing them may involve the removal of some structural members, and then doubling up across the opening to pick up the support. The stairs are very self-contained units, and come complete with detailed directions and hardware. It's fairly important that you buy the right stairs for your home.

The units come in two widths. A standard unit will install when the ceiling joists are sixteen inches on center, or typical frame construction. This involves removing one joist the size of the opening and doubling up the supports around it. The second size is designed for a truss support attic and fits exactly between two trusses. They are twenty four inches on center. Do not cut into a truss system and try to frame around it as you would with standard frame construction. They are engineered systems and any variation in them can drastically compromise their strength. The stairs must run parallel and between the trusses. The right stairs for you can vary. The best units are complete stairways that roll down and provide an actual stairway complete with railing. They cost $800 to $1,000, and may be more than some Home Owners can tackle as a weekend project. They weigh about two hundred pounds and installation can require several people. If you go with these stairs, hire somebody. The most popular units involve a three section folding stairway. These stairs require far less space, but are far less sturdy. They are generally rated at about 250 to 300 lbs. This means only one person on the stairs at a time. Also, carry small boxes up the stairs. The installation requires some finished trim work or drywall repair in the living area once it is installed. These stairs are most often installed in the center hall. If space allows, installing it in the master bed room closet may be safer as these stairs can be viewed as an attraction to curious children. There are some things to consider when installing these stairs. If you install it in the garage, they create a break in the fire protection built into your

 garage. Garage walls built today have a minimum of a one hour fire rating to isolate a fire in the garage from the house. If you install pull down stairs, the board on the bottom of the stairs is normally 3/8" plywood. Fire will eat through this in no

time, and the fire will be drawn to the oxygen source in the attic, and soon engulf the house. Install a piece of 5/8" drywall on the bottom of the stairs if they are installed in the garage.

The better pull-down stairs come with insulation. The R value or the resistance to heat flow rating is usually less than 10. The rest of the attic is rated R30 to R40. This creates a "chimney effect" and the heat is pulled out of the house through those attic vents that should not be closed off. When you have the stairs open, take a close look at the perimeter and you will see little black lines. These are dust particles caused by the air racing through the gaps around the edges. The solution is to build an insulated box over the stairs. (See previous page). Climb up into the attic and put the stairs up. Have someone below to pull them down when you are done, or opening them from above may be like a scene from a Chevy Chase movie. Build the box with plenty of room for the stairs inside it. A few inches of Styrofoam should work. It has a much higher R value than fiberglass and it is rigid. It is easily glued or screwed to line the box. The finished box will be heavy, and a bit cumbersome to get into the attic. If you have the room, cut your pieces of wood in the garage and build the box in the attic. Once assembled, you can slide it over the opening as you leave the attic. See the next section for more information on this. Now you have room to store all those things that were of little value when you bought them and of less value the longer we keep them. But, we keep them for their great ambiguous self-assigned worth known as "sentimental value."

Maintenance tips:

1. Check the pull down stairs once a year. Be sure the bolts are tight and the rails haven't cracked.
2. Put weight on only the bottom step first and work your way up slowly.

3. When closing it, put the pull down string back up into the attic so the children aren't tempted to pull down the stairs.

WINTERIZING YOUR HOME

We have been told that heating bills will not be as severe as in the past. My feeling is that heating bills are just like the price of gasoline. They are seasonally affected. The season that causes them to drop the most is the election season. Regardless of the price of fuel, it makes sense to reduce your usage any way you can. One way most home owners can conserve energy is adding insulation to your attic access.

Just about every home has access to an area above the living space. It is often accessible from a small hatch located in a closet. Newer homes have small access hatches and they are tucked away so access is difficult. This is done for a reason. They don't want you going up there. If you have a small access panel, insulating it is pretty simple. Buy some weather stripping. The type you put around an exterior door is fine. The access panel is often a piece of 3/8" plywood or drywall. Remove the panel and clean off the ledge on the inside of the access area. Then install the weather stripping just as you would insulate a doorway. While you're at it, take a look at the access area. If there are dark streaks, that evidence of heat loss in the past. The streaks are caused by dust traveling in the heat as it says good bye. This access hatch is through a wall into a partial attic area.

Next, pick up a 4' x 8' sheet of 2" rigid insulation and construction glue. You will also need a utility knife and a caulking gun. Cut at least two pieces of the insulation and glue them to the top of the panel. This will give you an R value of between 15 and 20 on the hatch. An R value is a rating given to materials to determine its ability to resist the flow of heat. Most of your attic should have an R value of 30 to 40. You can add more pieces of insulation to the panel if you like, but be sure you can still tilt it and get it back into the hatch. If you climb up into the attic to add the insulation to the hatch, you can build it up more and just lower it down over the opening. The access to your attic has been acting like a chimney allowing heat to pour into your attic. No insulation on the hatch is a little like leaving a window open in a bedroom. The heat loss is significant. Don't seal the opening with caulk or tape. You may need to get up there in the future and removing it can damage the hatch or the ceiling around it.

If you have pull down stairs for your attic, it gets a little tricky. Pull the stairs down and get into the attic. Now, have someone fold up the stairs and close the access. Make sure you are on good terms with this person or they may decide to leave you up there for a while. Measure the height of the stairs and the size of the opening. Now take the same type of insulation I recommended for the small access hatch and make a box to cover the stairs. Be sure to make the top piece several inches wider and longer than the opening to allow for the insulation on the sides of the

 box. You will need long screws to hold the sides together. You can try gluing the edges together but when you cut the insulation, the edge is often a little uneven and glue is not very effective. If you want to give the box some rigidity, make a frame from 2" x 3"s and screw the insulation to the wood. This will do two things. It will make the box more permanent, and it will add weight to press down around the sides. You can caulk the seams in the box to make them more air tight. Now climb down out of the attic and slide the box over the opening. The stairs should fit inside the box without lifting it. Obviously, making the box a few inches bigger is fine. There is a picture of a well-made box in the Pull Down Stairs section of this manual.

Here are a couple of tips for those who never venture into the attic. WALK ONLY ON THE WOOD CEILING JOISTS! This is very important. If you walk on the insulated areas, there is only drywall supporting you and you will fall through. We performed a home inspection where the home owner fell through his ceiling when he went into the attic to change the filter on his A/C unit. He fell eight feet and landed on his bed. If he had fallen about five feet to his left, he would have fallen over his front door center hall. The fall there was about thirty feet onto a tile floor. A tragedy!

While you are in the attic, don't insulate the vents to the outside. You need these vents open more in the winter than you do in the summer. Closing them off will trap 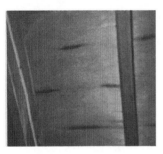 moisture contained in the warm air that works its way into the attic. This moisture condenses and rots the wood in your attic. If you have rust on the nails coming through the roof deck, you may need more ventilation in your attic. Are you looking for something to do on Thanksgiving weekend? I thought so. It's a great time to clean your gutters. Just about all the leaves are down and the gutters haven't frozen yet. But once again, be careful. Most home accidents involve a home owner and a ladder. The picture above shows nails rusting from condensation in the attic. That's right. They [17]were caused by internal moisture not leaks.

How much insulation should I have? This is a question that often comes up when I am dealing with home owners. The amount of insulation required by Codes varies depending upon your geographic location. For many areas an R value of R40 is considered adequate. An "R" value is a material's

[17] Home Tune-Up, Doris Ikle, CMC Energy Services

ability to resist the flow of heat. This varies considerably from product to product. The most popular insulation used today is fiberglass. The insulation value of the fiberglass comes not so much from the material itself, but more from the air pockets contained in the loft or fluffiness of the material. Adding insulation is a great idea. Going from none to 8-10" in your attic can drastically reduce your fuel usage and add a great deal of comfort to the 2nd floor. There is a point of diminishing returns. More is not always better. There is a point at which the payoff for additional insulation is negligible. (See the graph below. I know it's tough to read, so I am about to explain it, Sorry.). If you have no insulation and you increase it to R 30 you can go from no savings to about $200.00. If you add more insulation and take it to R 50 you will only save about $20.00 more in a heating season.

Where do I put it? As discussed in the attic ventilation

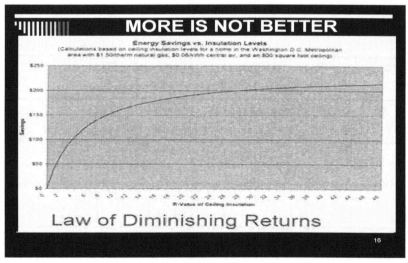

section, you want a nice clean air flow from the eaves to the ridge. Therefore, the insulation should be on the attic floor. If you are finishing off your attic, and you want to have it as a heated or conditioned space, leave at least a 2 inch space between the insulation and the underside of the roofing. This area can be sealed off from the heated area but it should have clear air flow from the eaves to the ridge. Achieving this clear air flow can be tricky for the average home owner so you might want to hire a contractor who is familiar with this type of insulation. If he doesn't think this air space is important, hire a different contractor. You might be surprised at how many contractors do not fully understand this concept. If you are insulating the attic, here are a few of tips. Get a HEPA rated respirator with replaceable filters. Wear goggles over your eyes, a long sleeve shirt, and gloves. Then shower as soon as you are done. Everyone reacts differently to fiberglass exposure, but my advice is to protect yourself and wash it off quickly after you are done.

Another approach to insulating the attic is to spray foam insulation on the underside of the wood deck. This will provide lots of insulation. It will also reduce the radiant heat reflecting downward, and it provides its own vapor barrier. (See Attic Ventilation section for more on vapor barriers). I will admit I have inspected a limited number of homes insulated this way. One that I inspected had a section with a cathedral ceiling where there was no access to install the foam. The moisture in the house was drawn to this area. The result was stains and streaks of water running out of the drywall and down the walls in this room in the winter. If foam is installed, it must be done to the whole house. If there is an area that is not accessible for the foam, this area should be very well ventilated to reduce the likelihood of this problem. From what I have read on foam being used as an insulator, it seems to work best if installed during original construction. There are some retrofit applications such as the basement or crawl space band joist areas where it seems to work well. My suggestion is if you are using foam to insulate an attic area for the purpose of making it a living area, or protecting it because HVAC equipment is there, leave this job to a professional with lots of experience. There are many little details that can create problems if not properly addressed. One last item, many shingle manufacturers will not issue warranties on roofs with "compact roof panel assemblies" or insulation right up against the underside of the roof. This can affect the surface temperature of the roof. Take these factors into account when selecting an insulation system for your attic.

On the second floor, the windows are the enemy. Reglazing single pane windows can greatly reduce heat loss. Carefully hold a flame near the windows. Go around the perimeter of the window and watch for the flame to flicker. This test works best on a windy day. If the flame moves, you have air infiltration. A thin bead of caulk can do wonders in reducing air flow. If the sashes are loose enough to shake, there is significant heat loss. Consider replacement windows if they cannot be repaired. You can replace a few each year and work your way around the house. If you replace one or two, you may pay a premium. Replacing four or more at a time will get you a better price. In the short term, tape at the junction of the sash and the frame helps, as do those clear plastic windows that you tear off at the end of the season. Don't laugh, they are very effective.

There is also a Plexiglas window system that is held in place magnetically. These are very effective, particularly when insulating metal casement windows that you may want to keep for architectural reasons. When checking your storm windows, clean out the space between the prime window and the storm window. Be sure the weep holes in the bottom of the windows are open. This is another opening that overzealous handymen want to close off. On the first floor, you can seal the windows, and also add weather stripping to all the doorways. Put your hand at the bottom of the doorway and see if you can feel a draft. There is weather stripping that can be put between the door and the frame, and you can also add a sweep to the bottom of the door. There is an item I see advertised on TV that insulates the inside as well as the outside of the bottom of the door.[18] I have one. My experience has been that keeping it in place is difficult. It also catches on the floor. We have it on a door that gets very little use, and it is very effective. It definitely was worth the $10.00. Now for the basement. Start by insulating the perimeter where the floor joists sit on the foundation. If you have an unheated crawl space, insulate the space between the crawl space and all heated areas. This can be difficult. Be sure any pipes or duct work in unheated crawl spaces are insulated. If you have insulated the crawl space properly, including the pipes and the duct work, you can leave the vents in the crawl space open. I personally don't see an advantage to insulating a basement ceiling if your central heating system is in the basement. Don't insulate your water heater. The manufacturers of the units discourage this for a variety of reasons.

While you are winterizing the home, check to be sure no one has moved into the fireplace flue during the summer. Raccoons love to nest in them. Tap on the damper loudly and wait a few seconds. If hear the scamper of little feet, don't open it. Give it a few minutes then tap again. If you had a critter move in, get a professional to clean it out. You are dealing with an open fire and your house. Don't take chances. Have your entire chimney cleaned once a year if you use it often. If you only use it on big holidays, get it cleaned professionally every other year. Turn off all the

---

[18] Twin Draft Guard, Taylorgifts.com

water to the outside. Then go outside and open the faucets. They have frost free faucets, but I have seen them occasionally freeze in severe conditions. Treat them as you would regular faucets. (There is more on freezing pipes in the next section). After all, you are not going out there to wash the car in January. Be sure your smoke detectors are working. Change the battery in October, its fire prevention month. A few other items to address since you are now thinking house: Drain a few gallons of water from the bottom of the water heater to reduce sediment build up in the bottom. Also, check the temperature setting on the water heater, and check the hood damper. It should be free of rust or corrosion. Clean the coils for the refrigerator. Hold a tissue at the base of the refrigerator. It should be pulled under the refrigerator on one side and blow out on the other, as you move it across the front of the unit. Clean the range hood of grease, and flush out the garbage disposal. And one last thing, clean the whole house! Vacuum out the heat registers as well. Everyone talks about spring cleaning. It is more important from a health standpoint to clean your house in the fall than in the spring. In the winter, houses are closed up, so dust, pet hairs, molds, and other air pollutants hang around in the carpets and every time you walk you stir them up. Clean all those irritants out now, and you may have a healthier winter. If you have gas or oil burning appliances in your home, or a wood burning fireplace or stove, get carbon monoxide detectors. The Night Hawk battery operated model is excellent. In purchasing a CO detector, get the kind that has a digital display so you can see if the amount of carbon monoxide is rising in a home before the alarm goes off. There are inexpensive cards that change color in the presence of carbon monoxide. Don't count on them. All they will do is make the coroner's job easier. Most CO deaths occur at night. Changing colors on a card won't awaken you. It's a good idea to have more than one detector. Run them next to each other for about 8 hours in the kitchen to cross check their accuracy. Other sources of

CO in the home are fumes from the garage, and the cleaning cycle on your self-cleaning oven. Even electric ovens can give off CO while cleaning the oven. Open a window during the cleaning cycle. Now it's time to stack the firewood off the ground, and watch football.

FREEZING PIPES

"Tis the season for pipes to freeze," is not exactly how the seasonal jingle was written, but it's true. Pipes freeze in the winter. And when they freeze, they split, causing untold damage. The first obvious job is to replace the broken pipe. The real problem is the surrounding damage. The water damages walls, ceilings, floors, basements can fill with water, mold can grow, and the damage, particularly in an unoccupied home such as a vacation home, can be catastrophic.

Have you ever pondered exactly what happens when the water freezes and the pipes fail? I have. I guess I need more hobbies. The water gets too cold and freezes. That sounds simple enough, doesn't it? The freezing action, interestingly, doesn't crack the pipes. It's slightly more complicated than that. The lateral pressure of the water freezing creates enormous pressure against the water. If the pipe cracked in the frozen area, and it was discovered before the thaw, there would be very little leaking. The pipe breaks where the water is still in a liquid state. This releases the pressure of the expanding water. The water starts flowing, and flowing. Another interesting fact is that it can be pretty cold outside for quite a while before pipes start to freeze and rupture. Pipes in well built homes in Canada did not rupture for 2 weeks with an average outside air temperatures of 18 degrees during power failures. The temperature inside the homes did not go below 39 degrees. The water in pipes often doesn't freeze until the water temperature is as low as 25 degrees. Once ice crystals form, the entire pipe then freezes quickly. This exerts thousands of pounds of pressure and the pipe bursts. The force exerted by a pound of water freezing is greater than the force of one pound of dynamite exploding. Ice shatters engine blocks.

Most damage from frozen pipes occurs in warmer climates where the homes are not adequately designed or insulated to handle an occasional prolonged cold period. How can you prevent freezing pipes in your home? First, shut off the water to the outside or garage hose bib. Most garages lack sufficient heat or insulation to protect pipes. Next, remove the garden hose. Now, open the hose bib and drain it, and leave it open till spring. They have "freeze proof" hose bibs that shut the water off inside the wall so all the water exposed to the outside air drains out each time. These too can freeze, given the wrong conditions. The best approach is shutting off the water inside the house.

Let's now look at your plumbing, and its' location. Any plumbing that runs up the outside wall of a building is vulnerable to freezing. My friends have a shore home with plumbing to the second floor kitchen on a west facing outside wall, and the pipes froze repeatedly. They finally installed a drain on the lines in the basement. They shut off the lines and drain them so no water remains in the wall. The faucets should be open during drainage to allow the water to run out. Any pipes in the crawl spaces? These pipes should be insulated. You should insulate the ceiling of the crawl space, the perimeter edge, any duct work in the crawl space, and any plumbing. There are several schools of thought on venting or not venting crawl spaces. If you leave the vents open in the winter, everything should be insulated. Some say a well vented crawl space is healthier. Most home owners find it easier to insulate the vents. You can buy foam insulation that snaps onto the pipes. This is a good start. A far better way to insulate them is to take R11 fiberglass batts with a Kraft paper backing, and cut it in long strips. Then wrap it around the pipes taping it with aviation grade duct tape. That's the real shiny tape. The flat grey colored tape dries out in a year and all your hard work will be wasted. Wear a respirator, gloves, and long sleeves when cutting and working with fiberglass. If you buy the cheap masks for breathing, which I don't recommend, get the kind that has two straps to secure it. If your water main comes up in the crawl space, insulate it.

If you have a vacation home, turn off the water at the main, and have drainage points installed in the system as well as right next to the main. If you have a particular pipe in your home that sometimes freezes, even when it is insulated, let the water trickle in the lines in very cold weather, particularly overnight. The pressure doesn't build up if the lines are left open slightly. Things not to do. Don't use heat tapes. I'm sure there are some out there that are safe, but I personally don't recommend them. Many are not Underwriter's Laboratory approved. Others state on the instructions they should not be in contact with metal. All of them dry out in time and are forgotten. When they are installed, people think of them as a lifetime fix. The insulation on them deteriorates. This is due to the heat they provide. There was a huge fire at the primate house at the Philadelphia Zoo in the early nineties, and the cause of the fire was attributed to heat tapes. A ground fault circuit interrupter or GFCI receptacle will not protect you against a fire caused by failed heat tapes. Don't use a plumber's torch and try and heat the pipes. Unless you are used to working with an open flame in a confined area near flammable materials with limited oxygen, don't use a torch in your crawl space. You can start a fire that smolders and reaches a flash-point hours later. Don't use a portable heat source with a flame, such as a kerosene heater, in a crawl space. Those heaters should be used only in well ventilated areas and kept in sight. Electric resistance heaters should not be left in unattended areas either. The oil filled heaters that look like radiators are fairly safe, but be sure the breaker and receptacle are adequate for the electric draw. Some shut off after 24 hours.

The bottom line is, insulate the pipes and drain any standing water in the lines. The best time to take these measures is on a mild winter day, before a hard freeze.

Better yet, make winterizing your water system part of your fall routine. After all, going in the crawl space is almost as much fun as raking the leaves. Nah, raking leaves is a lot more fun.

ATTIC VENTILATION

Perhaps the most misunderstood concept of home maintenance is attic ventilation. Most people feel the gable vents that were installed when the home was built are adequate. They also believe it's a good idea to close them off in the winter to save heat. Along with closing off the gables in the winter, many home owners believe you should cover over the soffits or eave area with insulation. They feel that seeing light there is a bad idea. "It will let in insects," is something I hear often. All of the above beliefs are wrong.

When houses were built in colonial times, there was no ventilation and there was no need for it. Early homes were very drafty and there wasn't any need for additional ventilation. Fuel was also very cheap so they weren't all that concerned about insulation. The truth is, the science of residential construction is really only about 150 years old. Prior to that there was very little change in the science of construction. The wealthy built bigger homes and used stone rather than wood when it was available, but they still had a path for plumbing and heated the rooms with multiple fireplaces rather than just one.

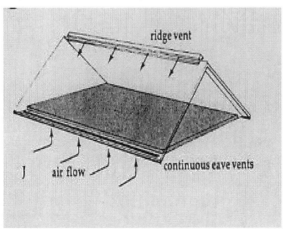

Let's start with the soffit vents. These vents are located all the way down where the roof meets the ceiling of the rooms below. Pull back the insulation so it doesn't block the air entry. You should pull it back so it is even with the outside wall. You may need a rake to get all the way down there. It's pretty tight quarters. In newer homes there are chutes or baffles that allow the air to pass above the insulation. Never close off attic vents for the winter. You want the cool dry outside air to enter the attic at the eaves, and pass over the underside of the wood deck taking moisture away. This air then rises and leaves through the continuous vent across the ridge. Ventilation works best when the air has a means of entry and a means [19]of exiting. Warm air rises. The warming of the air in the attic causes the air to rise and leave through the vent. As it leaves, it pulls the air in at the eaves. You don't want it to pull the warm heated air in the house up into the attic. You paid a lot of money to heat that air. The last thing you want to do is dump it into the attic. It's bad enough that the heat you paid for leaves through the attic. You don't want the air to go with it. You are now wondering, how is the heat leaving but the air staying? Heat passes through everything! Nothing stops the flow of heat. If you put two objects with drastically different temperatures next to each other, the heat will equalize between them. This is the 2nd Law of Thermodynamics. [20] So the heat passes from the living area, through the insulation, and into the attic. If you

allow air to flow into the attic, the heat loss will be greatly accelerated. You want a nice tight barrier between the attic and the living area. You want lots of insulation to hold the heat in the living area, and you want lots of ventilation in the

[19] Sketch courtesy, Airvent.com
[20] NRCA website

attic. You want the attic to be as close to the outside air temperature as possible. Once the heat has passed through the insulation it is of no use to you. Heat is like beer. As Archie Bunker used to say, "You don't own beer, you only rent it." The same can be said for heat.

There is another material that travels into the attic with the warm air. It is water vapor. Warm air can hold a lot of water. Air at 75 degrees with a relative humidity of 35% holds a specific amount of water vapor. We're not going to get too scientific here because the actual quantity of water is contingent upon the volume of air but for the sake of this explanation the important fact is the air remains in a vapor state at these numbers and will not condense out of the air. That warm air is now drawn to the attic. We want as little of the air to find its way into the attic, but no matter what you do, some of it gets up there. Openings like the gap in the attic floor on the left allow huge amounts of household heat and moisture into the attic. You can install a vapor "barrier" but it is not a barrier. They are more appropriately named vapor retardants because they slow or impede the flow of vapor, but they don't stop it. Now that warm moist 75 degree air is in the attic. The air in the attic is much colder. If you cool that air with 35% RH down to 47 degrees,[21] the moisture reaches its' dew point temperature and condensation occurs. The "Dew Point" is always a

temperature. It is the point at which water vapor changes state and becomes a liquid. This temperature is always contingent upon two numbers, the

---

[21] Same

temperature and the humidity. Humidity is always referred to as "relative" because it is always relative to the ambient temperature.

You now have a wet attic. There are some obvious telltale signs that the home has a moisture problem in the attic. Rust forms on the nails on the underside of the roof deck. There will also be stains on the floor of the attic as shown in the picture on the previous page. When I was in the roofing business home owners would swear this was evidence that "every nail in the attic was leaking." The stains are the result of the moisture dripping off the nails. If you go in the attic in the winter under these conditions you may actually see small icicles hanging off the nails. These stains are the result of excess moisture in the attic. A ridge vent will surely help, but if you have these stains, you have to take a look at moisture sources in the house. Venting is not enough, dealing with the excess moisture is often recommended. In reality, most homes are about 70 degrees in the winter, and attics are much colder than 47 degrees. If the air is cold and moving, the water vapor continues to move with the cold air and vents out through the ridge vent. It's sort of like the windows fogging up in the car in the winter. If you open a window, the vapor leaves through the window. If you turn on the defroster, it blows cold air on the glass and prevents the glass from fogging up. Now if you close off the vents in the attic to save the heat that is now worthless, you trap the moisture in the attic and rot out your attic. This is the equivalent of closing the windows in the car. You want nice even balanced continuously working ventilation to carry out the moisture in the attic. It should be working round the clock and not running off electricity. Continuous soffit and ridge venting will give you the best defense against moisture damage in your attic. There are other variables with attic moisture. If the home has more moisture than the system can vent out, you may have a perfectly working ridge and soffit venting, and still have moisture accumulate in the attic. A humidifier, a wet basement or crawl space, are a few examples of conditions that can put too much moisture in the home and create problems. These conditions are covered in more detail in other sections of this book. So that covers attic ventilation in the winter. Let's take a look at ventilation in the summer.

We ventilate in the summer to let out heat, AND reduce the surface temperature of the roof. The most efficient form of attic ventilation in my opinion is continuous ridge venting, and continuous soffit venting as stated above. This will allow the most air flow over the underside of the roof. A well ventilated attic can help to keep your roof cooler. Heat is the enemy of your roof. I climb on roofs all year round. I travel with a laser thermometer. I take roof temperatures occasionally. (Okay, so I'm a little different). I have recorded temperatures in excess of 160 degrees on the surface of the roof. The roof is 160 degrees on a hot summer day and a hail storm rolls in. The hail is 32 degrees. It's ice. The hail pelts the soft asphalt shingles and chills them down 130 degrees in a matter of minutes. Roofs have a tough job! This change in temperature and getting pelted with ice can cause the granules to dislodge, the mat to blister or crack, and drastically shorten the life of the shingles. There is not a lot you can do about the hail, but you can reduce the surface temperature of the roof. A well ventilated attic will help reduce the temperature

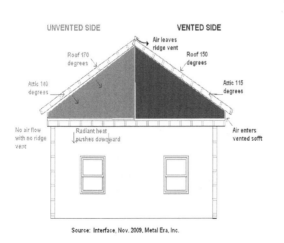

Source: Interface, Nov. 2009, Metal Era, Inc.

of the shingles. Studies have shown you can reduce the surface temperature of the roof by 20 degrees by having proper attic ventilation. So the roof is happier. It still has to deal with a lot of heat, but 20 degrees is a significant reduction in surface temperature. Another thing that happens with a well-ventilated attic is it cools down better at night. The attic builds up heat during the day. If the attic is not properly ventilated the heat just sits there at night. The next morning comes and the attic is already hot. It has a running start on building up heat the next day. If it's properly ventilated, it will cool at night. This cooling will reduce the heat on the 2nd floor and in the attic. This will make it more comfortable to sleep and reduce your air conditioning load. A well ventilated attic is very close to the outside air temperature just before dawn in the summer. A poorly ventilated attic stays hot right through the night.

We all are familiar with the concept of heat rising. Actually what happens is the air gets heated, and it rises. Warm air is thinner than cold air and therefore lighter. The heated air rises and takes the heat with it. Heat can travel in various directions and comes in several forms. Radiant heat is the heat that leaves an object and you feel it on the surface. The radiant heat from the sun heats paved areas. If you walk barefoot on an asphalt driveway on a sunny summer day, you will feel the results of the radiant heat from the sun, heating up the driveway. In the summer, your attic gets hot no matter what you do. A lot of this heat raises the temperature of the underside of the roof and the shingles. But a lot of the heat reflects back into the living area. The radiant heat from the attic raises the temperature of the 2nd floor. The 2nd floor is generally about 5 degrees warmer than the first floor. If the roof is poorly ventilated, the 2nd floor may be 12 to 15 degrees hotter. Studies have shown the attic temperature to be as much as 25 degrees hotter in a poorly ventilated attic [22]compared to a well-ventilated

---

[22] Interface Magazine, Publication of RCI, Raleigh, NC.

attic. This heat then transfers down into the living area causing the occupants to be warmer, uncomfortable, and costing more in cooling bills. A well ventilated attic saves you on cooling, and it saves not by extending the life of your roof, but by not shortening it through too much heat. Most shingle manufacturers will void the warranty of a roof if it is not properly ventilated.

So what is proper attic ventilation? Building codes and shingle manufacturers have accepted the number of $1/150^{th}$ of the flat attic space as proper ventilation. The ventilation should be balanced equally between high and low areas, or eave and ridge as discussed. This translates into about one square inch of ventilation for one square foot of attic spaced. This number was actually based on no scientific study but was adopted for housing during World War II. It has become the standard of the construction industry. This is not always easily attained. There are hip roofs, roofs with dormers, and a variety of other conditions that can make getting to this number difficult. There are a variety of products on the market that can address unusual conditions. If you have a home where you don't have an open clear easily ventilated attic, you can do your own research. Air Vent, Inc. makes a whole host of products to address specific conditions. They have a website, www.airvent.com. Their phone number is 1-800- A-I-R-V-E-N-T. Another company that has specific materials for specific applications is DCI, Inc. They have some nice products that can be used when there is no soffit area to vent. They can also provide in roof ventilation for specific conditions. They are very willing to work with you on your particular issue. Their phone number is 1-800-622-4455. One more thing, for a properly installed ridge and soffit venting system to work, it is recommended that you close off all other attic ventilation. This means removing the fan in the roof or at least covering it over. Also cover the gable vents. Openings such as the gable vents and fans will allow air to enter the attic and short change the soffit venting. Rather than the air entering at the eaves, it will enter through the other openings and the attic won't get the full benefit of the balanced system.

While we are on the subject of attic ventilation, let's talk about ice dams. An ice dam is the ice that forms in the eave area of the roof after a snow fall. The dam is caused by the melting of the snow on the upper part of the roof. The water then runs down and refreezes on a lower part of

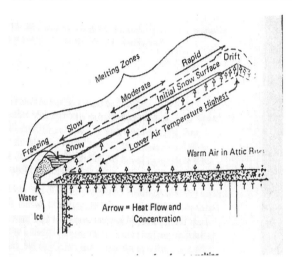

the roof. They are most common at the eave but can occur in the field of the roof. They are a [23]ventilation problem. There is ice dam protection that can be installed when the roof is installed and they are fairly effective. It is a self- sealing membrane that should be extended up the roof a minimum of 24" above the inside wall line. Removing the gutters will have no effect on them. As a home owner, the best thing you can do is be sure the attic ventilation system is functioning. If your home does not have a ridge vent, my suggestion is to add it, and also add vented soffit panels to the overhangs. Both of these ventilation products can be added without adversely affecting the roof. Properly installed insulation and insulating the access hatch to the attic will also help. Do not go up on an ice covered roof and try and shovel it off. Walking on a dry roof on a warm sunny day is a

---

[23] Roof-Snow Behavior and Ice-Dam Prevention in Residential Housing, University of Minnesota

hazardous activity and should only be done by those very comfortable on a roof. The comfort is gained by experience. Climbing on an ice covered roof in 20 degree weather with a shovel is a bad idea on so many levels. And if you need just one good reason, you will damage the roof and have a leak when it rains as well. DO NOT SHOVEL SNOW OFF THE ROOF! Also, don't make the wife do it. There are other approaches to ice dams such as heat cables which I also discourage.

The cables dry out in the sun and can short out. The cables in the picture are less than five years old. If you decide to use them, have them installed by a licensed electrician.

 Also, check them every year for drying, cracking and fraying. I saw heat cables used in Dillon, Colorado and they were very thick, about the size of a 100 amp electrical service. Dillon gets 200+ inches of snow every year. If you are in that kind of climate, you may need drastic measures. Another solution I saw in Colorado was installing the self-sealing membrane over the entire roof. Ice dams can occur in the field of the roof and installing the membrane over the entire roof will address that. Obviously, this must be done when the roof is being replaced. Let's say your roof has just started leaking. The roof is covered with snow, it is 22 degrees out and you know it must be an ice dam problem. Go to the attic access and check to see if the access is insulated. You want to make sure the attic is as cold as possible. If you have gable vents, you may be able to position a house fan so it is blowing cold air into the attic. This might be tough to do, but if you can lower the

temperature in the attic to below freezing, you can stop the thawing action that is fueling the ice dams. The best time to address ice dams is in the spring or fall. Insulating the attic and ventilating it are the best line of defense against ice dams.

Maintenance tips:
1. Keep attic vents open including soffit vents.
2. Don't close off attic vents in the winter.
3. Have a balanced ridge and soffit venting system installed if possible.

WOOD FLOORING

You just moved into your dream home. The fresh smell and the clean walls fill you with excitement. Then you look down, and wonder, what is happening to my new wood floors? Wood floors take some time before they get comfortable in your home. Let's start with a basic property of wood. Wood expands and contracts with moisture. It is either absorbing moisture or releasing moisture depending on temperature and humidity. You wood floors are installed in a very tight pattern. There is very little room for movement. If the humidity rises in the home, the wood expands, and it will buckle. Lower humidity in the winter causes squeaks and gaps. You want to blame someone for this, but it's the nature of wood.

There are some things the Contractor can do to protect your floors. When your home is being built, the wood should be kept dry. Have you ever driven by a construction site and see large pallets of wood stored out in the pouring rain? The bottom of the pallet may be several inches in mud. The wood used in your home is kiln dried. It should have a moisture content of about 9%. In the construction boom of the late 1980's they extended it to 19%. The theory is that mold grows at 20% and the house will only get drier as people live in it. There are lots of exceptions to that rule. Suffice it to say, 19% has been accepted, but lower moisture levels are always better. Any wood left out in the rain is affected by the rain and will move excessively. I have never seen wood flooring stored in the rain, but I have seen the truss systems and joists that support the floor left exposed to the elements. These structural members can be seriously damaged. If you are having a home built and you see the trusses for you roof or floor lying out in the rain, demand different wood be used. You will probably get a major fight over it. If the wood is laying the mud and exposed to rain, hit it with some spray paint. Tell the Builder you don't want it, and that you are going to check to see if any of the painted wood is in your home. What you can't control is wood that is soaked before you see it. The wood is delivered in open bed trucks. When the day starts, that load of wood is delivered, rain or shine. You can deliver wood in the rain; you just have to cover it. When your home is being built, the goal of the Builder is to get the home under roof protection as quickly as possible. Often the roof gets installed, but the gutters and grading around the property is done much later. These conditions lead to water in the basement. Large amounts of water in the basement raises the humidity in the structure. Have the Builder pump any standing water out of the basement. Excess moisture can increase settlement cracking and contribute to health problems for people allergic to molds and fungus.

Let's say you own an older home and you want to install wood floors. Have the wood delivered, and store it in your home for sixty days. The Contractor may not like that idea, but it's the best way to install the wood. Wood floors should actually have a lower moisture content than the structural members. When you are selecting a wood-flooring Contractor, ask him if he uses a moisture meter to check the wood before he installs it. If he doesn't own one, thank him for his time and call someone else. When they are ready to start, check the wood. The moisture content should be about 7 to 8%. Getting these conditions for new construction flooring is just about impossible. That's why movement in the wood flooring is to be expected. If the floor has buckled, it's best to wait before you sand it or take any drastic measures to repair it. Let the wood go through the four seasons. The wood will be a different dimension in summer than in winter. If you are dealing with new construction, notify the Builder in writing of the conditions that occur and take pictures. Overreacting by sanding and pulling boards can lead to unevenness when the wood changes in the next season change.

Wood floors, as you can see, are sensitive. Clean up any spills quickly. A damp basement can damage your wood floors. Keeping the humidity in your home too high in the winter can damage your floors. Humidifiers adding moisture to homes that are already tight will damage the floors. Do you wear high heels? A dainty 100 lb. woman wearing spike high heels with a tip of 1/4 inch exerts a pressure of 1600 lb. per square inch on the floor. This exceeds the compression strength of red oak, a very hard wood, by 400 lb. It's will sink into pine floors like a nail. Wood floors should not be installed everywhere. Laying them over a damp concrete floor often results in buckling. The manuals for installation tell you to install them over a vapor barrier of heavy plastic or roofing felt paper. My feeling is there is no such thing as a vapor barrier, only a vapor retardant. Moisture, which is water, always wins. There are several man made floors that have grown in popularity. Some are made with a laminate over a hard or press board backing. These products have a thin veneer finish and can't be refinished if they become damaged. A friend of mine, who bought one of these products, took a nail and a piece of gravel from her driveway, to the store and ground them into the samples to test their finish. The Bruce manufactured flooring held up the best to her test. Some of these products are very attractive and designed to "look" like wood. If you think they do, then they do. But as Joyce Kilmer said, "Only God can make a tree."

HAVING A DRY BASEMENT

Perhaps nothing is more frustrating than water in the basement. Dampness can deteriorate the home's heating system, the water heater, electrical panel box and can even trip electrical circuits on ground fault interrupters. A damp basement is also the breeding ground for molds and fungi that can affect the health of the occupants. If your basement has been dry, the best suggestion is to try to keep it dry.

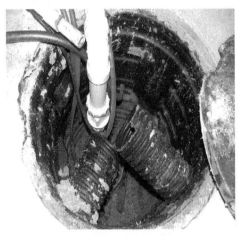

If you have a sump pump, test it. Lift the float device, or pour a bucket of water in it to be sure it works. It's better to know if it's broken on a dry Saturday afternoon, than at 3 A.M. in a driving rain storm. The sump pump on the left lacks a float device. Pour a bucket of water in it to test it. (The hoses were overflow lines from the two humidifiers on the heating system. This house had problems.) Now, check the roof's drainage system. Be sure gutters are clean and functioning. The best time to see how your gutters are working is during a heavy rain. If the gutters overflow, you may want to clean them on the next dry day. If you need to use a ladder when cleaning the gutters, be sure the ladder is level. Ladder safety and gutters is covered in detail in other sections.

Next, check the downspouts. Tap on them. They should sound empty. A couple of taps can often free items stuck in the elbows of the spout. Cleaning a clogged downspout from the top with a hose can be tricky for someone not comfortable on a ladder. Leave that job to a professional, such as a handyman or a local roofer. If the downspout goes into an underground system, be sure it is clear. Run a hose in it for a few minutes. If it overflows, the system should be flushed with a hose, or a mechanical snake.

If a downspout drains onto the ground, it should extend away from the house until there is a natural slope of the ground away from the home. Downspouts should be extended with an additional length of spout, a concrete splash block, or PVC piping. Roll up plastic drainage devices are rarely effective. It may extend a few feet or a few yards, depending on the home. If the downspout drains onto level ground or ground sloping towards the home, there is a high likelihood it will back up into the basement under adverse conditions. Frozen soil, or soil hardened by a prolonged dry spell, followed by a heavy rain, can cause flooding in a basement with no history of a water problem. How do I know? It happened to me. Our first summer in our home and we went above 25 days with above 90 degree temperatures and no rain. We then had a downpour getting about 2½" in about 90 minutes. The water kept coming, and coming, and coming. Our living room is slab on grade construction. We ended up with about 2 inches of water across the living room floor. Fortunately I had 2" x 4"'s for a project I was doing. We lifted the furniture onto the wood and kept if off the wet floor. We bought a shop-vac and kept vacuuming and dumping, vacuuming and dumping. I called my insurance company and they said I wasn't covered for a flood because I wasn't in a flood plain. This incident pre-dates flood insurance and predates me being in the home inspection profession. I highly recommend flood insurance if you are anywhere near a running body of water. Flooding is less of an issue with lakes. The insurance company told me to set my air conditioning very low, about 62 degrees. They said by running continually it will dehumidify as well as cool. That was good advice, as air conditioners both cool and dehumidify. The air conditioner seemed to run continually for about two days. The rugs were drying out. The next morning I came downstairs and the rug was completely soaked, as it had been a few days before. The condensate line for the air conditioner had clogged and re-flooded the carpets. I called the insurance agent back and he said we cover that. The end result was we got new carpeting. I digress. Back to keeping your basement dry.

Check the drainage around the home. Look for worn areas or grooves in the soil near your home where water may be standing or running close to the home. These areas shift and expand over the years, and the Home Owner will have to redirect them periodically. When redirecting the water, it is best to dig out a new drainage path around the home rather than mounding soil against the home. Soil above the foundation line can provide easy access for termites and other forms of infestation. Cut back plants and trees close to the home so the sun can dry the soil close to the home. You should be able to walk comfortably between your shrubbery and your home. If you do develop a water problem and you have a large tree near the home, check with a landscaper to see if that particular shrub has a large tap root that can damage the foundation. The root may be providing a direct channel funneling water to the foundation. If you do get water in your basement, you may try running a garden hose in the suspected area. It is best to do this immediately after the rain has stopped. I have had some success tracking down the location of water entry areas this way.

So I get water in my basement. What do I do next? As we have stated so far, the best remedy is prevention, keeping the water away. There are basement waterproofing companies. Many of them are very effective. The most effective method is to trench out the exterior of the home and seal off the exterior of the foundation. There is a Delta MS system that is used in new construction and may also be retrofitted to the home. The installation may run several hundred dollars a linear foot. If you have 80 linear feet of foundation at $500 a linear foot, you can see how the costs climb quickly. There are some more reasonably priced approaches but there are tradeoffs. You get water in your basement and you get it often. Not in every heavy rain, but in most. One approach is to dig a sump or hole in that corner. This will not be easy and you may want to hire a contractor. Go down about 18" to 24" and seal the sides with concrete. The hole should be about two feet across if round, or about 18" sides if square. You then drop a sump pump into the hole. You will want to get it plumbed to the outside. I also recommend a professional electrical connection with ground fault protection since it involves electricity and water. If the problem is chronic, get the pump put on a battery backup so it works when the storms knock out the power. If you have a 2nd location that's a problem. You may try adding a 2nd pump. If the water seems to enter along one wall, digging a small trench and sloping towards the sump can also be very effective. You only need to go down an inch or two for the trench. The water will take the path of least resistance. If you are getting seepage through the walls, have a parge coat installed on the wall. That's a thin layer of concrete that goes on like stucco. If you do it yourself, be sure the wall is clean and free of all loose mortar and dirt before you start. Allow the wall to dry for about a week. Putting a fan on it will help. Then seal the wall with elastomeric paint. This is paint designed to waterproof masonry surfaces. Most home centers will have some variation on this. Some of these products can be fairly strong smelling so prepare the family for it. Open windows in the basement and run fans. The whole project will take about three or four weekends depending on your house and your ability. The wall area and the number of pumps will greatly affect the price. If you can do it for $500 to $1000 dollars, it is a far cry from the seven figure amount contractors will want to dig up the outside. Also, if water is running in around openings in the wall for plumbing, clean them out and seal them with Great Stuff. This is fairly effective at sealing these openings. Last, but not least, put a dehumidifier in the basement and run it continually. Have it plumbed so it drains. You may want to drain it into the sump and have the sump pump the water out. Also, once you are done, cover the sump so the water in it isn't constantly evaporating back into the house.

Even though your basement has never had water in it before, there is no guarantee that it will not get water in it. The storms and the freeze-thaw cycles of the winter of 1994 in the Philadelphia area put water in many "dry" basements. There can also be changes in the drainage elsewhere in the neighborhood that can affect your basement. A fully functioning roof drainage system, a well-graded yard, and neatly trimmed shrubbery set prudently away from the home can all go a long way towards a dry basement.

What about crawl spaces? Everything I just said about keeping water out of basements also applies to crawl

spaces. The conventional wisdom on crawl spaces was to insulate the ceiling which is the floor of the living area above. Put a moisture barrier down on the floor and leave the vents open. This is a safe system if you have radon, as it vents the radon to the outside. Having done many seminars throughout the United States I had the opportunity to speak with other inspectors who have inspected many more crawl spaces than I see in northeastern US. They all recommend closing them off. If you have a dirt or gravel floor, the system most recommended is covering it with a very heavy ground cover. The picture above shows a damp crawl space with a dirt floor. The walls, you may notice, are both cinderblock and stone. This is usually evidence of an addition being built onto the home over the years. Heavy weight plastic can be rolled out to completely cover the floor. It should then be secured around the perimeter and on all seams as well as possible. Any seam should overlap about 10 inches and weighted down with ballast. Run the plastic up the side walls a few inches. A concrete floor eliminates the next step. I insulated the perimeter walls of my crawl space with 2" Styrofoam insulation used for roofing. It came with an asphalt skin on it that served as a waterproofing material as well. I wedged it in as tight as possible from top to bottom. The plastic can be rather slippery when you set the panels. The edges of the sections were also very tight. Once the panels are set, you can then go back over all the seams and seal between them with Great Stuff.[24] It's a foam insulation. You should also seal any small holes to the outside with this as well before you put the plastic down or insulate the side walls. Now close off the vents. Some may have a small damper type mechanism on them. You may need to cut a piece of the insulation and fit it over the vent. Make sure it's secure. Wind can pop it off the vent. This system will provide insulation and keep the moisture down. While you are in the basement or crawl space, it's a good idea to inspect for cracks. See the section titled "Will It Fall Down?" in the book for more information on cracks. If water is entering through any crack, have a structural engineer examine it. If you want to know if the crack is expanding, you can buy a gauge to put on the crack from Avongard. Their number is 1-800-319-9827. The gauge is about $30.00.

---

[24] Manufacturer trade name

Maintenance tip:
1. Test your sump pump once a year.
2. Get a battery powered back up system if you have water in the sump.
3. Cover the opening to the sump pump. They have covers you can buy. They often have a slot in them for the sump pump. Cove the slop with plastic and secure it with ballast.
4. Keep your gutters clean.
5. Be sure the downspouts extend away from the home at least 3' or until the ground drains away naturally.
6. Check the grading on the side of your home annually.
7. If the parge coat on the basement walls is failing, hire a contractor to repair it.
8. If you just can't stop water from entering your basement, you may need to hire a professional. Your best bet is a referral from several satisfied customers. Check the Better Business Bureau as well. There are a lot of horror stories when it comes to basement waterproofing.

RADON

One day, back in 1981, in a land called Pennsylvania, Stanley Waltrus went to work at the Limerick Nuclear Generating Plant. He walked in through the front door, and suddenly the alarms in the plant went off, indicating he was contaminated with radioactivity. They checked Stanley and thought this was strange because no one ever set off the alarms on the way into work. They usually set them off when leaving if they somehow were exposed to elevated levels of radioactivity. They couldn't find any radioactive material on him so they went to his house. They found the levels of radioactivity were incredibly high in his house. They spent the next several months examining and testing his house and concluded that Stanley brought radioactivity from his house to work, rather than the other way around. They continued to check his house, his neighborhood, and the homes of other workers and realized that there were a lot of homes in the area with very high levels of radioactivity. They then discovered that a lot of homes in Pennsylvania had very high levels of radiation present. They expanded their study and found that homes all over the country had radioactivity in them. The amounts varied, but in many cases, it was dangerously high, and they decided that it would be best for the people who lived in them to have the radiation removed. Thus was born the radon testing and mitigation business that has spread across the country.[25]

Radon. What is it? It is a colorless, odorless, tasteless gas. It is the second leading cause of lung cancer in the United States behind tobacco. Radon is everywhere. If you went out in your backyard with a shovel, you will hit uranium. Radon is caused by the breakdown of the uranium. Radon becomes a health concern when you are exposed to high

---

[25] Radalink Training program for radon testing.

151

levels of it for an extended period of time. It can be accumulatively fatal. How can you be exposed to it? If your house is built on soil that has a high level of uranium in it, and there is an opening in the basement floor that can allow the radon to enter, then you can have high levels of radon. Radon can enter other ways also, such as from well water. Your next door neighbor may not have it, your friend down the street who had his house checked may not have it, but you may have it. The only way to know is to have the house tested. A Home Owner is permitted to test their own home. Testing devices are available at many home centers. Professional testing companies also test. There are various methods and devices used for testing. The test can be as short as 48 hours, and as long as 6 months. The Surgeon General has determined that radon in the home is a serious health concern. Every home being bought should be tested for radon, including new homes. If a Realtor tells you not to bother with the test, they are contradicting every professional organization in the real estate industry, as well as the Surgeon General.

Radon activity is measured in a unit called a pica curie, and these breakdowns are measured in a specific volume of air. The most common term for measuring radon is in pica curies per liter or pCi/L. When uranium breaks down it emits tiny particles that damage the soft tissues in the lungs. Prolonged exposure to these breakdowns increases the risk of developing lung cancer. The higher the amount of radiation, combined with longer the exposure, the greater the risk of cancer increases. If you combine exposure to radon with smoking cigarettes, the risk of lung cancer increases dramatically. Exposure to 1 pCi/L for a day is considered to be about as damaging as smoking one cigarette a day. The level at which the EPA recommends steps be taken to remove radon from a house is 4.0 pCi/L. The EPA has published statistics on cancer risks for those who smoke and those who don't. The table does not mention the amount of smoking but in simplified terms, if 1,000 people smoke and are exposed to 20 pCi/L per day, 135 of these people will get lung cancer.[26] Another 1,000 nonsmokers were studied, and the rate of lung cancer was 8 people with the same radon exposure. People who never smoked have died from lung cancer from radon.

Radon is most damaging to children because their lungs are very tender. The highest concentration of radon is almost always in the basement. Many children have playrooms in the basement. This combination can be very damaging to their lungs, and the damage may not appear for years. Radon exposure is greatest in the winter, because we close up our houses and spend considerably more time in them. The amount of radon recorded in this area can be very high. The highest count our company discovered while testing was 427 pCi/L. However, in many homes it is less than 4.0. Pennsylvania licenses radon testing. Ongoing training is also required to remain approved by the state and it requires more hours of continual training than are required to be an x-ray technician. Radon emits particles that are more damaging than x-rays. For information on radon in Pennsylvania call 1-800-237-2366. They can provide you with literature as well as a list of individuals and firms licensed to test for radon. There are also radon mitigation companies that can remove the radon from your home. This process is relatively simple, and is very effective. A list of these contractors may also be obtained from the state.

There are those who don't "believe" in radon. (I have literally been asked that exact question by a Realtor). My response was, "It's not exactly the tooth fairy". The fact that radon gas damages the lungs is irrefutable. The quantity and duration of exposure is often debated. The United States is leaning towards lowering the exposure level.

---

[26] Pennsylvania's Home Buyer's and Seller's Guide To Radon

Canada had a much higher level of tolerance but recent discussion indicates they may be rethinking their number above which mitigation is recommended. Another argument I have heard was from a doctor who said they have no real scientifically documented studies with a control group and an exposed group. One of the reasons why this is difficult is the migration of people and who's to say the radon in this house got them when they may have been exposed to asbestos 50 years ago when they were children. The closest they have been able to come up with a study that addresses this is Iowa housewives. Iowa housewives tend to stay at home. They don't work outside the home. Many of them don't move. They lived in the same house 20 years or more. Also, interestingly, Iowa has the highest radon count in households of any state in the union. They did a study of 1,000 women in Iowa.[27] There were over 600 women who came down with cancer. They examined their households. They also examined the households of the other women who did not have cancer. While the radon counts were elevated in many of the homes where the women did not contract cancer, "overall, these results suggest that cumulative radon exposure is a significant risk factor for lung cancer in women. " If your house has not been tested for radon, you are running the risk of the equivalent of smoking cigarettes every day and not knowing it.

---

[27] Heartland Radon Research and Education Program (HRREP)

Shown below is a sample report similar to the reports I provide when I do a radon test. The column on the right shows the radon levels measured by the hour. Another page on the report shows the temperature, humidity, and

barometric pressure by the hour. They can all affect the radon count. When testing for a client, the test runs for 48 hours. The report is generated by Radalink, Inc. in Atlanta, GA who provides me with the continuous monitor system I use. With all the data that the report provides, including hourly results, I feel a continuous monitor system like this is the most accurate testing system available.

Maintenance tip: Have your home tested for radon.

MOLD

The latest feeding frenzy for the television and print news media is mold in your home. It will completely destroy your dream home, make it totally uninhabitable and the only solution is a bulldozer. This sounds pretty scary. Has it happened? Yes. Does it happen often? Absolutely not.

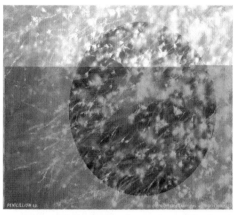

There are a few basic facts about mold you should know. First, your house has it. Every house has it. Molds are tiny organisms that facilitate the breakdown of plant and organic matter. (I'm not sure exactly what they are. I am not a biologist, but I called them plants once in a newspaper article and some anal retentive expert wrote me saying they weren't plants.) Wood, paper, and food are organic matter. Everything you need to know about mold you can learn from a piece of bread. Leave bread in your bread drawer for about two weeks and take a look at it. It will develop a pretty shade of green. What do you do with the bread? You throw it out. This is a miniature case study in mold. You left a food source for mold in a warm dark location with ample moisture. The mold had everything it needed to grow: food, water, and darkness. So, the spores took root and blossomed. In most cases this is penicillium, which is considered less toxic than other molds. However, all molds are [28]considered toxic, and removal is recommended.

It is estimated that one third to one half of all homes have some form of mold growth present in the house. Before you tear down the house and move into a tent in the back yard, let's take a rational approach. Unless you have a strong medical concern and a health care professional says that mold may be creating a health risk in your house, there is no reason to test your house for mold. If you test, the answer will be yes, you have mold. There are no guidelines for "safe" amounts of airborne mold in the home. Testing will only keep you up at night, and not solve any problems.

The best way to approach mold is to remove conditions that are conducive to its' growth. First and foremost, reduce the humidity in your home. Do not use a humidifier. If not operated properly, they are a health risk. If you read the EPA guidelines on a humidifier, they recommend using distilled water. If your humidifier is running off your tap water, it's not distilled. There are so many problems that an improperly maintained humidifier can create, I feel they are not worth the risk. Get a hygrometer, monitor your humidity, and keep it below fifty percent in the basement. They say molds grow at sixty percent. Fifty percent is safer, and it's still very comfortable. (That being said, I've seen roof decks rot in homes with 50% RH). Get a dehumidifier that is draining constantly. Clean the dehumidifier pan every few days with bleach.

Next, ventilate, ventilate, and ventilate. The vents for the dryer and the fans for the bathrooms should vent to the outside. Older homes often had kitchen fans that operated on a pull string. They took the cooking moisture outside. If you have one, use it. Be sure to clean it regularly. Every month is usually sufficient. I have seen some that looked

---

[28] EMSL Analytical, Westmont, NJ

like a science project. If you don't have one, open a window slightly when you cook. Be sure your attic has lots of ventilation. A balanced ridge and soffit venting system is best. Never close off attic vents in the winter. You will destroy your house. If your house is above a crawl space, insulate under the floor of the living area, and vent the crawl space. Put a sheet of heavy weight plastic or roofing felt paper over all dirt areas in the basement or crawl space under the house. If you have a basement, insulate the perimeter band joist area of the basement.

Aggressively attack any water source, or source of dampness in your home. Any areas damaged by plumbing or roofing leaks should be dried immediately, and removed if saturated. No water entry in the basement should be tolerated. Keep your gutters clean. Drain your downspouts several feet away from the home, and re-grade so the home is higher than every point at least eight feet away from the home. In many cases, only a few inches of re-grading are all it takes to make the water run away from the foundation. Check all caulking, roof flashings, gutter end caps and seams, and keep them sealed and tight. A roofing professional should check flashings. Home Owners and nonprofessional roofers seem to think that the more roof cement you use, the better the job. Check these areas annually.

If you are thinking, I have a new home, all of this doesn't apply to me, you couldn't be more wrong. You are far more likely to have mold problems in a brand new home than in an older home. Be sure all of the preventive measures listed above are in place and working in your new home. New homes are very tight. This tightness traps moisture in the home, which leads to mold growth. If your new house has a problem with mold, the Home Owner, through poor maintenance, is far more likely to be the cause than the builder. I personally would not buy a home with an Exterior Insulation Finished System, (EIFS). This is a stucco system that can work very well. However, the tendency towards human error creating insurmountable problems and mold concerns with the product, lead me to advise new homebuyers to ask for a traditional stucco system instead.

Lastly, if buying a home, don't expect the home inspector to be able to tell you if the home has molds at an unhealthy level. Mold is a health issue. Talk to your doctor about it. Some people with weak immune systems, asthma, or other health conditions, may react to the presence of molds, and others will never know it's there. If there are obvious moisture problems such as a wet basement, leaky roof, or visible evidence of plumbing problems, these conditions can create mold concerns, but it's not a reason to panic. Go to www.EPA.gov and you will find all the information you need about molds. Mold grows out of sight more often than in visible areas. Remember the bread? Often, homes will have a roof leak that's repaired. The stained area is painted and forgotten. The mold on the other side of the wall or ceiling is never cleaned off. No home inspector can find every area that may have gotten wet in the history of a house. Mold is everywhere. The chances your home will develop unhealthy amounts of it are very remote. There are many ways to address it short of a bulldozer. Most involve common sense, good maintenance, and checking the home on a regular basis for warning signs. Condensation on windows, a black film in damp areas such as basements, bathrooms, attics, or cold closets, and rust or black rings around nails in the attic are all indications of too much moisture and potential mold problems.

The picture above shows mold that had grown on the paper backing of the insulation. It was present on the insulation nearest the outside wall. Apparently, the cold air from the outside wall was getting between the insulation and the ceiling of the heated area below. There was no evidence of mold under the insulation in middle or other areas of the attic that were inspected. The cold air caused the condensation that was sufficient to provide enough dampness for the mold to grow.

Maintenance Tips:

1. Clean up and dry everything thoroughly after any spill or leak.
2. Run a fan on the wet areas to dry them.
3. Follow clean up instructions at EPA website.
4. Test for mold if someone is symptomatic.
5. Don't just test for mold. You have it. Check for moisture levels throughout the house. A mold test should be part of a rather through inspection of moisture present, and items in the home that can raise moisture levels.
6. I recommend a dehumidifier for every home with a basement or crawl space.

CHECKING YOUR FIREPLACE

Candy is dandy and liquor is quicker, but a fireplace works pretty well too. (Apologies to Ogden Nash). Nothing can change the mood of a room quite like a fireplace. The crackle of the burning wood and the glow of the heat can transform an ordinary room into a cozy environment. Before you use it, it's a good idea to take some precautions. Fireplaces can kill people! But that is not a reason to weld the damper shut, block it off, and not use it. It is, however, a very good reason to treat it with the greatest respect.

Prior to lighting first fire of the season, brush down the firebox area and give it a good visual inspection. Use a nice bright light when you do this. Is there loose mortar? Pick at it. Run a stiff brush or even lightly test it with a screw driver. Repair any small cracks in the firebox. Be sure to use fireclay. It will withstand the heat of the fireplace. If you have a metal firebox and flue, I recommend you have the firebox checked professionally more often than with mortar. While the metal is built to withstand the heat, fireplaces often exceed 1,000 degrees. This amount of heat can fatigue the metal. At the top of the firebox, the box tapers into the flue. It's here that the heat converges and can fatigue the metal. A chimney expert should examine metal fireboxes and flues every year.

After you have cleaned and checked the firebox thoroughly, examine the damper. The first time you open the damper to start the winter season, shake the handle a few times, before you open it. Then wait and listen for a commotion. Birds and animals may find the chimney perfect for their home, and move in during the summer. If they are in there you want to scare them so they leave through the top. If they fall into your living room, they get very upset. A squirrel dropping into the living room usually changes the mood of the room. If you saw Chevy Chase's

Christmas Vacation you know what I mean. The damper should open easily and close tightly. The fireplace is a major source of heat loss in the home. Fireplaces are energy hogs, not heat sources. Mythbusters[29] did a study on a fireplace in a home and while it raised the temperature in the room with the fireplace, the remainder of the home cooled off. A tight damper is helpful in keeping cold from falling down the flue into the living area when the fireplace is not in use. Those glass doors for in front of the fireplace also help. Between the two closure systems, you can keep heat loss to a minimum. Next, shine a flashlight up the chimney. The shiny black crust in the chimney is creosote. It is a by-product of burning wood, and it is flammable. If it has built up to about 1/8 inch, have the chimney professionally cleaned. Clean out all leaves and other debris. If clay falls out when you open the damper, have the chimney checked. Mortar falling from the smoke chamber is not as great a concern as the clay liner breaking down. Now turn the flashlight off and see if you can see light from the top of the chimney. Next, hold a tissue near the damper. If it is cold out, the heat from the house should pull the tissue up. If this happens, the draw is normally adequate.

Examine the outside areas of the chimney. The chimney will sometimes pull away from the house. In most cases this is not a serious condition, but the cracks that appear between the house and chimney should be sealed to keep water out. If the chimney is leaning more than about a half inch in eight feet, have it checked. The flue of the chimney should extend above the top of the chimney. Examining the top of the chimney should be left to professionals, unless you are very comfortable on your roof. The top of the chimney or crown should be in tact, and should be tapered to allow for water runoff from the top of the chimney.

---

[29] Mythbusters Show, Discovery Channel

The chimney crown flues and chimney cap below it are very well done. Chimney caps reduce airflow slightly, but they keep animals, water and debris out of the chimney. I would suggest every chimney have one. If everything has

checked out and is working, let's test the chimney. Roll up a newspaper very tightly and get a bucket of water. (You remember newspapers). Light the newspaper on fire and stick it up the flue. Does it draft well? If it doesn't, the house will fill up with smoke very quickly, hence the bucket of water. If it drafts well, you are ready to go. If it doesn't draft well, try opening a window a crack in the room with the fireplace. The influx of cold air under the fire can help lift the smoke out the chimney. For best results, use well-seasoned dry hardwoods. Fireplaces that are essentially boxes built on the side of the home, particularly the north side, will draft slower in the winter until they heat up. A chimney is a static column of cold air. The cold air needs to be pushed out of the way. When you are starting your fire with a cold flue, get your fire ready to go in the bottom of the fireplace. Next, roll up the newspaper. Now open the damper, light the paper and hold it as far up the flue as you can reach. When you can't hold the paper anymore, light your fire and the flue should be drafting nicely by now.

Look for gaps in the mortar and cracks on the crown, (top), if you can safely get up there. That cute little sapling growing out of the side of the chimney can allow water to enter, damage the mortar and result in leaking into your home. If you really like it, pull it out and transplant it to the back yard.

The damper. Most fireplaces have a damper located in the living area at the top of the firebox. It is heavy steel or cast iron; it is hinged, and has some form of handle operation. Lyemanco[30] makes a damper that is mounted on your chimney top. It is spring loaded. The spring pops it open. There is a cable that comes down through the flue and is hooked at the opening for the fireplace. The way to operate it is to pull the cable off the catch and release it. The damper pops open. To reset it, you pull the cord back down and hook it. This is the best damper system I have seen. It keeps out animals, leaves, and the weather. It also keeps the chimney full of heated air in the winter. The advantage of that is the chimney will draw much better when it is first ignited. It is also not as cold when the fireplace is not in use. Many new homes have small vents on the side of the fireplace. It's a little door you open when the fireplace is

---

[30] Lyemanco is manufacturer's name.

burning. This enables the fireplace to pull make up or combustion air from the door rather than from the house. That way the fireplace doesn't cool off the rest of the home by pulling the heat out of the other rooms. This vent also allows for some make up air as the fire is burning down. A deficiency in air can cause the fire to increase its output of carbon monoxide.

And now for the last most important item: **GET CARBON MONOXIDE DETECTORS!** Carbon monoxide is fatal. And fireplaces can increase the quantity of this deadly gas in your home in a couple ways. The first is the fire itself. As the fire dies down, the smoldering logs give off more carbon monoxide than the raging fire you had earlier in the evening. As the chimney cools, the draft of the chimney decreases and the smoke, with the carbon monoxide, can back up into the home. Glass doors over the fireplace reduce this condition. The other condition that occurs is the raging fire is stealing air and oxygen from any source it can find. If your home is tight, the only source of makeup air for your fireplace may be the flue for your gas appliances. The heat from the fire will create a negative draft and cause their exhaust to be pulled into the house. This is like driving with your exhaust pipe in the window. Two small children died from carbon monoxide poisoning in January of 1996 in the Midwest and one theory is that this condition caused it.

For this reason, opening a window slightly is a good idea, so the fire will pull outside air from the window rather than from the flue for your gas appliances. Fireplaces are romantic, cozy, a conversation piece, but they are also a system that must be respected or the consequences can be deadly. There is a new generation of fireplace referred to as unvented gas fireplaces. They run on natural gas or propane and give the look and warmth of a fireplace. There are some limitations with them. They should only be used in a large room with lots of air. The manual that comes with the unit will give you the recommended open space required for one. They are relatively inexpensive. You can have a decent quality unit installed for less than $500.00. They run off a pilot light so once the pilot's lit, you just turn a knob and they come on. Built in gas fired fireplaces in areas where a normal fireplace would be are sometimes operated off a remote control or wall switch. You can't beat the convenience. The built in gas fired units do not have a down side in my opinion. They don't have the smell of a real fire, but they also don't have the mess of a real fire. The unvented gas units do have some downsides. They leave soot on the walls in time. Expect to repaint every other year with them. I know gas burns clean, but they often get deposits in the jets that effect the burning. They also give off impurities such as carbon monoxide. If you have one, be sure there is a carbon monoxide sensor in the same room. They can also greatly elevate the moisture in the home. This moisture rises with the warm air and can damage the underside of the roof. If you have one or decide to get one, my recommendation is to use it sparingly for special occasions. Using it regularly will take its toll on the home.

Maintenance tips:
1. Keep your wood stored off the ground and season it at least one year before using it. Burn hard woods whenever possible.
2. Clean the fireplace area thoroughly throughout the season. Get the entire chimney cleaned once a year if you use it weekly or more.
3. Get it cleaned out every other year if you only use it about once a month or so during the heating season.

4. Check the outside of the chimney and be sure no trees have grown over the flue during the summer.
5. Check your carbon monoxide sensors and be sure they are in working order.
6. Keep the damper open until you can put your hand in the coals. Smoldering coals can be fatal.

HOW DOES MY HEATER WORK?

Before we get started on your particular heater, a brief discussion about heaters in general is in order. There are a variety of heating systems in the home. Some heat the air, some heat water; some heat the floors under your feet. We'll start with the most common. That is a forced air fossil fuel burning heater. The main unit consists of a burner apparatus, a fire area, a heat exchanger, and a plenum connected to a distribution system. In the simplest of terms, the thermostat calls for heat. An igniter begins ignition in the fire area. A valve then opens that allows the fuel to rush in over the igniter. The fuel ignites. The heat exchanger begins to heat up. Once it has reached sufficient temperature, a fan kicks on and distributes the heat. While it is pushing the air over the heat exchanger it is also pulling the air through a filtration system that removes dust and dirt from the air. The unit continues to run until the thermostat is satisfied that enough heat is in the house. It then tells the unit to shut off. The flame expires and the unit runs a little while longer to distribute the last of the heat through the house. There are a few variations in this cycle depending upon the unit, but this is the basic operation. The fuel for this unit can be natural gas, propane, oil, electric and even some forced air units are run off coal, or wood. The system is pretty basic. There is one central area where the air is heated. A distribution system takes the air through the home. A second distribution system returns the air to the unit where it is filtered and reheated. The precurser to this unit was a central heating system that distributed the heat based on gravity. There was a distribution system that took the heat through the house, but no return system. These units lacked a fan in most cases and just depended on the hot air rising to heat the home.

Next is a hydronics heating system. Hydronics heat works in the same manner. The major difference is the water is heated, distributed throughout the home, and then returned to the boiler. Rather than a fan, a boiler has a circulator pump on it. The pump distributes the water, once the water in the boiler is hot enough to supply heat to the house. Hot water heat tends to be a rather uniform heat. The rooms don't seem to get as cold when the thermostat call for heat. The rooms also don't seem to get as warm when the heat shuts off. Another form of hydronics heating is steam heat. Water, in a gaseous state, is distributed through the home. As it cools, it runs back to the boiler as water. The fuel for a hydronics system can be any of the above mentioned as well. A steam system does not have a circulator as the pressure of the steam provides distribution. Once the water turns to steam, the steam rushes to create uniform pressure through the entire line. The basic concept with most heating systems is that a medium is heated; it's distributed through the house, and then returned to the unit.

A third common form of heat is electric resistance heat. Electricity is run through a conductor that retards the flow of the electricity. When electrical flow is impeded but permitted, heat builds up. This heat is then used to heat the home. This can be done with a central unit that is a forced air unit. The difference between this and the fossil fuel units is the heat source. In this unit, electricity is the fuel. Contained within the unit are electric resistance heaters instead of a fire or burner area. They are located in the plenum. The fan pushes air through the plenum area where it is heated. Electric resistance heat is common in baseboard heat and temporary space heaters as well. There are some areas where no gas line exists, making electric heat the most practical system. Electric heat is also very practical if you finish off an unfinished area of a home or add an addition. Often there are too many complications with connecting to the existing heat source and running electric heat to the new area makes more sense.

There is also radiant heat. This can take on many forms. The most common radiant heat systems are located in the floor. The may be hydronic or electric. The theory is they heat the floor. This heats your body from the feet up. This system was very popular in the 1950's. They installed copper lines in concrete floors in Levittown, PA developments. It failed miserably as the copper lines failed and the heated floor attracted termites. The newer systems have lines that don't react with concrete and modern homes have treated wood and termite shields. The universal response of people with radiant heat is they love it. It has to be set into the floor during construction or renovation. It is particularly effective in rooms with high ceilings such as great rooms and barn conversions.

There are other variations on heating systems. Central wood burning stoves, coal stoves, pellet stoves, as well as fireplace inserts, and many other means of heating your home. I guarantee you I will miss at least one. My goal here was to familiarize you with the variations in the systems and the basic functions of some of those systems. We will go into more detail on each unit including simple maintenance and home owner tips to help keep your unit running through the winter.

INSPECTING YOUR CHIMNEY

IMPROPERLY WORKING CHIMNEYS KILL PEOPLE!

I can't emphasize this enough I find it very frustrating to inspect homes that have replaced the heater and the chimney was never discussed. The chimney has failed and I tell the potential buyer that the chimney has to be relined and everyone says, "Why didn't the Heating Contractor say anything about it?" I can't answer for the Heating Contractor but I suspect it may be a fear of not being competitively priced. (See the section on fireplaces for additional information on chimneys).

If you have replaced your heater or converted from oil to gas heat, the chances are extremely good that your chimney is not sized right for the present heating system. Also, if you upgraded your oil heater and now have a more energy efficient heater, your chimney should be relined to allow for the new heater. There are several ways that a Home Owner can check the system before having it professionally examined. Start with the clean out at the bottom of the chimney. This is generally a round piece of metal with the handle on it directly under the  chimney. With the heater off, pull it out. It should not be sealed shut. When you open it, you should see daylight. It may contain leaves or a dead bird. If a bird can live in your chimney, your chimney is malfunctioning. Gasses easily damage bird brains. (Remember the miners that took a bird into the mine with them? If the bird died, they got out of the mine!) Clean out the bottom of the chimney. If there is dirt from clay, brick or mortar breaking down the sides of the chimney, clean it out. Now, hold a tissue over the opening. (See next page). It should be pulled into the chimney. Next, put a small hand held mirror in the chimney. The sides should be clean, and smooth. It may be tough to see up the chimney. If the clean out was full of debris from the lining disintegrating, get the chimney relined. If all you see is brick, there is no lining in the chimney and I recommend it be relined. After you have cleaned it out, put the clean out cover back, and turn on the heater. It should fire smoothly and without odor. If the area smells from the exhaust, leave the area, and have it check immediately. Now that the heater is running, put your hand around the chimney flue, but don't touch it. It gets very hot. Move your hand slowly over any seams or openings in it. Oil heaters will often have a hole in it. That's fine. What you don't want to feel is the exhaust coming back into the house. Oil heaters should have a flapping door like opening in the flue. This is called a barometric damper and it should swing free. If it was wired or screwed shut when the unit was serviced, call another Heating Contractor to check the unit and never call back the mechanic who secured it shut. If you feel hot air coming out of any openings in the flue, you should have a professional examine the unit. If you are not sure, hold a lit match over the opening. Don't worry, nothing is going to blow up if the unit is firing, and producing heat. The flame should be pulled into the opening. If it blown out or the air is coming out of the opening, have the unit serviced. Also, hold the match in the opening in front of a gas furnace just below where the flue pipe is attached. With the unit heating, there should be a strong draft up into the unit. If the flame turns down, have the unit examined immediately. Also, check the clean out opening that you just closed. No air should be coming back into the home from around the door. All of these tests should also be performed on your gas or oil water heater as well. Gas water heaters have an opening on top of the water heater called a hood damper.

While the appliance is on, hold a tissue near the edge of the damper. The tissue should get sucked into the damper from the updraft.

Now, let's check the chimney outside. Examine the outside walls of the chimney. If there is white powdery material appearing on the sides of the chimney it is not functioning properly. If it is causing the paint to peel off the stucco on the sides, or the mortar to chalk or spall, it is malfunctioning.

The chimney on the left had the top section of the flue replaced. Rather than mortar the sections together, they dropped the new top piece in on a makeshift brick ledge. This will allow moisture to accumulate on the bricks where there is no liner to protect them. The outside walls of the chimney had some spalling. A gas fired heater produces a little over a liter of water per hour for every 100,000 BTU's of heat it produces. You don't want that water condensing in the chimney. You want it to vent into the atmosphere. If it is condensing in the chimney, you will see stains from it. This moisture will cause the chimney liner to fail. If it's staining, have it serviced. Both oil and gas burn cleanly. If you see smoke coming out of the chimney, your heater is malfunctioning. If there is soot at the top and stains running down the sides of the chimney, the heater is not working properly. These stains are far more common on oil units than gas. The stains from oil often are reddish in color. People think that is rust when it is actually soot. These stains may be from the old heater. If you have an attic, go up there when the heater is running.

If you smell the fumes from the heater in the attic, you have a problem. Also, if there is a white residue from moisture on the walls of the chimney in the attic, the chimney is not venting properly. If you have stains up at the junction of the wood for the roof and the mortar, the chimney flashing may be leaking. If the white stains start further down on the side of the chimney, it's a good chance the problem is with the chimney. By the way, I see evidence of active or past leaks or water entry around 9 out of 10 chimneys I inspect. The chimney below has moisture damaging the mortar joints from openings in the lining.

The last item to consider with chimneys is to have separate chimneys for gas and for oil appliances. It is not a good idea to have two appliances running on different types of fuel venting into the same chimney. For example, a gas water heater and oil burner should not be sharing the same chimney. Both operate at different temperatures, and the result can be long term damage to the chimney liner. This might be difficult to arrange logistically. It's not easy to add another chimney. How this happens is the Home Owner has an oil boiler to heat the house. Gas is run to the house sometime after the home is built. The Home Owner then adds a gas water heater. It's cheaper to run than an electric water heater, and there is less wear on the boiler if it is not used for domestic hot water in the summer. So the gas appliance gets installed and run into the same flue. If you have oil heat, now have gas available for your home, and want to get a gas water heater, get a high efficiency unit. They can be vented out the side wall. Their "chimney" is actually a PVC pipe that rarely gets to more than 100 degrees. This is a simple solution and it saves you money. Be sure it is vented properly with relation to doors and windows. You don't want the exhaust backing in through a bedroom window.

If you have any of the symptoms mentioned here, or if you are at all doubtful about your chimney's performance, have the chimney examined by a professional. Remember two things: Some heating contractors never look at your chimney during their annual service to the unit, and improperly working chimneys kill people. This is not a good combination.

Maintenance tips:
1. Check the clean out to be sure the chimney is drafting well
2. Look for clay dust in the clean out or other debris that can indicate the chimney liner is failing.
3. Open the barometric damper on your oil burner while it is running. The smoke should not be visible. White or black smoke is not good. Call a heating repair person.
4. If you have a PVC chimney for a high efficiency heater or water heater, be sure no birds have nested in it over the summer.
5. Check for growth on top of the chimney. Seeds get trapped in the cracks in the mortar and soon you have saplings growing out of the chimney.

HEATING SYSTEM CHECK UP

The vast majority of home heating systems break down into three categories based on the fuel they use: gas, oil and electric. These fuel sources run heaters that heat the air or water that is distributed through the home. If you have oil heat, have it serviced every year. Usually the company that provides the oil will perform this service for less than $100. Ask them to also check the chimney. Fossil fuel heat, if not drafting properly, can damage the chimney liner. An improperly functioning chimney CAN KILL YOU! If there is an area of the heating system that I have seen not given enough attention, it is the chimney.

If you have gas heat, remove the panel that covers the burner area. The first check is with your nose. If you smell gas, don't fire the unit. Call for service. This smell can be strongest if the unit has not been run for several months. If you have the type where the burner area is in complete view, turn the heater off. There is often a small plate that can be unscrewed. In many newer units, this entire area is sealed and should only be opened by a professional. If the plate is connected to the burner apparatus, don't remove it. If you can remove the plate, remove it and reach into the heater area and feel the metal just above the burners. This is the heat exchanger. Often there is rust on the metal. You should not feel any holes in the metal. Look over the rest of the unit with a flash light, and look for any holes or cracks. If none are visible, reinstall the plate. If you find any holes or cracks, call a heating contractor and do not use the heater. Holes in the heat exchanger can allow carbon monoxide to enter the living area. This can be sickening and even fatal.

If no holes were noted, no gas smell is present, or if you couldn't remove the plate, sit back and have someone turn on the unit at the thermostat. Watch the burners ignite. You should keep your face at least five feet back from the unit. The burner should light smoothly. If the flame is erratic, or lights with a pop or sudden burst, have it serviced. The color should be blue with a touch of orange on the tips. Now watch the flame. After a few minutes the fan should start. The flame will move slightly from the vibration of the fan. If the flame gets pushed down, or jumps when the fan starts, have the unit serviced. If the flame remains even, and the fan is running, the unit is probably ready to go.

Next, shut the unit off, open the area where the fan is located, and vacuum the area. Install a new filter. Filters should be changed monthly on forced air heating and cooling systems. Keep a supply of filters near the unit. Close up the unit, and while you have the vacuum out, clean the heating registers throughout the house. Remove the covers and vacuum inside the duct as far as you can reach. Clean off the cover and check the operation of the damper on the register. It should open and close freely. If you have electric central heating, about all you can do as a Home Owner is the vacuuming. If you have electric baseboards, vacuum the heating fins thoroughly, and be sure no paper or debris has fallen into them.

If you have hot water heat, check the gauge on the unit. If the water pressure is zero, don't fire the unit. On most homes, the water pressure should be above 10 to 15 lbs., and should always be less than 20 when the unit is cold. If the water pressure goes above 30 and stays there, or if the temperature pressure valve on the unit begins to give off water, have the unit serviced immediately. If the temperature pressure relief valve goes off, have the unit serviced. If it keeps going off, turn the unit off and leave it off until the technician gets there. Also, look around the base of the unit for evidence of leaking. Leaks will sometimes leave a white powdery deposit, a sign of leaking that is evaporating as it leaves the unit. The job of the air conditioning system is to remove heat. Through the compression, (the compressor is outside), and the evaporation, (the evaporator is the inside unit), of a liquid, (refrigerant), your air conditioner takes heat from inside and puts it outside. The maintenance of the unit is the same as the heater. The main difference is you need to see how much cooling the unit is providing. A very easy way to do this is get a small pointed thermometer at a heating supply store. Some home centers also carry them. Turn the air conditioning on, and let it run for about 5 minutes. Now stick the thermometer in the cooling register closest to the unit. Leave it in there for a few minutes. Now take a temperature in a return register on the 2nd floor or as far from the unit as possible. The difference between the two readings should be between 15 and 25 degrees. If the difference is below 15 degrees, the unit will run forever to cool the house. If it is too high, (above 25) the coli may ice up. Too high can be caused by a dirty filter, dirty coils, or a blockage in a register. Either way, I would suggest you have it serviced. There is a lot more on both air conditioning and heat pumps in the next section. They actually work the same way.

In general, if your heater is over ten years old, have it checked at the start of the heating season. If you have oil or gas heat, get carbon monoxide sensors, and install them according to the directions on the box. A good heating system can service a home for a minimum of ten years and in some cases twenty five to thirty years with a minimum of care and service.

Maintenance tips:
1. Change the filter every 90 days. Get filters with a MERV rating of 8 or higher or 1000 ppm.
2. Vacuum out the entire filter area once a year.

3. Have gas units serviced every 2 years, oil units annually. Also, clean out the "clean out" every year.
4. The flame sensor and the valve that releases the gas are the most common failures on gas fired units.

HEAT PUMP, GOOD OR BAD?

You moved into your new home and you have a heat pump. You have heard horrible things about them. "It's always cold," is one I have heard. "They are no good in cold climates" is another. We'll get to both of those issues, but first let's talk about how a heat pump works. A heat pump pumps heat. Well, now that we have that covered, let's move on. Just kidding! A heat pump is really an air conditioner that runs backwards. If this sounds confusing, it really isn't. An air conditioner contains a refrigerant such as Freon or Puron. Freon is a trade name for Dupont's brand of refrigerant. Puron is a new refrigerant that is more environmentally friendly. They both basically do the same thing. They start as a liquid. They are pumped into a coil where the pressure on them is reduced. This allows the liquid to become a gas. As this physical transformation occurs, the liquid absorbs heat. This heated gas is then pumped to the condensing unit. Once there, it is spread over coils and changed back into a liquid. As it changes back into a liquid, the heat that it picked up when it became a gas is now released. On both ends of this process, fans move large amounts of air over the coils to accelerate the absorption or removal of heat. In a standard air conditioner the evaporator is inside and it cools the house. In a heat pump, the two coils can perform either process and either coil can pick up or release heat. So a heat pump picks up heat outside and pumps it inside.

There is an old expression, "You can't pump what you don't have." If it is too cold outside, there is not enough heat to pump inside. You then need another heat source inside to provide additional heat. A heat pump, like an air conditioner, can "move" fifteen to twenty five degrees of heat. It all comes down to mathematics. Heat is measured in btu's or British Thermal Units. Twelve thousand btu's equals one ton of air conditioning. You may have heard an air conditioner referred to as a two ton unit and then you see two servicemen pick it up and carry it out of the truck. It does not weigh four thousand pounds. The two tons refers to its cooling capacity. As a rule of thumb, in the Mid-Atlantic region, where I live, one ton of cooling will cool about 800 square feet of living area. This number may be much different in Butte, Montana or Palm Coast, Florida. There is a whole range of variables that can affect that, but for the purposes of this chapter we will use that number. A residential home often has somewhere between 1600 and 2400 square feet of living area. Therefore many residential central air conditioning and heat pump units are rated for two to three tons of cooling. Larger homes frequently have two systems. It is very unusual for a home with forced air heat to have the duct worked in zones, but some do. We won't get into those systems here. In most cases, when the home has two "zones" it is done by separate units. Some air conditioners/heat pumps also have fans that operate at variable speeds depending upon the heating or cooling load. I mention them just so you are aware of them. If you are replacing your unit, look into this system. They are more energy efficient.

Back to your heat pump or air conditioner. A heat pump, like an air conditioner, can provide a temperature difference between the air entering the system and the air leaving the system of about 15 to 25 degrees. If it's 90 degrees outside, removing 20 degrees of heat takes you to 70 degrees. That's a good range for most homes. Southern Florida and Yuma Arizona may need more cooling. Now let's look at winter. If its 40 degrees out, adding 20 degrees of heat to the home may take you up to 60 degrees. You will probably want more heat. Your house has other sources of heat such as people, pets, cooking, and most importantly incandescent lighting. Lights provide a lot of heat. If you combine all these heat sources, you will often be comfortable with the heat pump providing enough heat when it's 40 degrees outside. Remember, its mathematics. You start with X amount of heat, you add Y amount of heat and you reach Z as a comfortable temperature. Neither you, nor your family care much how you get there.

So you can see with our example, a heat pump producing 20 degrees of heat when its 40 degrees out works fine. What happens when it's 20 degrees out? Good question. Many newer heat pumps actually provide more heat in the heat pump cycle so they can keep up with the demand for heat below 40 degrees. When it gets down to 20 degrees, they may need help. So, heat pumps come with a secondary source of heat. The vast majority of them come with electric coils inside the unit that come on based on demand. If the heat pump can't keep up, the electric heat kicks in and everyone is comfortable. There are some that have a wide range of supplemental heat sources, such as gas, oil, or even wood pellets. The goal is to get as much heat as possible from the heat pump source before the unit asks the other sources of heat for help. The reason is the heat pump is your cheapest form of heat. When the electric resistance heat coils in the unit start, the unit uses considerably more electricity than the unit was using only running the heat pump. There were two statements I started this article with. The first was "It's always cold with heat pump." A heat pump will heat the discharge air to somewhere between 85 and at the most, 95 degrees. Most people are around 98 degrees. The air blowing on them is colder that they are. Therefore, it feels cold. If you had gas heat before, the air was much warmer. If you had radiators, they were A LOT warmer. So, you are not cold, the air has been adequately heated. This takes some adjusting. When the electric resistance heat comes on, the air is warmer than you. It should be greater than 100 degrees. This will feel good, but it's expensive in comparison to the 85 degree air.

So, how do I check my heat pump? Back in the previous section we talked about taking temperature readings on your registers and looking for a 15 to 25 degree range. The same applies here. This is where it gets tricky. Turn the thermostat to heat, not emergency heat or auxiliary heat. Set the thermostat two degrees warmer than the temperature in the room. Go check on the outside unit for the heat pump, which is also the outside unit for your air conditioner. It should start. Now take that same thermometer you used for checking the air conditioning temperature and check the temperature for the heat pump. The unit should produce about the same amount of heat. It is just "pumping" heat from outside, inside. The discharge air should be about 20 to 25 degrees warmer than the temperature of the return air. It is fairly important that you check this every year. Things break. You will turn on the heat and you get heat. You won't think about it but suddenly the electric usage is much higher than before. The only way you know if the unit is working properly is by checking the temperature.

Now, turn the heat up about five more degrees. Let it run for a few minutes and again take the temperature. The output temperature should be over 100 degrees. I've seen as high as 115 degrees. The electric heat should come on without throwing the switch on the thermostat to auxiliary or emergency heat. If the temperature doesn't spike up over 100 after several minutes, you are running on the heat pump only and you may find the home tough to heat in the winter. Now if you switch to emergency or auxiliary heat, I have seen the outside unit shut down. The heat should rise to over 100 degrees without the outside unit running. Ideally, you turned the heat up the five degrees I mentioned, the compressor keeps running, a little light on the thermostat came on indicating the emergency heat was on, and you didn't have to switch the thermostat over. If the unit didn't operate in this sequence, I would have it serviced. The most common reason heat pumps don't operate as designed is the controls were not properly wired to the unit. If you turned the thermostat up two degrees and air coming out is over 100 degrees, there is a good chance both the heat pump and the electric heat are now heating your home. This is comfortable but expensive. This is the most common defect I find when inspecting heat pumps. When I inspect a unit, I pull the cover off the electrical panel and put a tool called an amp probe on the electric lines to the heat pump. I then watch the electrical draw as the resistance heat starts. The draw usually spikes twice as there are often two heating elements. Some only contain one, and others may contain three, but two is the most common I find. I am not asking you to pull the cover off the main panel. This book is about simple home owner maintenance.

One more thing, don't turn the heat down at night and the up in the morning. You will waste money. Get a programmable thermostat that is made for a heat pump. They cost more than the same thermostat for a regular gas furnace but they know to get your heat from the heat pump as long as possible. The other thermostat will just run on the heat and you will be running on electric heat, not the energy efficient heat pump. The bottom line is newer heat pumps will heat your home, and they will save you money over regular electric resistance heat. They work well in most climates.

How do I know if I have a heat pump or just electric heat? Well, I could be a wise guy and say something about getting an inspection and your inspector will tell you, but I won't go there. The first place to look is the thermostat. It should have a setting for emergency heat or auxiliary heat, but you can't always go by that. In some cases, the thermostat you get is the one the mechanic had on the truck. I have seen thermostats with a fan control on hot water heaters and there is no fan in a hot water heating system. Next, look at the name plate on the unit. That should tell you. The plates on the outside units often fade with the sun and are very difficult to read. People often ask me if the unit is the right size for the home. I don't get into sizing the units because the size needed can vary greatly depending upon the construction of the home, number of windows, exposure to sun, etc. I usually determine it by the output of the unit. People often look at the outside unit and if it's big, they assume it has high capacity. The newer units are big. The bigger the outside unit, the more heat the coils can displace with the same amount of energy. Larger units have a lot more surface area. The increased surface area gives the heat in the coils greater area to release heat in the summer and pick up heat in the winter. So, you can't go by size. When you run an air conditioner, you cool the air and dehumidify it. Because of this, there is a pipe that comes out of the unit that drips water when it is running. This water may go into a pump and be pumped to the outside, it may drain under the basement floor, or it may drain into the sump. You will hear the pump kick on periodically if you have a pump. The line gets black and moldy in time. If it's clear plastic, you can replace it every few years. It is often connected to the refrigerant lines that run outside, so it's a little bit of project to replace it. Use wire pull ties or electrical tape to attach the new line. If the line is PVC and comes off the unit and runs to a pump or under the floor, you can sometimes pull it off at the unit, and pour about a shot glass of bleach into the top of the pipe. That will kill most molds. It may pull a bleach smell into the home for a while when you run the unit.

Maintenance tips.
1. Change the filter as mentioned so many times in this book. (Ever 90 days during the running season. If the unit is heat AND air conditioning, that means year round).
2. Take a temperature reading on discharge and return registers and look for about 20 degree difference with just the heat pump running.
3. Turn the thermostat up five degrees or more and take another temperature reading. The discharge air should be above 100 degrees.

4. Simple rule. With just the heat pump running, the air coming out of the register should be between 85 and 95 degrees. With the electric or whatever form of supplemental heat you have, the discharge air should be greater than 100 degrees.

HOW IS YOUR DUCT WORK?

If you think of the house as a living entity, the ductwork for the heating and air conditioning might be compared to the lungs. The ducts, like the lungs, are responsible for distributing air. The air is pumped through the house by a fan. It circulates through the rooms. There, it picks up dust, dirt, animal hairs, dander, mold spores, pollen, water vapor, and more air suspended particles than I can list. It is then sucked through the return ducts and back to the central

heating and cooling system. It is filtered, heated or cooled, and it starts the whole process all over again.

It's a pretty nice system, but it has some basic flaws. The first is there is no outside air mixed with the inside air. In commercial buildings, outside air is introduced, so the air is replaced with fresh air every hour. Another basic flaw is that the air slows down at different points in the ductwork. Every turn, bend or ripple causes the air to slow down. Long lengths of duct also cause the air to loose velocity. Every right angle elbow or bend in the

system adds the equivalent of ten feet to the run of ductwork. The registers that keep objects, such as curious cats, from going into the ducts, also slow the air. The system has to work harder to move the air. When the air slows down, those particles fall

inside the ductwork. Often mold spores can fall in the same

cracks and crevices where the water vapors fall. They are warm, moist, dark habitats that molds just love to call home. Both molds and dust are unhealthy. Homes with forced air heating and cooling tend to be less user-friendly for people with allergies. The filtering systems for residential heating systems are far less sophisticated than those used in commercial buildings. These conditions combine to make commercial buildings healthier than your home. Note the gaps in the duct work in the picture on the previous page. When you see gaps like this view them collectively. Gaps mean heat loss and obviously money loss.

What should a Home Owner do? Begin by checking the airflow through the house. The duct on the right was wide open in the attic. It was not connected to any register. The woman had a well heated attic with no snow on her roof. The home was two years old. By checking the air flow through the registers she may have discovered this sooner. She said her upstairs was never comfortable. She had the builder back several times and he said nothing was wrong. So much for buying a new home and not getting it inspected.

Now, here's how you can check your heating distribution system. On the thermostat, turn the fan control to "On" so the fan runs continuously. Now go into each room in the house and place a tissue against the return register. The suction should hold the tissue there. If it doesn't, the airflow through the house is poor. Now go to the basement and open the door about an inch. Does it slam shut? If so, your heater is pulling basement air rather than the air from the living area. This is another sign there are openings in the ducts in the basement. Next, examine the ducts. All those little holes at the corners of the ducts should be closed off with tape. (See picture previous page). A group of small gaps equal one big gap. Basement air often has more dust, dirt, mold, humidity, radon and other undesirables than household air. Go to a heating and air conditioning supply house and buy commercial grade tape. "Duct" tape from home improvement stores fails off in about a year.

Change the filter in your heater every month. Most people change it every heating season. Some pleated filters are described as ninety-day filters. They are better than the cheaper fiberglass filters, and you can get away with changing them every ninety days. The filter on the left is the right filter. Too bad it's the wrong size. That gap in the top of the filter opening will pull lots of basement air into the unit, thereby negating the return system built into the home. Next, take the registers off the heating system and vacuum inside as far as you can reach. Be careful, the metal edges can be sharp. Also clean off the register itself. Now open the fan housing area on the heater. Clean everywhere in this compartment. By manually cleaning all of these areas you can get a good start on reducing dust and mold. New homes often have loads of construction dust and sawdust all through the ductwork. Many new homes have large gaps in the ductwork in the basement, particularly in the return ducts. If you have a humidifier, disconnect it. Unless you maintain it perfectly, it puts far more moisture into the home than you need. This added moisture, fuels the mold growth, rusts the ducts, destroys the heater, and rots the underside of the roof. You don't need all that moisture in your home. Homes built today are very tight. Just by living in our homes we are humidifying them. The humidity level in the home stays between twenty and thirty percent through the winter. Humidity levels of forty to fifty percent are fine for green houses, but unhealthy for humans. If the measures mentioned are not enough, there is professional help available. There are duct-cleaning services that will put a video camera in your ducts and show you how bad they are. They clean all the accessible areas with HEPA filtered vacuums. They then seal off the return side and power brush, clean and scrub it. Now they clean the other side in the same manner. They have special brushes to clean your fan, the heat exchanger, and the entire heater. They scrub and clean the entire system. They will spend six to eight hours cleaning a three to four bedroom home. The cost is about $500.00. If the duct cleaning service takes an hour or two, you could have done it yourself.

Once you have it cleaned, there are more options on filters. The filters mentioned are low cost simple systems. They catch a lot of the big particles. If you have a serious health concern, there are very elaborate, expensive systems that are similar to those used commercially. The January 2000 issue of Consumers Reports goes into detail about filters and air cleaners. They also recommend that if you are going to hire a duct cleaning service, check the EPA web site before you hire someone. The site's address is www.EPA.gov/iaq/pubs/airduct.html. There are spores and molds showing up in homes that have rendered the home uninhabitable. These conditions are the extreme. I have seen poorly maintained heating distribution systems cause heaters to fail prematurely and negatively affect the quality of life in many homes. Evaluate your own condition. Decide how bad things are, and how much you need to invest. Those constant runny noses you and your children have may be traced to an unhealthy environment that can be corrected.

Another form of gas heat is a boiler. It heats hot water and then circulates it through the home. The original units operated on gravity. Hot water rose, and the cool water fell back to the unit. All modern boilers have circulators except steam heat. Steam heat is distributed by the pressure of the steam. We will stick to hot water heat here. The burner area is about the same as a gas fired hot air unit with a pilot or ignition system, lines for fuel, and a burner area located below the boiler as opposed to it being below the plenum in a gas unit. It heats the water and the circulator sends it through the home. Modern boilers are very efficient and many home owners prefer them to gas heat. The heat distribution is more uniform with less cooling felt before the unit fires again. The down side of a boiler is if you have central air conditioning you need two distribution systems, one for heat and the other for cooling. The heat in the rooms is most often provided by baseboard radiation or radiators. These give off a warm comfortable source of heat. The boiler in the picture is about 50 years old. End of useful life, recommend replacement.

Maintenance tips:

1. Vacuum out the ductwork at the registers annually.
2. Vacuum out the return air plenum in the heater annually.
3. Get filters with a MERV rating of 8 or higher and change every 90 days.
4. Bleed radiators at the start of the heating season.

RADIANT HEAT

Do you have cold feet? My feet get cold a few days after Thanksgiving, and they show no signs of thawing until the first day of spring. There is a heating system that addresses this problem directly. Radiant heat. It is a heating system installed in the floor. The theory is it heats the floor, not the air. Your feet get warm, and so do you. It heats in a manner similar to the sun. We don't feel the heat of the sun in the air, we feel it as it "radiates" off of surfaces. Radiant heat was a very big item in the post WWII building boom. Levittown, PA had copper piping installed in the floor as the concrete was poured, the pipes connected to a boiler, and that was your heat. Great concept but it failed miserably. The biggest problem was the impurities in the concrete reacted with the copper, and disintegrated the pipes. Leaks began to appear, and repairs were costly. The leak would create a hot spot in the floor. Cats were put in the room. They would lay on the hot spot and locate the leak. This was the first actual "cat scan." [31]Tearing up the carpets, chopping away at the concrete and repairing the leaks were costly and the systems were eventually bypassed. Baseboard hot water heat was then installed to replace it. The system was shelved for many years. Today radiant heat and air conditioning are extremely popular in Europe and growing in popularity here. Europe places a high value on energy efficiency where we do not. We place no regard on energy use as a nation, and continue to use heating systems that are banned in most European countries. Our leaders love when we use lots of oil. The downside of radiant heat is the front end costs are higher. Builders in many cases are reluctant to incur these costs on products like radiant heat. Builders like to put money into flashy impractical items that sell, and we buy as consumers. You can't blame them,

---

[31] Dan Holohan, Steam and hydronics heat expert's joke.

they have houses to sell. Radiant heat is the best kept secret in construction.

The major change in radiant heat from 40 years ago is the piping is not copper. The tubing is polyethylene. Plastic does not react with the concrete. The plastic used today has an extremely low rate of expansion and contraction with heat change. This eliminates the problem of abrasion damaging the tubes as they were to move in the concrete. The energy source for these systems can be natural gas, oil, solar, or electric. The medium carrying the heat in most cases is still water. The water is heated, circulates through the system, and returns to the boiler. The heat in the tubing heats the concrete and creates a passive warm distribution system that dissipates uniform comfortable heat. By slow heating, the air is not heated quickly. This reduces air currents and reduces stratification. Continual air movement and uneven temperatures in the layers of air are major sources of discomfort in heating a house. The house is cooler and healthier, but you are warmer. Cooler air has higher humidity so your skin won't dry out as much in the winter. Less outside air is sucked into the house which also lowers the humidity level in your home in the winter.

So simple, why isn't everyone doing it? There are some minor considerations. The National Wood Flooring Association advises against it, but the National Oak Flooring Manufacturers Association approves it with special installation guidelines. It can be a problem in a bedroom. The bed traps the heat under the bed creating a hot spot and a small fan may be needed to distribute the heat. The system should be zoned. A proper installation includes a manifold that allows water to only run to the zones demanding heat. This is slightly different than a zoned system with a traditional boiler and circulators for specific zones. The biggest problem with radiant heat is it does not lend itself easily to a retrofit installation. It's most cost effective if done as part of the original construction. It can be installed as part of a renovation, but it can be considerably more expensive than another existing system being modified for the renovation. There are also electric and ceiling mounted systems that heat you but not the air. Heat does not rise. Hot air rises. Therefore, radiant heat can be put in a ceiling and the heat will come "down" to the occupants. There are some applications where radiant heat is absolutely the best system. If you are renovating an old barn where there are very high ceilings that create massive amounts of dead air. Heat the floor where the people are, not the air 30 feet above them that no one ever occupies. Forced air heat will have the ceiling air at almost 80 degrees while the air at the floor is 70 degrees if you have a 25 or 30 foot vaulted ceiling. Who's using that heat up there? Churches, halls and office buildings would be best heated by radiant heat for the same reason. The system can also be installed to provide air conditioning through the same tubing. The air conditioning is far more efficient than traditional forced air cooling systems used here. But then we will use less oil, less electricity, less fossil fuel, and create less pollution. How would all of those people making millions of dollars off of our energy use survive?

Maintenance tips:

1. Often these systems are run off a boiler. See that section for tips on maintenance.
2. You can pick up a small thermometer at the hardware store. Radio Shack has a nice one also. Once a year. Lay it down on the floor in a variety of areas. The temperature should be constant throughout the system.

GAS OR OIL?

The question I am often asked is, what is cheaper for heating your home, oil or gas? Or, should I get a heat pump? Let's take a look at the first two options. The answer is quite simple. The cheapest heat source is the one presently in your home. Deciding which fuel source is cheapest is often a question of one thinking the grass is always greener on the other side of the fence. When the price of oil rises, the distributors of natural gas always seem to notice. They will then raise their prices. There may be a slight lag between the two, but they are rarely far apart. Recently oil jumped significantly in costs, and soon the natural gas distributors began ratcheting up their prices. The problem I have is that natural gas is primarily from domestic sources and the world market fluctuations that effect oil should not affect gas, but they raise their prices anyway. In other words, you get gouged either way.

There are some decisions regarding your home heat that do often arise. If your heater is in need of replacement, you then might consider the various options. Or, you just bought a house, and it does not have natural gas on the street, and you are used to living with gas. People often want natural gas for other reasons besides heating. Many people find gas the preferred heating fuel over oil or electric. A gas water heater is significantly less money than an oil water heater. A gas water heater is cheaper to run than an electric water heater. A gas dryer runs slightly hotter and is cheaper to run than an electric clothes dryer.

If these are concerns, a propane tank can be installed. In many cases, the tank is installed at no charge if you agree to buy all of your gas from the supplier. There are other considerations if you switch from oil to propane. The most overlooked item is the chimney. A chimney is an engineered structure that is built specifically for the fuel and appliances it vents. Switching from oil to propane will cause the lining in the chimney to fail. Faulty chimneys burn houses down, and kill people. Be sure your chimney is sized right for the appliance. A frequent defect I observe in homes is the "orphan water heater." The Home Owner buys a new high efficiency heater. High efficiency appliances vent through a PVC pipe out the side of the home and do not use the chimney. Now the water heater is the only appliance vented into the chimney. The reduction in exhaust gases into the chimney leads to considerable condensation. This moisture destroys the lining and the chimney fails. The solution is to change to a high efficiency water heater at the same time, and close off the chimney.

When purchasing a new heater, the contractor rarely discusses the chimney. I am not sure of their logic, but I am often asked, "Why didn't the heating contractor tell me this might kill me?" You will have to ask the heating contractor that question. If you have natural gas in your home and convert from oil to gas, all of the conditions described above also apply to your new gas appliances. Converting from gas to oil is another story. I am rarely asked about it, but the biggest concern with gas I hear is safety. Some people fear the explosive nature of gas. Again, changing fuels requires changes in the chimney system that should be addressed.

If you presently have electric heat and want to change to propane or gas, your best option is a high efficiency appliance. Basically they are called high efficiency appliances because they use more heat from the fuel being consumed. They contain a second heat exchanging system that pulls additional heat from the exhaust. This greatly reduces the temperature of the exhaust. The exhaust leaving the unit is about 100 degrees. This can be vented through a plastic pipe and does not have to vent through the top of the house. They can save you 10% to 15% each season in fuel. The PVC pipe is also considerably cheaper than relining the chimney. The unit itself is more expensive, but if you are there for the long haul, they are the best investment.

The last heat source is electric. Electric heat gets a bad rap. You only heat the rooms you are occupying and shut it off in the rest of the home. If done judiciously, this works very well. Children seem to struggle with this concept. Turning off the light when they leave a room is enough to remember. Also heat pumps get a bad rap. New electric heat pumps work very well. The secret is don't touch the thermostat. Set it at one temperature and leave it there all winter. They can be a competitively priced source of heat. Don't turn it down at night, and don't turn it up when you get a slight chill. "Put a sweater on," as Mom used to say.

What's the best system? If I was building a house, and had all the options in front of me, I would install a heat pump with a gas fired back up heat source. A heat pump is a good source of cheap heat for about 35% of the winter. With gas as a backup system, you get the best of both worlds. If you don't have gas in your home, they also make excellent oil fired heat pumps. If you have hot water heat, obviously a heat pump isn't considered. In general, your best bet is to stick with the fuel source you are presently using, get the most energy efficient type of appliance for that fuel, set your thermostat a little lower and put a sweater on.

HUMIDIFIERS

You moved into your new house and everything was fine until winter came. You walk across the carpet in your slippers and turn on the light. ZAP! You get struck by static electricity that feels like a miniature lightning bolt. It feels like a lightning bolt because it is a lightning bolt-just scaled down a bit. I was told when I first purchased a home computer that those little static electricity charges could damage the computer. That's just what I need, one more thing to worry about when I use my computer. Well, I haven't damaged the computer yet, but there were other issues with static electricity. My wife bought me a new robe for Christmas. It was loaded with static electricity. I put my robe on and went over to set the alarm clock and what seemed like a huge bolt of electricity jumped from my hand to the alarm clock. It knocked out the LED screen. All the alarm settings had defaulted back to 12:00. I couldn't believe it. I unplugged the alarm, waited ten seconds, and then plugged it back into the wall. I reset everything and it still works. From that day on, I believe that static electricity can damage computers as well. But this section is about humidifiers.

We will start by saying homes have humidity. There is lots of it caused by people living in the home. Cooking, showering, running water, and all our human functions such as breathing put moisture in the air. Humidity is relative. It is always listed as a percentage of how much moisture the air can hold at a given temperature. This is covered in detail in the attic ventilation section. A comfortable level of humidity in the winter in your home is about 35% to 40%. Even at those levels, there is the potential that you can damage the attic. The moisture rising into an unheated attic area in the dead of winter can condense. The attic ventilation section covers venting it. People add humidifiers to their heating systems to raise the humidity level. Very often they set the humidifier at 45% or higher. They complain about their nasal passages being dry, their skin being dry, and the static electricity. With the humidity set at 35%, you can still get shocks in the winter. My advice, deal with it. It won't kill you.

Let's take a look at what humidifiers do. They add moisture to the air in living space. The moisture rises with the warm air and damages the attic. It also follows the warm air out through the side walls. It then hits the cold surfaces beyond the insulation and condenses. Once the  insulation is wet, it becomes less effective. This makes this area colder and actually aggravates the situation by pulling more moisture into the area. This area becomes a breeding ground for mold. So the humidifier can damage the roof, the walls, the insulation, and create an unhealthy environment. And, that's just what the moisture will do. The elevated moisture levels can encourage the growth of biological organisms such as dust mites. Humidifiers also fill the air with microscopic mineral material. Homes with high humidity can get a white film on material. Most people think this is dust, but it's actually mineral deposits. The young, the elderly, and those with pre-existing lung conditions are the most vulnerable to respiratory problems from humidifiers. Wait a minute. Didn't you get that humidifier so you could breathe better? The Federal government has not concluded that using tap water in humidifiers poses a serious health risk. However, tap water does promote the growth of scale and crusty deposits in the humidifier. These materials provide a breeding ground for microorganisms. Therefore the use of alternative water sources such as distilled, or purified water is encouraged. I have been inspecting homes since 1994. The next humidifier I see using distilled water will be the first. They ALL use tap water. The use of water that has run through a reverse osmosis treatment is also encouraged. (I have seen that in homes, but it is usually only for the drinking water). There are specific instructions for the cleaning of humidifiers as well. You should empty the tank or reservoir in the bottom of the unit. Wipe it down daily. Use water with low mineral content. Clean portable humidifiers every third day by scrubbing it with a brush to remove any scale. The recommended cleaning solution is a 3% hydrogen peroxide solution. It is also recommended that you follow the manufacturer's instructions for cleaning them. The information in this article was obtained from the EPA Website, "Indoor Air Facts No. 8: Use and Care of Home Humidifiers. My suggestion is, before you buy a humidifier, go to the EPA website and read the entire article. If you have a humidifier, follow the instructions with the unit relative to materials used for cleaning and the frequency of cleaning they recommend.

Let's take a look at a problem home I was asked to inspect. The home had water running on the walls and ceilings. The attic had stains on the wood and drips of condensation off the nails for the shingles. There was evidence of excess moisture throughout the home. The house was six years old. The builder has spent in excess of $90,000 redoing

walls and ceilings in the home. The house was rotting away from moisture in the home. This house was extreme. The picture on the left is the heating systems for the home. They had two heaters and, voila, two humidifiers. They set the heat at 74 in the winter and the humidifiers at 45%.

Most humidifiers come with a humidistat. In the summer they set the air conditioning at 68. (I couldn't figure that one out either). They had a 175 gallon aquarium, a Labrador retriever and five adults living in the home. The combination of all these conditions was causing water to literally run down the walls. The first step I recommended was disconnecting the humidifiers, and cleaning them out. The cleaning should include descaling with a stiff brush and vinegar or hydrogen peroxide, then a second cleaning with a fungicide such as a mild bleach solution. (See the picture on previous page for an example of moderate scaling on a humidifier). Next, shut off the water supply and set the humidistat at zero. All of the problems relative to moisture in the home were life style related. By setting the temperature high, you fill the home with warm air. Warm air holds more moisture which will increase the amount of condensation formed when the air hits colder surfaces. By setting the air conditioning lower in the summer, you create a greater temperature differential which causes condensation to form on the cold surfaces. In our home in Florida, we keep the thermostat at 78 when the air conditioning is running, which is about 8 months out of the year. Even at that setting, the windows completely fog over. The condensation is forming on the outside of the windows. If it is forming there, it is also forming in areas where can't see where a cold surface is exposed to the warm humid outside air. No matter what part of the country you live in, if you have a need for air conditioning, set it as high as you can and still be comfortable. It's cheaper to run it  and you reduce the potential for mold growth and damage form moisture in areas that are inaccessible. Any vents in the home that remove moisture to the outside should be kept clean and working. This includes bathroom vents, and particularly dryer vents. Drying a load of clothes can put a couple of gallons of moisture in the home if the appliance is not properly vented. Clean bathroom fans regularly. If they vent into the attic, go up and be sure they are venting to the outside. Many times, bathroom vents are blocked by insulation and the moisture from showering stays in the attic, and in many cases, stays in the living area.

Maintenance tips:
1. Throw out your humidifier. If you want more humidity, get any or all of the following: Dog, cat, or other pets, (Larger pets create more humidity). Get house plants. They are a very healthy source of humidity. Consider an aquarium, or an indoor waterfall or fountain system. If you get one of the last two items, they require considerable maintenance.
2. If you have a vaporizer or room unit that you use for a sick child, completely drain it every morning and wipe it out completely. Every third day wipe it down with a hydrogen peroxide or vinegar solution. This will help reduce the buildup of any scaling.
3. Once a week, wipe it down with a mild bleach solution. Then run it to get any bleach smell out if it. Drain it and wipe it down before you use it for the child again.
4. Be sure the dryer vent is clean and venting to the outside.
5. Clean bathroom fans at least once a year and be sure they are venting to the outside as well.
6. Pick up a hygrometer at the local hardware store and monitor the moisture in your home. You never want it above 40%. (The government says 50%, but I have seen too many roof decks damaged by humidity to accept that high a number.

ELECTRICAL INSPECTIONS

How safe is the wiring inside your home? Many homes burn down because of electrical problems created by one owner and inherited by subsequent owners. In the past I have written about inspecting the exterior electrical system up to the to the main panel box. Let's take a look at the rest of the system. As I mentioned before, electricians are neat. Are there loose wires hanging in the basement ceiling or laying around in the attic? A Home Owner or "helpful" brother-in-law probably installed those wires. Wires should be secured every four and a half feet. If the wires are hanging loose, don't secure them. You want to have an electrician check the work.

When checking the system beyond a visual inspection, use a plug-in circuit tester. You can get one at any good home supply company. Get the type that also contains a ground fault circuit tester. They cost about $12.00. The tester has three lights on it, one is red and two are yellow. There is a button on it for testing the ground fault circuits. It also has a small chart on the one side that explains the different combinations of the lights. The second tool you will need is called a voltage sniffer. It looks like a fat ball point pen. It will make a noise or flash a light when it is near a live electrical line. You may have to go to an electrical supply company to get one. The sniffer will run about $25.00.

Take a look at your receptacles. Do they have two slots with a round hole? The small hole should be on the top, but about one in ten residential electricians install them that way. Three-hole receptacles are capable of being grounded. If they only contain two slots, you will need an adapter to get the three-prong tester to work. Let's go through testing the three-hole receptacle first. Simply plug the tester into the receptacle. The two yellow lights should light. If anything different happens, you should check the chart on the back of the tester. Now, write down the results, and the location of the receptacle. When you check the receptacles in the bathrooms, garage, exterior, and the receptacles above the counter area in the kitchen, push the test button on the tester. If the receptacle is grounded, the power should cut off. If the receptacle is not grounded, it won't trip or cut off the power. My suggestion is that you get the receptacles grounded. They are safer if they are grounded. If the power doesn't shut off, look in the main panel box and check all the receptacles in the house. If you find a receptacle or breaker with a button on it marked "test," push it. Go back and the power should be off at the receptacle. If it hasn't shut off and you have no other receptacles with the test and reset buttons, that receptacle is not on a ground fault circuit interrupter. Get one installed. If the GFCI has tripped reset it with the reset button and continue testing the remaining receptacles in the house. The GFCI will work on an ungrounded outlet. A GFCI can also protect up to five receptacles besides the receptacle where it is installed. A whirlpool should be on its' own GFCI.

You want GFCI protection on almost all receptacles near water. This includes bathrooms, above the kitchen counters, on the exterior, and in readily accessible areas in the garage. You should not plug a freezer or refrigerator into a GFCI protected receptacle. People often make this mistake, particularly in garages. The GFCI can trip in high humidity, during a thunderstorm, or from the surge of the motor starting. This can lead to a sad surprise when you get those steaks from the garage freezer. The receptacle for the sump pump should not be on a GFCI either. Although this does involve electricity and water, you don't want it tripping during a thunderstorm when you may need your sump pump. The second result you want is all the remaining receptacles to be properly wired. Improperly wired receptacles can indicate nonprofessional electrical work. Nonprofessional electrical work burns down houses. The second type of system, found in older homes, is the two-prong or two slot system. Plug the tester into the adapter you purchased. On the adapter is a small round piece of metal that lines up with the screw on the plate covering the receptacle box. Plug in the tester and push the metal against the screw. The ground light or second yellow light should light. If it doesn't light, the receptacle box inside the wall is not grounded. If any other lights on the tester light, the receptacle is improperly wired. I would be more concerned about improper wiring than the lack of a ground wire, however both are important. Write down the location of all the receptacles that did not test properly, and the defects observed on them. GFCI's are a very high priority, and you should have them installed as soon as possible. Remember those hanging wires? Hold the voltage sniffer close to the wires. If they are live, it will go off. Any live uninsulated or improperly protected electrical connections should be corrected immediately. At this point, show everyone in the house where they are so they may avoid them. Someone could be killed if they touch them before they are corrected. Practice using the sniffer on a cord for a lamp so you can see how it works. Next, run the refrigerator, the washer, dryer, and all the ceiling fans. Hold the voltage sniffer next to them. If it goes off, they are not grounded and should be on grounded circuits. Your highest priority is a safe electrical system. First, get the GFCI protection installed, and all live unprotected or unsecured wiring corrected. Next, ground the major appliances, and last, get the branch circuits grounded. Now, call and electrician and recite your "laundry list" to him. Hint: The bigger the job, the faster they seem to respond.

Maintenance tip:

1. Trip each breaker in main box one at a time each year. The first time you do it, label the breakers. If they are labeled, check them. Never believe the label. Don't worry; the breaker switches are as safe as any wall switch in the house. You are only touching plastic.

ARC FAULT INTERRUPTORS

We have all read or heard about a house fire that starts when no one was home or flares up in the middle of the night when everyone thought they were safe. The culprit is often an electrical fire. How can an electrical fire start at a time when most appliances are turned off or in a very minimal electrical demand? Another often asked question is how can a fire start when we have a perfectly operating electrical panel with a bevy of breakers to provide us with safety?

Many experts asked these same questions and began studying the problem. The solution begins with an understanding of how electricity is distributed, and how it operates. First, electricity will continue to flow through a wire at the same voltage, regardless of the draw. In simple terms, the wire to your clock radio has 110 to 120 volts of electricity flowing through it when the clock is running. It doesn't need the radio to be on. The current through the line is the same. The second consideration is when electricity runs into resistance, it gets hot. The heat builds up, and the gradual accumulation of the heat causes the fire. It's not the action of a single spark, but the constant flow of electricity creating a series of tiny sparks that cause the fire.

Let's take a look at the first part of the problem. Electricity is flowing along, happily minding its own business. The electricity actually travels along the surface of the copper wire, not in it. Suddenly, it comes to break in the electrical line. This can be caused by the wire being cut, bent, twisted, or impeded in some way. Often it is caused by a plug not being fully inserted into an electrical receptacle. This is most likely to happen in the bedroom. We plug in an appliance, and push the furniture back against the wall as close as we can. In doing so, the wire bends the plug, and now the receptacle is in the socket on an angle. The plug is close to the connecting terminal but not making full contact. The electricity then "jumps" from the plug to the terminal. This jumping action is called an arc. It can even be viewed as a tiny lightning bolt. The space between the plug and the terminal causes resistance, and electricity doesn't like resistance. The jumping action creates heat. This heat builds up. The heat is very gradual and is not enough to activate the safety device back in the main electrical panel. That device responds to an excessive draw of electricity. Too much electrical demand can create heat, but that's not our problem. In reality, it can happen when it's drawing very little electricity. Fires can start with low load electrical appliances.

This heat eventually accumulates to the point that materials around the receptacle begin to heat up. Remember where this is taking place, behind a piece of furniture. There is very little air exchange to cool things down, and the slight crackling noise that the electricity is creating is muffled. This is a formula for a fire. Enter the arc fault circuit interrupter or AFCI! The arc fault interrupter is a brilliantly designed safety device that responds to a combination of conditions. It senses that arcing is taking place. Have you ever plugged in an appliance that was turned on, and witnessed a tiny spark? That is an arc. That little arc usually won't trip your AFCI.

The AFCI knows that spark is nothing and ignores it. If the spark continues to occur, the AFCI springs into action and cuts off the flow of electricity to the entire branch circuit. It operates on a combination of sensing an arc, determining the size of the arc, and lastly, measuring the duration of the arc. The combination of these elements will trip the device. How does it work? I don't know. You will have to ask an electrical engineer. My advice is to be seated comfortably when you ask them. Most engineers I know will graciously provide detailed answers to these types of questions. The important consideration is that it does work.

How do I know I have them, where do I see them, and how can I check them? Arc fault circuit interrupters were added to the Electrical Code on January 1, 2002. If your home was built after that date, the chances of you having them are better, but it's not automatic. Your house may have been built to comply with an older code. If your home was built before that it may have them, as they have been on the market for several years. Look in your main electrical panel for breakers with a small blue button on them. The Code required them for bedroom areas only. To test them, push the blue button. Now go to the bedroom served by that particular circuit and test for power. Use a light or electrical tester, and plug it into the receptacles. There should be no power to that branch. Go back to the panel and reset the breaker. Push the breaker all the way to the opposite side of all the other breakers, and then push it back to the same side as the other breakers. You should hear a click when you push it back. You should now have your power restored.

This is the best way to test them. Testers are available, but they are several hundred dollars. How often should you test them? The experts feel you should test the ground fault circuit interrupters in your bathroom once a month. In theory, these should be tested with the same frequency. What's important is that you test them regularly. A second thing happens when you test them. You pull the furniture away from the wall and examine the connection and the receptacle. If the wire is damaged, replace it. If there are burn marks on the plug or receptacle, have a licensed electrician check it. Electricity is a powerful force that should be respected. Be aware of its dangers and regular inspections of outlets can protect you. The newest Code will require either Arc Fault Interrupters or Ground Fault Interrupters on ALL outlets in your Home. That is a drastic but realistic change.

Maintenance tip:

1. Test your ARC Fault Interrupters once a month by pushing the test button in the panel. I know it's a hassle to reset the digital clocks in the bedrooms, but you want to be sure these safety devices are working.

A TRIP TO THE BATHROOM

Let's take a look at the bathroom in terms of regular maintenance. We will start with the sink. Sinks get clogged. You may try a very basic approach. Pour boiling water down the drain. Generally that works better in the kitchen where some type of food blockage or grease might be the culprit. Bathroom sinks are often clogged by an accumulation of foreign objects. Hair and other smaller debris then catch on the larger object and soon you have a pipe's version of a log jam. Sometimes a plunger will do the trick in opening them. If that doesn't work, you have to break out some real tools and go to work. Under the sink is an S shaped pipe called a trap. (The "S" is turned sideways). Its' job is to hold water. The water keeps sewer gases from backing up into the house. It also holds a lot of other things on occasion. You will need a large adjustable pair of pliers or a pipe wrench. Ideally, you always want to use a wrench that is exactly sized for the item you are loosening. Remove everything from under the sink. We often keep paper products there and wet toilet paper cannot be saved. It is a good idea to have a bucket or pan under the trap. Having a couple of rags or a chamois handy is also helpful. Remember, the reason you are taking it off is there is water in the sink that won't go away. That water will now come gushing out of the trap. Turn the slip nut to loosen it. You remember the old saying, "Righty tighty, lefty loosie." (I have no idea how to spell those words). You may want to hold the pipe with the off hand. Sometimes they tend to move as you try and loosen them. Once you have started it, it should turn easily by hand. Loosen the top one first. It is between the S trap and the sink. Now loosen the bottom one between the S trap and the floor. That way most of the water will run in the bucket. By loosening both nuts you have now freed up the trap which is really a J pipe. You are hoping it is full of debris. Clean it out. Run a rag through it if necessary. In reassembling the connection, you might want to change the washers. If you bought a new J pipe, it comes with new washers as well as nylon bushings. When you put the trap back together, be careful. Pipes do not require you turn them down with a lot of force. They should be tight enough that you need a wrench to loosen them, but not too tight. They can snap off and the threads can also bind or strip easily. I tend to use slightly more force than needed. If everything is clean and there is no blockage, you may have problems "further on down the road" to quote a blues song whose author I do not know.

Cleaning out the drain from the trap down can sometimes be done by a Home Owner, but it can get complicated. We had a sink we just couldn't get to drain. I bought a cheapie snake to clean the drain. A snake is a long wire with kind of a head on one end and it is connected to a crank on the other end. You feed it down the pipe and turn the crank as you force it down. The wire clears debris from the drain. I pulled the trap apart, after numerous attempts at clearing it with plungers, hot water, and assorted drain cleaning products. When all that didn't work, we went to Plan B, or more appropriately, Plan P. We finally brought in a plumber. He had a snake that attached to a drill. He fed it down the line and ran the drill. He was at it for about twenty minutes. It sounded like very painful dentist work. He cleared the line, but the job was far more involved than most Home Owners can handle, at least this Home Owner. (Remember, this is *not* a how to book, it is a maintenance book). The plumber said the snake he used costs about $1,000.00. When he was done he ran water and came downstairs and looked at the ceiling. I thought he was checking to see if he came through, but he was afraid he may have punctured the drain line. When you empty the trap you may find some unusual items. We found tooth brushes. You might also find jewelry. You can try the Home Owner snake. They are under $50.00 but you may still end up with a $200 plumbing bill.

Replacing a washer in a leaky faucet is relatively simple. First, shut off the water with the shut off valve under the sink. If you live in an older home and don't have shut off valves, it gets complicated. You have to shut off the water at the main. If you are working on the first floor, shut the water off at the main, then open the water lines in the basement laundry tub to drain all the water in the house. If you are working on the highest floor of the home this is not an issue. Once you open the faucet you are repairing, all the water above it in the house may drain out through the missing faucet. Next, close the stopper in the drain in the sink. Murphy's law says if you don't, the first screw you take off will fall down the drain. If that happens, refer to trap repair described above. There is usually a cap on the top of the faucet you can pry off. Then remove the screw and pull the handle off. You may need to pry it with a screw driver. Be careful not to scratch it, some are shiny chrome and scratch easily. The washer is usually rubber and compressed under a nut. Take the washer off and the whole assembly to the hardware or plumbing supply with you. You will need to get the right size. It slides back on and just reverse the whole process. In a pinch you can sometimes flip the washer over and reinstall it and get a good seal, at least for a while. There are washerless faucets with a handle that is sort of like a joy stick. This type of faucet very rarely needs repairs. A leaky faucet can be a very expensive minor defect. They can easily put $50.00 to $75.00 on your water bill in a month. That sounds high, but I have seen people with that much of an increase. It is a whole lot worse if the leak is on the hot water side. Your water heater will keep turning on so you are paying for fuel as well.

The stopper for the drain sometimes breaks. There is a rod that comes up through the top of the sink. You pull it up and the stopper goes down. It is connected to a horizontal rod that goes into the drain. There is often a nut and bolt that holds the first two rods together. They come apart and are easily reconnected. If the stopper comes off the rod inside the drain, you have to remove the slip nut off the side of the drain. These pieces fit inside each other. Piecing these two items together can be a little tricky. It often takes a few tries to get it to go together. You may have to replace the rod and the rubber washer inside it. This connection may leak on occasion as well. The rod slides inside the opening in the bottom of the stopper itself. The bottom of the stopper can also crack. If the stopper comes off the rod, the stopper falls and closes the drain. The stopper won't go up. You have to pry it with a small sharp edge. A Swiss Army knife works well, as does a screwdriver for eyeglasses. The most common item to break in this assembly is the base of the stopper itself. This breaks off and the horizontal rod has nothing to grab. We had a problem with the stopper in our master bathroom. It was on my "Honey Do" list. My wife, bless her heart, wrapped a rubber band several times around the stopper, then stuck it in the drain. It didn't operate but it stayed up so the sink would drain. The truth is, who actually uses this stopper anyway? If you use, write me. I'm curious as to how many people use it. In performing home inspections since 1994, and asking people, no one admits to actually using the stopper.

The faucet on the sink will sometimes spray sideways. There is a small screen aerator in the faucet. Turn the base of the faucet and it unscrews. There is a screen that you may be able to clean off. It too, gets sediment in it. Have you noticed a pattern here? Sediment and basic build up in the dishwasher, toilet, sink, and the humidifier. A water softener or in line filter for the entire water supply can help. Generally when people get a water softener or filter, they sometimes have the outside water isolated from it. There is no need to soften the water for the lawn, or used to wash the car. People often think of these items with private well water. The truth is in line filters and softeners are not a bad idea for any water system. Softeners replace an ion in the water with a salt. It is such a small amount that it doesn't alter the taste of the water. A softener is good for the pipes as it cuts down on corrosion in the lines. It also cuts down on sediment. You may have heard of the term hard water. Hard water contains various ions that the water softener replaces. Without getting into a chemistry class, softened water lathers better so you use less soap. It reduces the streaks and soap scum you can get on plumbing fixtures. It adds salt to the diet so if you are on a low salt diet, consult your doctor before you have one installed. They are not at all harmful to the environment, and they help reduce build up inside your plumbing lines. There are also salt free softeners. If you are having a problem with sediment build up, or any of the conditions mentioned above, consider adding a softener and inline filter. Most homes that have one have both. The filter is a lot cheaper. In terms of maintenance, the filters are often in a clear plastic assembly. The top comes off with a plastic wrench that comes with the filter. You change the filter when it is dirty. This can be a few months in some homes, to once a year in a home with one occupant. Turn the water off at the main before you change the filter. Softeners require a back wash cycle every few months, and again that depends on usage. The most common softeners I see are from Sears. I suggest you hire a plumber to install them. Then read the manual and follow the instructions for use. You will also have to buy salt for it which I am told is relatively cheap. Remember, you see the sediment in the faucet filter, the dishwasher and other visible areas. Most home owners have no idea what's going on in the water lines where they can see sediment and deposits. Back to the bathroom.

The toilet. You want the toilet to be steady, with no rocking. You want the handle to operate easily and everything to go away with one flush. You want the tank on the back to fill up and shut off when it's filled. Sounds simple enough doesn't it? When I was growing up in the 1950's my father used to tell me they didn't have flush toilets in Russia. I was glad I was born here when he said that. Let's start with a steady toilet. The base should not rock, nor should the tank. If the tank rocks, the first thing you need to do is shut off the water to the toilet. Now flush it. Now with no water in the toilet, there are two screws at the base of the tank. They usually have a cap over them. The walls may be a little slimy, don't worry, it won't hurt you. Flip the caps off, and tighten the screws. Then reinstall the caps and turn the water back on. Don't tighten them too much!

If the bowl rocks on the floor, this can be a little more complicated to fix. The principle reason toilets rock is there has been some slow leaking that has not been addressed. If it's on the first floor and you can get under it in the basement, go down and check the area around it for leaking. Sometimes, the leak rots the floor. This is a little more than a maintenance issue. You have to remove the toilet, fix the floor and reinstall the toilet. This project can be involved. There are two nuts that hold the toilet in place. They usually have caps on them to hide them. Flip off the caps and try and tighten the nuts. If you are really lucky, they will tighten down and the problem is solved. That rarely happens. In some cases the slow leak has rusted the nuts and bolts. The bolt snaps off when you try and tighten it. In this case, you need to pull up the toilet. First things first. Turn off the water to the toilet. When working on any plumbing fixture, turn off the water to it first. Then disconnect the water line to the toilet. You will need a small wrench. I strongly suggest, again, using a wrench that fits rather than pliers or an adjustable wrench. They can slip and strip the fastener. Now flush the toilet to empty the tank.

Next is the yucky part. Get a small paper cup like the one they give you at the doctor's when they want a sample of a particular body fluid. The smaller the cup, the easier it is to use. Scoop as much of the water out of the bowl as possible. You want it lighter and you don't want to spill it.

Be careful. A toilet is top heavy with the tank attached. You are actually much better off if you remove the tank from the bowl. Remember those two screws we just talked about? Lift it just enough to move it off the drain. The bolts hook on two holes on the sides of the flange. If the bolts have rusted away, you will need to get new bolts. If the flange is rusted away, add that to the shopping list at the hardware or plumbing supply store. Once you have removed the toilet, stuff a rag in the drain line. These openings are magnets for items like glasses, pens, etc. or whatever is in your top pocket. You lean over, the item falls, and you begin sounding like a plumber that thinks there is no one in the house. (Sorry plumbers, it's a joke!)

Once the toilet is lifted off the drain, you can clean the drain. If you had leaking, the wax seal is probably damaged. Either way, add a wax seal to the items you will need. Be sure you get the right one. 4X3 is the most common. Measure the opening in the drain. You want the inside dimension as well as the outside dimension. Have both with you just in case. If you have a camera phone, take a picture of the opening and take it with you. The clerk at the plumbing supply should be able to guide you through the wax seal buying process. Now clean the opening. Clean everything as well as possible. Set the seal in place. Now lower the toilet onto the opening. This can be tricky. First, the toilet is heavy. Secondly, you need to fish the two bolts that hold it in place up through the holes in the base of the toilet. If these holes are cracked, you need a new toilet. You will never get it tight. Feed the bolts up through the base and set the toilet. Now sit on it! Get the heaviest person in the house to sit on it. If that's not you, don't tell them why you asked them to sit on it. Next, push down on the bowl on all sides so the toilet is firm and level. Now tighten down the bolts. Careful, not too tight! Firm, but not too tight, you don't want to crack the porcelain base. Now, reconnect the water and voila! You have a toilet that doesn't leak. Do not caulk around the base of the toilet. If it's leaking, you want to know about it so you can fix it. As far as fixing the guts inside the toilet, the most common failure is the chain, and the next is the flapper. The connection between the chain and the lever often rusts away. Hardware stores have the right parts to fix this. I see a lot of paper clips used to reconnect the chain, as well as a diverse list of make shift repairs. When you connect the chain, you want it to lift the flapper, but be careful the lever doesn't hit the lid on the bowl. Carefully, bending this rod sometimes works. The flapper can easily be replaced. The good thing about toilets is most repairs can be done with pliers and a couple of screw drivers. A lot of the internal parts are now made with nylon rather than metal so they are easier to work with. Changing the seat is rather simple. The new seat has all the parts, the nylon fittings come off easily. WD40 is very good at loosening things up if they don't co-operate. When you use it, put it on the uncooperative bolts, nuts, fittings, etc. and leave it on there. It sometimes takes time to seep down into the joint before it actually loosens it. Once it's on there, you may want to wipe it off the area where you put the wrench. It can make it slippery.

TILE REPAIR

When was the last time you thought about your grouting? There is a tendency in Home Owners to feel grouting is forever. Now you are wondering, "What is grouting?" Grouting is the material found between the courses of tile in your bathroom or kitchen. It is usually white. Gradually, over the years, mold grows and darkens it. There are several products designed to clean this area. The most effective cleaner I found is "The Works." It cleans away the mold as well as the residue left by hard water drying on the tile and grouting. When using a tile cleaner follow the directions carefully. Some may not be suited for color grouting. On the label, all of these products warn you to ventilate. They are not kidding. Open the window, and if possible set up a small fan to keep the air moving.

While cleaning the tile, now is the time to examine it. First, check for leaks. Run water in the shower with the water directed at the wall for about five minutes. Check the ceiling below for any stains. Now remove the wood panel on the wall behind the tub. Using a flashlight, check everywhere you can see for water stains. You may have a leak that hasn't worked its way to the ceiling yet. If the stain feels dry, mark it with a pencil line and check it in six months to see if the stain is spreading past the mark.

Next, get into the tub or shower and tap GENTLY on the tiles. If some of them have a hallow sound, they are beginning to work their way loose. Loose tiles leak. Start at the bottom and work your way up. If the tile are going to be loose anywhere, it is almost always in the bottom few courses. Pay close attention to the tiles below the faucets and the soap dish. Now take a close look at the grouting. Tiny hairline cracks will begin to appear long before the ceiling is damaged below. No hairline cracking is another good sign. Next, you may want to consider sealing the grout. There is a material called Tile Lab that reseals your grouting. Get a small paintbrush, and carefully go over all the grouting. If you use too much and it runs, there is a product called Grout Haze Clean Up that will clean up the haze that the seal can leave behind.

If you found loose tiles and cracked grouting, they should be repaired. Often, a dab of caulk works well. Be sure to get caulk specifically designed for the repair. If you are losing tiles, check the wall behind it. If the wall is severely damaged, repairs can be costly. Not repairing it will allow water to penetrate the stud cavity behind the wall and your problems will increase dramatically. Another condition frequently found is grouting repaired by graduates of the "More Is Always Better School of Home Repairs." The grouting is out of the joints, and raised above the tile. When installing grouting, the goal is to have it recessed, or slightly lower than the tile surface so it accents the beauty of the tile. In either case, you're faced with rebuilding the grouting.

To remove the grout, I use a screwdriver and a utility knife. Be very careful. A slight slip can scratch the tile. There is an inexpensive tool called a grout saw that is designed for the job. Clean out as much of the grout as possible and prepare the surface according to the directions. Apply the new grout with a small putty knife and try to keep the grout inside the joint as much as possible. When I did it, I worked the grout in with my finger to get the recessed look I desired. When doing this, clean up the excess grout right away. If it hardens on the tile, it can be a very slow clean up and the chance of damaging the tile with a scratch increases considerably.

When checking the floor, a major concern is a crack that runs right through joint after joint and through the tile between the joints. Tile is like glass. If there is no support under it, it will crack easily. A crack running through several course of tile is usually an indication of the floor failing below the tile. This can be a major expense. Failure to repair it will result in the wood rotting and eventually, someone will be standing there drying themselves and suddenly "drop in" on the floor below.

If you are getting leaking from a stall shower and the tile looks good, the lead pan may be damaged. Stop up the drain and run water in the shower. Let the water get one inch deep, but no more. Shut off the water and leave it in there for about fifteen minutes. If the pan is bad, you will get a leak below. If it doesn't leak, check the door area. Shower doors are installed by drilling holes in the tile. The caulk on these openings fails, and periodically has to be resealed. Occasionally, this testing system won't work. Sometimes the crack only opens when there is weight in the shower. Don't suggest to your wife that her weight is causing the shower pan to leak. This can have severe consequences. But by performing a test without a person in it, then with a person in the shower, it will tell you that the pan is cracked, or the joints around the sides are opening with the added weight. Another unusual scenario for tile leaking is what I call the 2nd shower syndrome. The first person takes a shower and it doesn't leak, then the next person takes a shower and it leaks. Everyone starts saying, "What are you doing in there to cause the leak?" Probably nothing.

One of two things is occurring. One is that the leak just needs more water to show up on the ceiling below. The leak is so small that not enough water accumulates with one shower. The other is the grout is very slowly absorbing water and finally reaches saturation with the 2nd shower. The repairs for these leaks are the same as discussed. Sealing the tile is often the solution to this problem. I do an extensive amount of leak analysis for roofing contractors. As you might expect, the smaller the leak, the less often it occurs, the more difficult it is to find. Same hold true for the bathroom. One last note about leaks, roofing leaks often appear under bathrooms. The water enters the home, runs down the studs or inside the outside wall, and then follows along the flooring to the lowest spot in the ceiling. This is often the bathroom due to the weight of the fixtures and tile.

If you haven't checked your grouting in the last five years, it's probably a good idea to do it. Be sure to clean the tile on a day warm enough to leave the window open.

Maintenance tips:

1. Tap on the tiles once a year to see if they are coming loose.
2. Re-secure them if loose as per the above article.
3. Pull the access panel off and check for any evidence of leaking behind the panel.
4. Clean the tiles annually with Tilex or another good tile cleaner. Ventilate! The fumes from these cleaners can be very strong.
5. Check the junction of the tub and the floor, as well as the tile wall around it. Re-caulk if the caulk is drying out and opening. BE NEAT! You can also use your finger to work it into the joint.
6. Don't caulk the base of the toilet. If that's leaking, you want to know it.
7. Get a squeegee for cleaning the glass door to the shower. Tell the clerk at the home supply what you want to do, and they will lead you to them. They are usually in the cleaning supply section.
8. Change the liner in your shower curtain once a year. They get very grungy gradually and suddenly they are covered with scum and possible mold or algae growth.
9. Use baking soda to clean the grout if you want to be kind to the planet and protect yourself from harmful fumes.

DRINKING WATER

"Plumbum" is the Latin word for lead, as in metal. Therefore the derivation of the word plumbing lies in the metal which was first used extensively to carry water to the masses. The Egyptians had plumbing systems as far back as 2500 BC. The Romans had sewers in 800 BC that are still in use today. Plumbing has a rich and long history. Humans need water. Our migration and growth is always centered on bodies of water, and flood stories are found in all ancient civilizations. We need it. But we need it clean, we need it in the right amount, and yes, we need it to go away when we are done with it. One more thing to note about water, water wins. Water breaks down the planet.

The drinking water we use today is a far cry from the "potable" water found in our cities as recently as one hundred years ago. At the turn of the century, (1899 to 1900), the principle source of water for the city of Philadelphia was a huge reservoir located at the present site of the Philadelphia Art Museum. The walls of the reservoir were as high as the walls of the museum. The water was pumped into it from the Schuylkill River. Philadelphia drinking water is still affectionately known as "Schuylkill Punch." The quality of the water varied greatly depending on the supply. A protest letter was written to the major Philadelphia newspaper of the late nineteenth century concerning the color of the water. The "ink" used for the letter was said to be the mud like water the resident had flowing from his tap. Fairmount Park was left undeveloped and designated as a park to allow clean run off water to replenish the reservoir. The factories of the distant town of Manayunk unfortunately, were the origin of pollution in the water. (Manayunk is now part of the city of Philadelphia and is about 5 miles from the present site of the Philadelphia Art Museum. This building gained considerable fame when Rocky ran up the front steps of it).

The water in today's modern cities is filtered, treated and tested regularly to protect the public. In smaller communities the testing and filtering may not be as vigilant. The lead plumbing may have played a hand in the fall of Rome as it has been linked to lead poisoning. This condition basically reduces the blood's ability to carry oxygen, and is a serious concern. Lead is still the number one contaminant found in water. Almost all houses constructed between World War II and the late 1980's used lead in the solder joints. The first draw of water in the morning may contain lead that leached into the water sitting in the pipes. If there is sediment in the lines, the water has a low ph level, contamination may still occur. Let the water run for thirty seconds or so before you drink it if you are concerned.

The Federal Clean Water Act of 1988 reduced the levels of lead in solder joints, but its enforcement may be inconsistent. It is estimated the United States dumps 400 million tons of toxic chemicals into the water each year. If you are very concerned about the quality of the drinking water, you can drink bottled "spring" water. I don't recommend this. The plastic in the bottles will be here for thousands of years to come. I recommend getting a pitcher with a filtering system and keep it in the refrigerator. This is much more environmentally friendly. Not all bottled water is spring water. Also, refrigerate the water after opening to reduce the possibility of bacteria growth in the water. Any individual filtration system can certainly help. Many advertise they reduce the lead content in the water. If you want to test your tap water, contact the following organizations for test information: Clean Water Lead Test, Inc. 704-251-6800, Environmental Law Foundation, 510-208-4555, or contact your regional EPA office. Go to EPA.gov and search for water.
There are presently over 1200 known contaminants listed by the Safe Water Committee of the National Academy of Sciences. No testing service tests for all of them. The

chemical composition of the water can not only affect human plumbing, it can also affect the plumbing in your house. The main water line entering the home may be lead in some home constructed before 1940. If your water line contains nice clean bends, is grey in color, and has no threaded joints, its lead. Change it, or drink bottled water. Replacement can be about $150 per linear foot from your house to the street. If the main water line is grey, has threaded joints, and turns at right angles, it is probably galvanized pipe. That is good news, and bad news. The good news is the iron and zinc in the water is beneficial to many people as it puts trace elements in our bodies. The bad news is these lines are old. They stopped using galvanized water lines in the mid 1950's. The lines rust internally, and eventually close off. Your water pressure will keep getting weaker and weaker until you need to replace the main line. Now you're back to that $150.00 a foot price we just mentioned.

The interior water lines can vary greatly. Most homes built since 1945 have copper interior water lines. They hold up fairly well but can fail. Hard water can damage them. Check the lines for small green spots on the lines. They may be starting to fail. Also check the fittings. If they are green and have a white powder building up on them they are starting to fail. The green can be caused by the flux used in soldering. The white powder is caused by small amounts of water leaking, evaporating off, and leaving salt and calcium deposits. In most cases, a water softener is a good investment. It's healthier for the pipes, and for you. If you have grey rubber plumbing in your home, that product may have been the subject of a class action law suit due to catastrophic failure of the joints. Production ceased in 1995. If you think you have this type of plumbing, you can call 800-876-4698, 602-966-0377, or 800-490-6997. Replacement of these systems can cost $5,000 plus.

Another rubber type water line system is PEX. It is pretty easy to tell if you have it. The water main goes into a central manifold with a row of shut off valves on each side. There is a little plastic wrench that comes with the manifold that you use to shut off the water in each line. The lines are two colors, red and blue. The red is for the hot water line, the blue are the cold water lines. PEX is easier to work with if you have the right tools. You run a dedicated line from the manifold to the fixture where you need water. This is fairly important. Have you ever had someone flush the toilet or throw in a load of laundry while you are in the shower? The water pressure can drop significantly resulting in scalding. It's usually the cold water pressure that drops. In older homes with older plumbing, these conditions can cause one to consider homicide. This doesn't happen with PEX. The water pressure remains uniform throughout the system. The lines are also very flexible. You don't have to stop, cut, and solder with each turn as you would with copper. This can greatly reduce installation costs. The material itself is also significantly cheaper. The lines are meant for interior use only. Copper can be used on the exterior. Copper can also be recycled, and PEX cannot as per what I have read about it. If I was building a home, I would probably be very inclined to use PEX based on my knowledge of the product at the time of this writing. Time will tell if there are unanticipated negative consequences with its use, but today, I think the positives greatly outweigh the negatives.

There are CPVC systems approved for domestic water today that are very good. They are white. The only downside is they crack easily when exposed to freezing temperatures. They crack much sooner than copper lines at the same temperature. Remember, water begins to expand before it freezes. This expansion in a stationary line can result in cracking.

The solution to all of this? You can test your water. You can contact you municipality and see their test results and how often they test. You can get home filtration systems that can be very sophisticated and filter the whole house, filter the water at the tap, or a pitcher that filters just the water you drink. Keep the pitcher refrigerated, and change the filter according to the instructions. You can also do nothing. Water contaminants have been linked to cancer, lead poisoning, and many other ailments. These events are isolated, but they cannot be considered rare. There is much we don't know about the human body and how it reacts to repeated exposure to various impurities. Damage caused by this exposure can vary greatly between two people depending on their own chemistry and immune system. Maybe someday the people in foreign lands will say the United States is a beautiful country but "Don't drink the water."

Maintenance tips:
1. Walk the basement and check the water lines for evidence of discoloration or white salty deposits on the pipes.
2. Get some form of water filter. The easiest is a pitcher with replaceable filters, and store it in the refrigerator.
3. If you are really concerned, ask your water company to supply you with the test results on the municipal water.
4. If you have a well as a private water source, get an inline filter for the whole house, and get your water tested every year.

WATER MAIN

Every modern home has running water. We take this for granted today but not that long ago and for most of history, this wasn't the case. The water enters the home through a water main. It is often located in the front of the home. It enters underground, anywhere from 3' to 8' below grade. Once it enters the home there is a shut off valve to turn it off. This is important. You should know where it is and anyone who is responsible for your home such as a baby sitter, adult children, grandparents, should know where it is. If there is a water emergency they should be able to get to it in a hurry and turn it off. That means you don't store boxes or put shelves in front of it. Water running at 8 gallons a minute on the 2nd floor can do enormous amounts of damage in a very short time.

The line itself is most often copper. If it is lead, you might want to replace it. If you don't, get your water tested for lead content. In many cases the lead has pretty much leached out of the line and the levels of lead coming out are acceptable. You should also get a filter for your drinking water. Many of  them, such as Brita claim to filter lead as well as many other less desirable elements in the drinking water. If your line is galvanized, it is actually healthier for you. The bad news is these lines fail. They gradually close off with rust and replacement cost can be significant. If you have a galvanized line, budget to replace. You will know it is failing by a gradual reduction in water pressure until there is no flow at all. Once the symptoms start, you are looking at about a year, before replacement is a necessity. Private water systems from a well are often rubber. If the water line is metal of any kind, there should be wire that is attached to the line on each side of the meter. This is called a ground jumper. It grounds your electrical system. Pull on it, it should be tight. The best type of shut off valve for your system is a ball valve. They have a lever on them to turn them off. There are often two, one on each side of the meter. Turn off the valve on the house side of the meter if you are going away for more than a few days, particularly in the winter. If the pipes should freeze and burst, you don't want the water running for days through the house. The other common type of valve is a hose bib type valve, (shown in picture). It is a good idea to test them once you move in and at least once a year even if you don't go away. They can seize and not turn off. This can also create huge problems in a plumbing emergency.

Once the water enters the home, if you have a private system you might want to consider some kind of filtering system. Private systems tend to have more dirt than public water lines. You may also consider a water softener. A softener adds trace amounts of salt to the water, but most medical professionals say it is not enough for a concern if you are on a low salt diet. If you are on a low salt diet, and are considering getting a softener, check with your doctor. Don't depend on my advice. They do require some maintenance and I recommend you have a plumber install it unless you are very adept at plumbing.

There is an important part of the electrical system that is located at the water main. If you have a metal water main in the home, the water line serves as a ground system for the electrical system. There should be two heavy clamps on the water main on each side of the meter. There should be a wire connecting them. In some cases this wire is thick aluminum or lead. In other cases, it looks like the battery cables in your car. This wire completes the ground circuit to earth in the event the home gets struck by lightning. If lightning strikes the house, it wants to go to earth. It often finds the plumbing lines in the house. (Don't shower during a thunder storm!) It then follows them wherever they go. You want the lightning to leave as soon as possible and as easily as possible. If the ground on the water main is tight and secure, the lightning will find this and hopefully leave without doing too much damage. 100 Million volts bouncing around the home has the potential to really cause some damage. Pull on the ground wire. It should be tight. You may not have this if the water main is rubber. Private well systems almost always have rubber water mains. Also if your meter seems to be hanging on the water line rather than in a straight line, and there are brass lines almost in a circle connected to the water line, this type of meter creates its own grounding system. That is acceptable.

Maintenance tips:
1. Clean out any obstacles to get to the water main. You want to be able to get there quickly if you have an emergency.
2. Turn the main off at least once a year. There are two valves normally. Turn off the one between the meter and the home first. It should turn off and turn back on. When you do this have a faucet running that you can hear. That way you will know if it shut the water off.
3. Now turn the other valve between the meter and street.
4. If you have an inline filter, change the filter when it is dirty. The filter will last different times for different people.
5. Back wash the water softener according to the instructions with the unit.

CROSS CONNECTIONS

The nation recently witnessed a tragic e-coli epidemic, and the experts were scratching their heads for some time trying to find the source. Somewhere in California they suspect, the sanitary chain of the distribution of spinach was violated and we may never know the where and why of how it happened. It is literally the equivalent of finding a needle in a hay stack. All it may have taken is some poor farm worker that, when nature called, couldn't make it to the proper facilities. The healthy distribution of safe food to millions of people is no small challenge, and we saw how fragile it can be. I won't get on my soapbox about buying locally grown foods. I do not do it as much as I should. My daughter makes a point of it and it is such a positive behavior on so many levels. You are supporting local businesses, the food is fresher, and the chance of you becoming a victim of some contamination along the food chain drops significantly. The distribution of clean water to the public is an equally daunting task, and unfortunately, just as fragile.

We take clean water for granted. The water leaving the filtration plants is run to us through clean lines in a sealed system. That system can be breached by a sequence of unrelated events resulting in contamination that can cause illness and death similar to the e-coli break out. Fortunately, this contamination is much easier to arrest as the area serviced by water companies is far smaller than a national food distribution system. Let's take a look at a possible sequence of unrelated events that can be a recipe for disaster. There is a large fire about a mile away in the valley. Mr. Home Owner's pool is low on water since the weather has been dry. He drops the garden hose in the pool, turns it on, and goes to the mall with his wife, (that part might be fiction). The fire rages for several hours significantly dropping the water pressure in the public water supply. Mr. Home Owner comes home and finds the water in the pool is lower than it was this morning. He's confused. That night the water company begins to get calls about the heavy chlorine smell in the water. The loss of water pressure caused by the fire has turned the hose into a siphon and pulled the water from the pool and deposited in everyone's drinking water down the street. The lesson to be learned from this is to hang the hose over the pool rather than dropping it into the pool when filling it. This or a similar chain of events occurs more often than you think.

Cross contamination is caused by the backflow of unwanted water, gases or other substances into the potable water supply. Another more severe way this occurs is when fertilizers or water used in industry back siphons in a similar manner. One way home owners leave their families and neighbors at risk is by leaving the fill line to their hot water heating system open. This is often done on older systems that have pinhole leaks. Rather than go to the expense of finding the leak and repairing it, people leave the feed line open. A drop in water pressure can pull the water out of the heating system and into the domestic water. This water has been sitting in rusty pipes that often have lead soldered joints. The water has been heated and reheated, so it just pulls all kinds of unwanted minerals out of the hot water heat distribution system.

How can a home owner protect against it? You really can't protect yourself against your neighbor's mistakes. Checking valves on all systems such as sump pumps and hose bibs are a great start. The sump pump doesn't affect the domestic drinking water, but often we see sump pumps connected to residential sewer systems. This connection is illegal in just about every municipality and without a check valve a blockage in the sewer line can flood a basement with raw human sewage. I'll spare you the details of how that can ruin your day. It can also result in thousands of dollars of cleanup costs. Dishwashers and bidets have air gaps between the water in the fixture and the fill lines. In the old days, the fill lines in tubs for example were down in the tub itself. Pressure in water supplies were not as uniform then and the tub water could be siphoned back into the supply water. Today, fixtures have an overflow opening between the fill line and the water line. The fill line is also often above the sides of the fixture. These design changes protect the water supply. When we wash our cars or mix chemicals for the garden, we often fill the bucket with water and drop the hose into the bucket. Never put the hose in the bucket. One unfortunate man was watering and fertilizing his garden with an aspirator device that attached to his garden hose. He finished the job, took the device off the hose and refreshed himself with a drink from the garden hose. The fertilizer contained arsenic. The chemical had back siphoned into the hose line. He died a short time later.

Our drinking water is basically safe. Philadelphia drinking water once was literally taken directly from the Schuylkill River. Municipalities are constantly testing the water and the results of these tests are available to the public. Private well water should be tested annually. There are many filtration and treatment systems for domestic drinking water. Some are rather basic, and some are extremely sophisticated such as a reverse osmosis system. A basic filtering system will not protect you against contamination caused by back siphoning.

Make a mental note. If there is a fire, if there is a major water main break in your neighborhood, the potential for cross contamination goes up. Often you will hear announcements that the public is urged to boil all water before drinking it, following one of these disruptions in uniform water flow. Or, you can do as so many are doing today, buy bottled water and hope that the bottler has been diligent in maintaining purity in their packaging facility.

Maintenance tips:

1. Never fill a bucket or the pool by dropping the hose into it. The water should spill into the vessel creating an air gap between the hose and the container.
2. Be sure the fill line to your hot water heating system is always closed.

WATER HEATERS

Many people never think about the water heater. They turn on the hot water and only look at the water heater on two occasions: when the water isn't hot and it should be, and when the bottom falls out and the floor is wet and it shouldn't be. Water heaters don't give you a lot of warning when they fail. What's the second thing people say when something breaks? It was working a minute ago. The first thing they say I won't mention here. Water heaters do require some minimal maintenance. If you have a gas unit, every six months drain some water off  the bottom of the tank. This will dislodge the sediment that develops there. Manufacturer's claim you can increase their efficiency by as much as 25% by this simple act. Run the water until cold water comes out. Then do it again about an hour later. When you get cold water, you haven't drained the tank. Cold water is denser and heavier than the hot water. It falls through the hot water and will begin to drain out after one or two gallons. This can help reduce the pinging noises that occur. The noises are caused by sediment build up inside the tank. It is less often a problem with electric units because they have two heating elements that agitate the water which results in less sediment. It is good to do this once a year as well for an electric water heater. It is also a good idea to completely flush the tank once a year.

How to flush the unit? First, turn it off. If it's electric, turn off the breaker to the unit. If it's gas, turn the control knob on the unit to off. It usually has three settings, on, off and pilot. It is often black. The newer heaters have a shield or cover over the controls and you will need a small wrench, screw driver or possibly a ratchet with a very small head to turn the fasteners. These fasteners vary depending on the unit. If you have a newer water heater, I'm going to ask you do to something that men resist. "RTGDM!" This stands for "Read the G D Manual." This will also contain relighting instructions. If you have a gas unit, the flame should go out when you turn the valve.

Now that the unit is off, close the cold water feed valve to the unit. Most water heaters only have one feed valve, although I have seen some installers put valves on both lines on the top of the unit. If you are not sure which is which, feel them. The cold line should get much colder as you move your hand away from the unit. The hot side will stay hot. Turn the water off, and open a hot water faucet somewhere in the house. Now connect a hose to the hose bib on the bottom of the unit. Some newer units require pliers or some kind of grip to turn the valve. Run the hose to a basin or drain. If you have a sump with a sump pump, that's a good place to drain the water. Open the valve and let it drain. If the hose is draining into a basin higher than the valve, you will have to drain the bottom of the tank with a bucket in order to get as much water out as possible.

Now reverse the process. Shut off the valve, close the hot water faucet, open the fill valve, and relight the pilot if you have one. Those real long fire starters you use on the barbeque work well to get all the way in there. There should be relighting instructions on the side of the unit. At least there was on everyone I have seen, and I've been doing this since 1994. Don't light it until you hear water running in the tank. You can damage the tank if you heat it with no water. The normal life expectancy of a water heater is about 12 years. Performing these steps can extend the life of it considerably. I have heard of and seen water heaters last twice that. It will also run cheaper and thereby save you money in your monthly budget. Setting the temperature on the water heater can be either very simple or a little complicated. If you have an electric water heater, back up a few steps here. Before you turn the electric back on, remove the two plates on the front of the unit. Don't do this with the power on. There are bare copper wires visible that have live electricity. There should be a small plastic knob with a screw driver slot in it. This may vary from unit to unit. There are normally notches without numbers that indicate the setting. These are the thermostats for the unit. There are normally two, one high and one low. Straight up and down is normal. Set them slightly lower, (usually to the left of center). If you have small children or elderly people living with you, you might want to set them down two notches. A safe water temperature is 120 degrees. 130 degrees can be fairly hazardous, 140 degrees is very high risk for scalding. That is a very dangerous temperature. It doesn't take being off by much to create a dangerous situation. My feeling is set it slightly lower than hotter. After all, what do you do in the shower? I know, you sing, but most people turn on the hot water all the way and then add cold. You will just add less cold if you set it lower. You should already be washing your clothes in cold water, and modern dishwashers often have a preheat system if you want your dishes real hot when you wash them. Setting it lower is cheaper and good for the planet. I know there are some people out there that argue with solid scientific facts about global warming, but I can't save the world with this little book. I can tell you it's stupid for many reasons to set the temperature high on your water heater.

So at this point, the water heater is full of fresh water and ready to go. If its gas and it is now firing, look at the burner area. It should be a nice even round blue flame. In time, the burner area sometimes falls apart and it burns uneven or has a yellow flame. Yellow means it's not burning cleanly and can often produce carbon monoxide. If the whole flame area is not lit, call a plumber and have the burner area cleaned or possibly replaced. If you have an electric water heater, put the covers back over the temperature controls before you turn the electric back on. The water heater should be supplying you with plenty of hot water in about 30 to 45 minutes. A 30 gallon tank is acceptable for a single person or most couples. A 40 gallon tank will serve a small family with small children. Once you have teenagers and adults, a 50 gallon tank is recommended. An 80 gallon tank is needed if you have a whirlpool tub that will use lots of hot water. Gas water heaters have slightly faster recovery than electric. For this reason, if you have an electric water heater, I recommend nothing smaller than a 50 gallon tank.

Now the unit is up and running. While the fire is burning in the burner area, light a match and hold it next to the top of the unit at the hood damper. That is the space between the unit and the flue on the top in the center of the water

heater. Move the flame slowly around all sides of the hood damper. The flame should be pulled into the flue. If the flame bends outward, wait about a minute and do it again. If it still bends outward into the living area, the exhaust from the unit is entering the living area. This is a potentially fatal condition. Call a plumber immediately. There is a blockage somewhere in the exhaust line causing the exhaust to enter the house. Symptoms of this condition are condensation on the windows in the house, and droplets of moisture forming in the attic on the nails. Those conditions can be caused by a whole host of conditions, one of which is improperly vented gas appliances. If you have this condition and can't locate the source of the moisture, having your gas appliances checked is a good idea. Unvented gas fireplaces will also cause the moisture on the windows and in the attic, but I digress. The picture on the left shows the hood damper on a water heater that is not venting properly. The exhaust from the unit has led to deposits building up around the damper. This unit had a serious ventilation problem. Note the rust on the nipple coming out of the top of the water heater.

The water heater is venting properly and everyone is happy. Check the unit monthly for any signs of water leakage from the temperature pressure relief valve. That's the small, often brass valve on the side of the heater. It should have a hose on it that extends to within 6" of the ground. Water should never come out of it. If it is leaking, or there is sediment built up on it call a plumber. Some experts say to press on the valve to test it. I am not of that persuasion. They sometime don't reset and now you have a leaky valve and you need to call a plumber. Replacement is  about $125 as of this writing. That may vary by area and unit. The valve on the left is missing its' hose and covered with sediment. This indicates it has been leaking. It should be replaced

The next question is how old is it? A.O. Smith puts the manufactured date on the information plate on the unit. It is contained in the serial number. The date is often given in the year followed by the month. Many other manufacturers will also put it there. Bradford White likes to be cryptic. Their date is in serial number but it's coded. The first letter stands for the year. I could include the whole chart here but the basic fact is they started over in 2004. 2003 started with the letter Z. If you have a letter near the end of the alphabet, just count backwards from that and you will have the approximate age. The letter A stood for 2004, B = 2005 and so on. The letter gives you a pretty good idea of the age.

You will want to check the unit periodically for leaking. The valve mentioned above is the most common source of leaking. The shut off valves as well as the nipple that attach the water lines on top of the unit will also leak on occasion. They will often get a bluish tint to them from water leaking and evaporating off. Sediment will build up on them. Be careful soldering them. Leave that to a pro. Often there are plastic tubes in the unit that take the cold water to the bottom of the tank. If you heat them, they may crack, and the cold water will come out at the top and run right out the distribution side. The water doesn't get heated and you end up with cold water when the unit is running. You may sometimes get a strong sulfur smell in the hot water. This is caused by the sacrificing anodes in the unit wearing out. This is more common in electric units than gas. I've been inspecting houses since 1994 and I have seen this condition once. The rods can be replaced. If the water is a rust color, the problem is not in your water heater. The most common source of rust colored water is galvanized pipes or fitting somewhere in the system that are failing. There are often galvanized connections in the tub in older home. The last question I hear often is, should I get an insulation blanket for the water heater? If the water heater is in the living area, you don't need it. If it is in the garage, an unheated attic or similar unheated area, then an insulation blanket is recommended. Be sure it does not cover the burner area or the vent area at the top of the unit. It should also be taped down at the top away from the hood damper. Feel the area where you are taping it on the top of the unit. You should be able to hold your hand there. It might be warm, but it shouldn't be hot.

Maintenance tips:
1. Check the temperature of the water. You should keep it at 120 degrees or lower. Water hotter than this greatly increases the risk of scalding.
2. Drain water off the bottom of the unit every six months.
3. Drain it completely once a year.
4. Check for leakage from the bottom as well as the TPR or temperature pressure relief valve.
5. When the unit is on, run your hand carefully around the hood damper on top of the unit. If you feel hot air and your hands get damp, the unit is not venting properly. CALL A PLUMBER IMMEDITATELY! I tell people to use a match to do this and if the flame leans outward you have a problem. The match or lighter makes some people nervous.
6. Replace the unit if it is over 12 years old. Avoid the flood.

TANKLESS WATER HEATERS

Our water heater is tired. Water heaters, (and please don't refer to them as hot water heaters, they get offended,) have a life of about ten to twelve years. Ours has just turned double digits in age and right on schedule, the pressure relief valve on the side of the unit has been leaking. In a newer unit, it makes sense to replace this valve, but in ours, it's not really cost justified. When a water heater fails completely, they leak severely, so you want to replace it before the flood, not after it. Water heaters are not one of those home items that you get excited about buying. It's not a fun purchase, at least not for me.

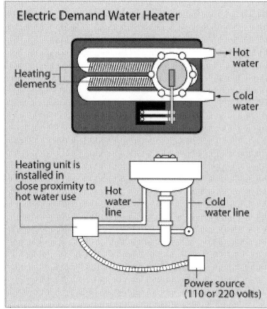

So we headed out to the store to see what is available. Once we go past the sticker shock we started looking at our options. If you buy an appliance every ten years, the price jumps a lot in that time. The latest concept in water heater is a tankless model.

Copied from website: www.tanklesswaterheaterguide.com/

The old concept in water heaters is to fill a large container with water, heat it, and store it. Then when you want hot water it's there waiting for you. As you pull water out, it refills, and heats the new water entering the tank. With a larger family and more demand, you normally get a larger model. Gas water heaters have faster recovery time which can be important in bigger families. Tankless models, on the other hand, store no hot water. They contain a coil that heats the water as it flows through the unit. The heater sits there cold, using no gas or electric until you turn on the faucet. It then heats the water instantly, and only heats the water on demand. You can actually set an exact temperature you want, and it comes with remote. If you plan it right, you can lean out of the shower and change the temperature with the push of a button!

These new units have a lot of advantages. They are small and fairly attractive, at least compared to the big tank models we are used to seeing. They look a little like the room heaters and A/C units you see in hotels, but they are much smaller. You can mount them on the wall. They require a slightly larger gas line than some of the older units. The gas jets in the unit will ignite based on demand and part of that demand is determined by the temperature of the water entering the unit. They will burn hotter and use more gas in the winter when the water entering the home is colder. They should be mounted on an outside wall and gas units must be vented directly to the exterior. They fit in the smallest places, so you can install it near where the demand for hot water is greatest. This will increase their efficiency. They are very popular in motor homes where every inch is a premium. They provide a lot of hot water per cubic inch of space allotted to them.

They come in several sizes. They are rated by demand. Some will allow two showers running simultaneously. The smaller unit costs about six hundred dollars and the larger units over a thousand. That's the price out of the box with installation being additional. The cost of the installation can vary depending on your home and what the plumber has to do. Paloma[32] has a video that shows how easy they are to install and explains how most home owners can install one in about a half hour. I watched the video. My suggestion is watch the video yourself before you take on this project. After watching the video, I personally would hire a plumber. You are dealing with gas, water, and electricity. I am not very fond of spilling or leaking any of these items in my home. If not properly vented, the exhaust from the heater can burn your house down, or allow fatal carbon monoxide to enter your home. So, you decide if the safety is worth a few hundred dollars.

One last thing about these units is they are energy efficient. If you are concerned about energy efficiency, and who isn't, get a unit with an Energy Star rating. You find both tankless and traditional units have very high energy ratings. I personally don't anticipate natural gas prices dropping any time soon, even though we have all the natural gas we need and it's not imported from the volatile Middle East. So my guess is these units will realize more savings as the years go by. Another consideration is, believe it or not, within the last five years there was a tax credit applied to these heaters as an incentive for energy conservation. I don't know all the details on this, I'm not an accountant. There was a tax incentive under the stimulus package that expired in December, 2010. I have read that you can receive up to fifteen hundred dollars in tax credits if you buy enough items and they are all Energy Star rated. It was for fifteen percent of the cost of the item for most appliances. The way I see it, that can cover the installation. It sounds like a win all the way around once you get past the fact they are about almost double the cost of a conventional water heater. It looks like the future of heating water will be a tankless job.

Maintenance tips:

---

[32] Manufacturer's name

1. If you change over to a tankless system, check the vent on the exterior annually for bees or other types of infestation. This is particularly important in mobile homes, or vacation homes where the system is shut down for months out of the year. With a home unit, firing several times a day, this shouldn't be an issue.
2. Keep plants trimmed away from the vents.

HOME REPAIRS

We are having a big party at our house right after Labor Day. When we have a party we look around the house and say to ourselves, "We can't have people over with the house like this." So, I looked around and realized just how much work has to be done. If I look at everything, I get overwhelmed. The key is to not look at all the jobs as one, but a series of little jobs. I looked at many of these jobs and came to the conclusion I can do many of them in less than an hour. The first job is to write down all of the jobs as you go through the house. As you write them down, detail them. List the tools and materials for each project. This is a one hour job all by itself.

Next, go to a home center and buy the items you need for several jobs. This trip is another one hour job. When I take on home projects, I have a tendency to look at the entire project, make one trip for that project and dedicate an entire Saturday or weekend to it. Many little projects that make the house more livable can be done in less than an hour with minimal costs. The basic tools are a couple of screw drivers, a hammer, a variety of nails, screws, fasteners, and lubricants such as WD 40 or CRC. Pliers and a few odds and ends can also be helpful.

You now have the tools. You now have the parts, or at least all the parts you think you will need for a few projects. Stop. Put on gloves. Tight fitting leather gloves work best. I was trimming palm bushes on my home in Florida and the saw I was using slipped. It slid down the shaft of the bush and proceeded to take a chunk out of the top of my left index finger. It created a little flap so you could look inside my finger. I went to the urgent care clinic in the area. (Palm Coast has a great emergency medical unit to handle just such problems at a reasonable cost and relatively quick service. I was receiving medical attention in about 40 minutes.) The attending nurse practitioner pulled the flap back and said, "See that little white cord, that's your tendon. If you cut that, it would be surgery to repair it. You are very fortunate you didn't cut in any deeper." The moral of the story, wear gloves. Let's start with loose doorknobs. Tightening the screws will solve the problem. Door knobs work their way loose. Is the door loose or tight when you operate it? Check the screws on the hinges. They sometimes loosen from wear. Take the screws out one at a time and put a tooth pick in the hole with a little white carpenter's wood glue on it. Then reinsert the screw. This will pack out the hole. Do each screw and then reinstall it before you do the next so the door doesn't pull off. If the door pops off at the top, you may pull out the screws at the bottom by putting too much weight on them. If there is a large gap at the top or bottom, or if the door rubs at the top or bottom, insert a business card or two between the hinge and the wall to adjust the opening. Then tighten the screws back down. Doors sometimes stick in the summer due to the increased humidity. In older homes, sometimes tapping on the door jamb can move it back a hair and the door will operate more easily. Don't use your hammer directly on the jamb; put a piece of wood against it so you don't leave marks from the hammer. Lubricate the locking mechanism with a lubricant designed for the door. Time of repair? Less than an hour if you have the tools and materials. Sometimes a little sandpaper on the side or top will also help with a sticking door. I have several clear plastic packages with screws of various shapes and sizes. I also have several boxes of nails in a variety of sizes. If that's not enough we have a cigar box filled with all kinds of miscellaneous hardware. Not sure how I got it, I never smoked cigars.

The windows need cleaning. You don't have to clean all the windows at once. Clean one room at a time. Use a good window cleaner and wipe them down with newspapers. They don't leave lint. Rub the outside of the window across and the inside vertically so if you leave streaks, you know which side has them. Doing one or two rooms, top and bottom, inside and out with tilt in windows is less than an hour. Don't remove tilt in windows to clean them, just tilt them. You might put a pillow between the two panes when you clean them. I have found many windows will come out in 3 seconds and go back in in about 45 minutes. Leave them in the tracks.

In one hour I replaced four or five broken slats in a stockade fence, fixed a hinge on the gate, and trimmed the bushes in the front of our house. I must confess that I went over the one hour rule with the cleanup of the cuttings. The slats come in bundles in various sizes. I used 2" exterior deck screws to repair the hinge that was loose. Trimming a tree can be a little trickier than it looks. If you are cutting a large branch, cut a notch out of the underside of the limb first in the direction you want it to fall. This operation usually involves a step ladder. Don't do it if you are not reasonably comfortable on a ladder. You can break an arm or ankle or worse with a relatively low fall. Once you have notched it, come in from above and be sure your ladder is safely on the side away from the notch. I have found most home owner step ladders to be an accident waiting to happen. Get a folding ladder that has a bar on the base that fans out and makes it much more stable. Have a helper steady the ladder. When sawing, drag the saw through the cut and let the saw do the work. (Something my father in law always told me, but I didn't do until I was older.)

There are many other little jobs that can be viewed more as maintenance than repairs but they can easily be done in less than an hour. Replace the filter on the heating and air conditioning system. Pick up a few at the home center, and be sure you have the right size. It's amazing how many improperly sized filters I see as an inspector. Get a filter with a MERV rating of 8 or higher and change it at least every 90 days, more often if you have pets or more than 3 people in your home. While you are in the utility room, take a few gallons of water out of the bottom of the water heater. This will reduce sediment accumulation in the bottom and extend the life of the water heater. Now is also a good time to test all of the GFCI outlets in your home. The small print tells you to test them monthly. Do you have sticking sliding glass doors? Clean out the track and use a little WD 40 lubricant. If you have vinyl windows that are tight, you may need to adjust the springs in them which can be tricky. You normally don't lubricate vinyl surfaces. The action of opening and closing the window will do that. The old school method of lubricating a difficult wood window was soap in the track. If you have casement windows, the set screw in the handles often work their way loose. This requires a small Allen wrench. Okay, the tool box just got a little bigger, but you can go through most homes and tighten all the handles in less than one hour. It never ceases to amaze me how little some people know about their homes. Many repairs are relatively simple and it's just a matter of taking the time and doing them. You need a very basic tool kit, and some time. The key is to take on small jobs, one at a time. Don't try and do them all at once. Getting doors and windows to work better improves your quality of life. In the movie, "Its' a Wonderful Life" a loose knob on the landing on the stairs put poor Jimmy Stewart over the top one day. A little carpenters glue would have tightened it up. But then, Jimmy Stewart was a banker in that movie. What do bankers know about simple home repairs?

THE GARAGE

Let's take a look at the garage. They say the woman gets the house and the man gets the garage and basement. I don't know how true that is in our modern world. I do know that junk expands to the size of the container and the garage is a large container. In many homes, it's a basement with a driveway. Originally a garage was a status symbol. You were not only wealthy enough to own a car, but, you also had a room for it. The garage also has a history in the entertainment business. The garage served as the incubator for many a rock and roll band. Advice to mothers, don't let your child be the drummer. They always practice at the drummer's house since there is too much stuff to move around.

The original garage door was a solid door that was split in the middle and had to be pulled open to each side, or it lifted overhead in one piece. The one piece door was heavy and clumsy to operate. The garage door later evolved into panels that folded as it rose on tracks. If you have an older home you probably changed to the folding doors at some point. The end result is the bedroom over the garage often became cold since the new folding door has very little insulating value and the garage ceiling was rarely insulated in older home. I often see drill marks in the garage ceiling where blown insulation was added after the door was changed.

It's a good idea to check the garage door opener regularly. I suggest the first day of every season. Check the tracks for it and lubricate them. The springs that pull the door up can be lethal. Check the connections on each end and lubricate them as well so they don't rust away and spring break loose. Newer systems have a cable inside the spring to catch it if it breaks loose. There have been incidents where the spring snaps off and the whip lash movement of the spring is extremely hazardous. Next, hit the button to close the door and stick your foot in the laser light that runs across the opening for the door. The door should stop smoothly and immediately, and it should then reverse. This system fails more often than you would think. The mountings for the laser can be hit accidentally and it throws it off. The garage door should also reverse on impact. In the 1950's there were incidents of children being crushed by the garage door coming down on them and trapping them.

Let's look at the floor of your garage. It should slope towards the outside door. It should not be concave, level, or worse slope inward. Garages are intended for cars and gasoline vapors come off the car. They are heavier than air and should roll out the door. Bays in commercial garages such as oil change facilities are very well vented to prevent vapors from building up in the wells under the floor. Boats with inboard motors are always run by diesel. Gasoline vapors could accumulate in the hull of the boat creating a very dangerous condition. Occasionally I will see a floor drain in the middle of a garage floor. I don't recommend this if a car or any gasoline powered tools are stored there. My suggestion is to seal it off. The slope of the garage floor also keeps water from running into the garage. Garage floors are often cracked. A garage floor is usually a 4" pour of concrete on a bed of crushed stone. It sits independent of the home. If you take the thickness of the concrete and multiply it by 2.5, that will give you the distance in feet the concrete can go without needing and expansion joint. So, your garage floor will have a crack about 10' in from one of the sides. Nature makes its own expansion joint. My recommendation is to not store gasoline or other highly flammable materials in the garage. Store them in a utility shed at the rear corner of the yard. Besides, buying a utility shed gives you more room and another place to store more "stuff." After you park the car in the garage, leave the outside door open for a few minutes. The exhaust manifold and pipe contain carbon monoxide. You want to give this residual gas time to vent to the exterior.

We had talked about having a fire extinguisher in the kitchen that is suitable for extinguishing cooking fires. It is also a good idea to have one in the garage as well. Here you will want one that will extinguish gas or oil fires. You don't want a water filled fire extinguisher in either location.

The electrical outlet in the garage should be protected by a ground fault circuit interrupter. It is an electrical safety device that cuts off the flow of electricity if you, electricity and water get together. They save lives. If you read the fine print on them it says to test monthly. If you test them on the first day of each season you are way ahead of the national average. They have a test and reset button on them. Plug a light into it and push the test button. The power should go off. Then reset it. Here's where it can get tricky. In many homes, there are multiple outlets run through the same GFCI protection so the test and reset button may not be there. They may be run through the same circuit as the bathrooms or the other exterior outlets. The reset often is in the main panel or possibly in one of the bathrooms. If so, trip it, and check the baths and the other exterior outlets to see if they are on the same circuit. There should be no more than five outlets run through one GFCI protection device. It bothers me when I find all of the bathrooms and all the exterior outlets run through the same GFCI. Many people keep a spare refrigerator or freezer in the garage getting its power from a GFCI protected outlet. This is not a good idea. The GFCI is very sensitive and can sometimes be tripped by lightning or the surge of the motor for the appliance.

Garages are considered more vulnerable to fire than the rest of the home and often have a fire wall separating it from the home. For this reason, a solid core wood or metal door is recommended between the home and garage. You don't want a door with any glass in it. The drywall on the garage on newer homes is 5/8" which provides a one hour fire rating. If you have an older home and are concerned about fire protection, add another layer of regular drywall over the existing wall to create a fire break. The old row homes in the city often have cement walls on the garage. Adding pull down stairs to the garage can afford you more room to store more of those things we just can't throw out. Keep a few things in mind if you go that route. First, the drywall in the ceiling won't support your weight. You will fall through if you stand on it. So you need a floor. Second, the garage ceiling is not built to support a lot of weight. Don't load it up with heavy things. Bulky light weight things can be stored there. Lastly, when you cut the hole for the pull down stairs, you just destroyed the fire separation from the home. The thin wood panel on the bottom of the stairs affords no protection. Cover it with a sheet of 5/8" drywall.

A garage is a very versatile room. It can be home to a car or bikes. It can be a workshop, or a three season play room. It can be a music room, or a storage room. A garage can greatly enhance the visual appearance of a home. It adds length to the home, making the home look much longer. Garages can be used as a nursery for plantings in the spring or a home for sensitive patio plants that you want to protect from the harshest cold weather in winter. Garages can be many things to many people. As I reminisce over the many homes I've had, I lament at the fact that I never had a garage. I have a car port on my home in Florida, but that's not a garage. A garage can be the "cave" where a man can "hide." Hiding in a carport is just not the same.

Maintenance tips:
1. Don't store gasoline cans, the lawn mower, or other gas run tools such as the weed whacker in the garage. Store them in a separate shed.

2. Test the reversing mechanism on the garage door once a year. When the door is coming down, hold the bottom of the door. It should stop and go back up. Most garage door openers have a reversing mechanism connected to a laser beam across the bottom of the door. Run your foot through the beam and the door should stop and go back up. It's not enough if it merely stops.
3. Trip the GFI once a month.
4. Clean out any rags or flammable materials that we tend to store in the garage.
5. Have both a carbon monoxide sensor and smoke detector in the garage.
6. Leave the exterior garage door open for ten minutes after you park the car in it. This will allow the car exhaust to dilute with the outside air.

ICY WALKWAYS AND DRIVEWAYS

Erma Bombeck once wrote, "The grass is always greener over the septic tank," but she never mentioned why. The reason is vegetation, in general, likes slightly acidic soil. The soil over the septic system is mildly acidic for reasons we won't discuss. This brings us to melting ice and snow.

In the winter the government uses 11 million tons of rock salt to melt the ice and snow from our roadways. This does not include the salt Home Owners put down on the sidewalks and driveways.

As we were taught in high school chemistry class, things can either be basic or acidic. The salt that is used to melt the ice is very basic and that brings us back to the septic tank. The salt that we use to melt the ice and snow is damaging our vegetation. This salt, used in these quantities, is also penetrating our ground water. While it is not as damaging as industrial leaks, the Gulf oil spill, and agricultural use of pesticides, it is a contributing factor in lowering the quality of our ground water. The jury is still out on the gas drilling into the Marcellus Shale operation. That greedy little grab could make most of the Mid-Atlantic region uninhabitable with the chemicals they are using. The jury is still out on the wisdom of that whole operation.

Ground water is the basic water supply to millions of people in private water systems. The storm runoff also affects the water quality in rivers that supply the rest of us with water. So what's the best way to melt ice and snow, making our walkways and travel safe, and having as little impact as possible on the vegetation and the ground water below?

Let's take a closer look at the materials we use in our own house to melt ice and snow. We use items with names like Winter Melt. The primary ingredient in these products is Sodium Chloride which is salt. On the bag is a warning that the material can cause spalling of surfaces, and that the slush it forms should be cleared away. It should not be used on concrete less than on year old. (Concrete takes a long time to cure, i.e. the Hoover Dam is still curing as per the documentary they show on the Hoover Dam on PBS). There is also the warning about grass and vegetation. It should not be used on wood surfaces such as wood decks, as it will be absorbed into the wood and damage it. The biggest problem they mention is that it can result in more frequent freeze-thaw cycles of the melted ice and snow. So let me get this straight, it can damage concrete, the lawn the shrubbery, and my wood decks, and it then refreezes more easily making the walkway slippery again. We use this, why?

Back when I was a child, there was this huge hill we used for sledding. (I go back to that neighborhood now and think, what hill?) The municipality used to put cinders on the road to give cars traction. We would wait for the truck to pass and then cover the cinders with snow so we could keep on sledding. This predated the use of rock salt today.

Some Home Owners save the ashes from their fireplace and use it on the sidewalks and driveways. Years ago, the ashes from coal furnaces found their way onto the walkways as well. This had its' down side. Ashes are messy. The burnt embers would soil the rugs and floors. From a vegetation concern, cinders and ashes are not very friendly for your plants and lawn either. So what is a Home Owner to do? There is a product distributed by Interstate Products, Inc. that is sold in both liquid and pellet form. It has a neutral ph which the plants like. It is non-corrosive and has no effect on the sidewalks or paved areas. The liquid form can be applied with a garden sprayer. The coverage they advertise is about a gallon for an average driveway, sidewalk and walkway. It is good to -35 degrees. That should be good enough for the lower 48. The bad news, are you sitting down? The price they quoted me for a gallon is $19.95 plus shipping. They sell it in cases of six bottles. My guess is this product would be excellent for commercial applications where they can make bulk purchases and reduce the cost. The packaging of small quantities makes many things more expensive. The best example of this is bottled water cost more than gasoline. The pellets cost $129.00 for two fifty lb. bags. The coverage on the pellets is one pound per four square yards. A fifty foot driveway has about 45 square yards so you would use about 10 to 12 lbs. You might double that usage when you factor in sidewalks and walkways. The way I figure, that one hundred pound supply would last you five or six storms. Three significant storms are about average for the Philadelphia area. We have had some brutal winters such as the ice storms of 1996 and the blizzards of the winter of 2009/2010. That winter we broke the record for snow fall by 160%. We almost doubled it.

While this is a little better than the liquid, it is still much more than the sodium chloride you can buy at the supermarket. A third option that is cheap and economically sound is sand. You can buy a couple of bags at a building supply and sprinkle it on the ice. You have to re-apply it as the water runs off and takes the sand with it. It will also track back in the house, but that happens with any product. The best approach to any of the melting products for any of these products is to read the instruction on the package and use it sparingly. An interesting side note to this, if you cleaned your gutters in the fall, you will probably have slightly less ice on the walkways. Melting snow on the roof and overflowing gutters can put a constant drip, drip, drip on the walkway that refreezes every night. In Colorado, they are using a material made from corn syrup. I'm all for this. They treat the roads before it snows, after it snows, and every week during the winter. I guess it's like shampoo. Apply, repeat. I hope they stop putting corn syrup in everything we eat and put it on the roads. I'm hoping it is not as damaging to the highways as it is to our waste lines.

Maintenance tips:
1. Be sure the outside water is turned off before winter. Turn it off inside, then open the outside faucet and leave it open. I don't trust frost free spigots. I would drain them as well.
2. Move the snow shovels from the back of the shed to the back door area so you can reach them without going out there and attack the snow in the front. If you have an attached garage, that's a great place to store them.
3. Keep a spade or hard blade type shovel handy. They are helpful with breaking up ice.
4. Get any old bags of ice melting material you have stored away and put it in an accessible area. Keep in mind that if the bag is open and you get blowing rain in the bag, the rain can ruin it.
5. Buy whatever ice treatment you will be using before Thanksgiving. Don't wait for the first storm.
6. Try sand on ice. It's cheap enough and you may find it works well enough for your uses.
7. Make sure the car has lots of windshield washer fluid in it. You use a lot of it in the winter.

8. Put a snow shovel in the car. Also, another bag of sand for traction is a good idea. Keep a blanket in the car. That, "snuggie" you bought on impulse last winter? Throw it in the trunk. Hours in a cold car can be fatal. Every little bit of heat becomes critical.
9. Keep food in the car. A couple of power bars, or packages of crackers is a good idea. Obviously, keep an eye on the expiration date.
10. Keep a full tank of gas in the car when snow is predicted.
11. Be sure your wipers are in good working order.
12. Jumper cables can come in handy.
13. Wire brush the corrosion off the battery terminals. The junction between the terminals and the battery cables is critical. Scrape this area clean with a screw driver.
14. Check your anti-freeze levels and be sure it's good for the temperatures in your climate. (This section had more tips than the pool section).

ANTS OR TERMITES

Is it an ant or is it a termite? Every spring, both of these insects take to the air and scare unsuspecting home owners. Both insects swarm for a very short time, usually only for a day or two. The date varies each year depending on atmospheric conditions. People think, "Ant good, termite bad," but how do you know which is which? The physical difference between the two insects is rather profound and telling them apart is quite easy. In the simplest terms, ants have segmented bodies. Their bodies are divided into three segments, the head, a thin abdomen, and a larger bottom section. Both species have antennae, however, ants have a bend in their antennae and termites have straight antennae. Now if you have a few dead samples to examine, the wings on a termite are the same length and the wings on a flying ant are uneven in length.

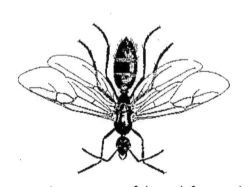

Winged carpenter ant: Courtesy Penn State Pesticide Applicator Training Manual

Why have they invaded my home? An army of ants or a colony of termites is very strong, powerful, and focused. The air force of both insects leaves a lot to be desired. They don't have very good flight plans. They are lousy flyers and drift with the wind. They head out of a tree or other wood areas and the wind carries them into the side of your home. If a few of them land there, they potentially can mate and start a colony, but those odds are less than 1,000 to 1. The female swarmer must land, mate, and make it back into the soil to start a new colony. There are plenty of birds, reptiles, and other predators looking for them. They eat most swarmers before they can nest.

You say you have ants and don't like them, what can you do? Let's start by deciding what type of ants you have. There are basically three species of ants that live in this area. There are house ants. They are small and black. They are sometimes referred to as sugar ants.

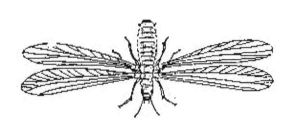

Winged Termite: Courtesy Penn State Pesticide

Applicator Training Manual

They are scavengers and are attracted to crumbs and food that is left out. They really like picnics. There are small red or orange ants that are called citronella ants. They give off an odor when crushed similar to the smell of citronella insecticide, hence the name. Both of these species can be classified as a nuisance, but not damaging, other than to the food they infest. There are many ant treatments available in retail outlets that will kill these ants. A topical treatment for visible ants that I have found very effective is rubbing alcohol. Dilute it with about half water and spray it on the ants. It stops them in their tracks.

There is another species of ants that is a more serious concern. They are large black ants called carpenter ants. At the picnic they are more interested in the picnic table than the picnic itself. Their job is to eat wood and they are good at it. They are particularly attracted to wet wood. When I was in the roofing business, we would often find them infesting the roof deck under the shingles near a leak. They can do extensive damage. Keep your trees and shrubbery trimmed around the home. They will follow the shrubbery into the home and create a long steady line eating your home. You often see them on the sides of big old trees. They are marching up to the dead wet wood throughout the tree. I replaced the roof on part of my home in Florida, I pulled off the old plywood near a leak and found the area infested with red ants eating the wood. They came up from the ground inside the cinder blocks in the wall. Once the wood is replaced and the new wood is dry, they will go searching for other wood to eat. Often, they will find it somewhere else in your home. A professional treatment for carpenter ants is recommended. Certified Pest Control of Horsham treats many homes for carpenter ants. Rich Salera, one of the owners of Certified, says they use a professional grade treatment called Suspend. It is an all-purpose insecticide that if used properly poses no threat to pets or humans. He also warns that once the property is treated, the ants pick up the insecticide, they take it back to the nest and it kills them in time. So you will see ants for a few days after the treatment. The rubbing alcohol is a little more fun to use, as you see the little guys drop dead in front of you. The professional treatment is the long term approach as it kills the nest.

Termites are always bad. It is a good idea to have your home professionally inspected once a year. There are two kinds of homes, those that have had termites, and those that will get them. Certified Pest Control can perform the inspection and once the home is declared termite free, they offer a one year guarantee against termites and will treat your home free of charge if they invade. Termites live in the earth and form thin brown tubes that serve as tunnels for them to get to the wood. If they are doing their job perfectly, they stay in the wood and you don't see them.

They do, however, often break through, or their tubes are on the wood.

We are quite fortunate in this part of the country. In other parts of the country, there are Formosa termites that are stronger flyers and therefore, more adept at forming new colonies. In Florida they have tiny red ants called fire ants that are brutal. Their nests are huge cones, sometimes six to ten feet tall. The problem is when they are forming their nests; it is a hole in the ground similar to any other ant colony here. If you step on it, they attack quickly and violently. Within seconds your leg is covered with thousands of vicious biting ants that leave red welts and bites. They are extremely painful. In the old westerns, they are depicted as a means of torturing people. Ants have quite a military profile. The common ant is often referred to as an army. The flying ant might be viewed as their air

force. And the red fire ants could certainly be considered their Marines. The main consideration with ants or termites is there are far more of them than there is of us, and the amount you see is a tiny fraction of how many you are really fighting.

Maintenance tips:
1. Walk the outside of your property annually and look for brown tubes on the walls coming up from the ground.
2. Walk the basement annually and pull back the insulation on the band joist where the walls meet the

floor. Look for brown tubes working their way up on the wood.

3. If you see brown tubes in either location, call an exterminator.
4. If you find flying insects such as the ones shown in this section, put a few in an envelope and have an exterminator check them if you are uncertain.
5. Consider an annual inspection for termites. It cost less than $100 and most companies will treat your home for free if you sign the inspection contract.
6. If your home has been treated, don't assume it is forever. You still need to check the perimeter once a year.
7. Homes built on concrete slabs are the toughest to check. Check every wall in the house for tubes once a year. They can literally come up right in the middle of the home.
8. Test the floor joists where they sit on the foundation wall. If you can put a screw driver into it as shown, you may have termites, you may just have rot. Either way, get it inspected by a structural engineer or equally qualified person. You need major carpentry work to stabilize the home.

SELECTING A BUILDER

You have made a decision on your next home. You are buying a brand new home. You thought about it and you have fallen in love with the crisp clean carpet, the pristine unblemished walls, and the fact that you can decide where you want your closets or that outside entrance. What do you do next? Many people then run out, trot through samples, get some mud on their shoes, and buy a home based on the sizzle, not on the chef. Actually the last thing you should do is pick the home. Let's back up a few steps.

There are the obvious considerations people make when selecting a neighborhood such as schools, job commutes, and convenience to shopping, etc. These items don't factor into the new home vs. old home decision. You have also taken a look at your budget and determined how much you can spend per month on your new home. New homes almost always have a higher assessed value than existing homes. This results in a higher tax bill and you may be paying several hundred dollars more each month to the local municipality, and all that money isn't going to get you tile floors in your kitchen. When looking at a new home, there are advantages and disadvantages to being the first one in the new neighborhood. Buying early in a new development can often be a good investment. The prices in most developments frequently rise as construction continues. A year later, as more homes are built, the price is often much higher than the price paid for the first home. There were speculators in Florida making a living buying early in developments and then selling six months or a year later and realizing a huge profit, and they never lived a day in the house. That whole market collapsed in 2008 and many of those people lost everything. The down side of doing this is living with construction noise, dust and workers showing up on your street at 6:30 every morning for as long as the development is being built. Backhoes are noisy neighbors. There is also the potential concern that if dealing with a small Builder that he might have financial problems and the development not finish. This again happened on a grand scale in the recent economic collapse. This is less of a concern in a hot Real Estate market. Another Builder will usually buy out the remaining lots and things keep rolling. Markets change. New construction in a development can be far more risky than buying a newly built home on an empty lot in an established community.

If you found a development partially completed and it looks appealing, knock on some doors. The best time to ask the people how they liked dealing with the Builder is on the weekend in warm weather. The new owners are often out working on the grounds. Ask if they had any problems and how the Builder handled them. In any construction job, there are going to be problems such as delays due to cabinets not being ready, weather delays, sub-contractors not getting there on time, etc. The key here is how they handled them. A major complaint I hear as an inspector is how the Builder treated them when problems developed. Ask the people if they remember the name of the superintendent that ran their project. I have inspected homes for Home buyers built by most of the major Builders in my area. I have found a huge difference between superintendents working for the same Builder. They all know how to build the homes the right way, but some of them are so far ahead in people skills that even if the problem isn't resolved completely to the Buyer's satisfaction, they end up feeling the Builder did everything they could to resolve it. One major Builder in the area told the people if they didn't like the way he handled them, "don't buy the house, I have a list of people waiting to get in here." If there were major problems with the construction, or with the superintendent, most people will tell you. Getting a particular individual to run your project may be difficult with a large Builder, but with a smaller Builder, that can often be arranged. One local family owned

Builder is run by three sons of the founder. One of the sons walks every buyer through the project. This company is known for their quality and customer relations. Small family owned operations frequently are committed to customer relations.

Check with the local building inspectors about complaints. They can't tell you who is bad, but any complaints to the municipal building inspector are public record and you have a right to see the Builder's file. One or two complaints every few years for a major Builder are not unusual. You can't please everybody. Ask if you can bring in a private inspector. One major Builder in my area tells the people he will only allow municipal inspectors on his lots. (I wonder what he's hiding.) I have inspected his homes on Sundays with the buyers, and then they put my findings in their own list. One of the principals of this company was convicted of criminal activity in the way he ran the business. Ask the Builder where he lives? Does he live in one of his developments? Is he comfortable having his customers as his neighbors? How long has the Builder been in business? Look for long term stability in one area. Check with the

County records for liens or judgments against him. The Builder may still be putting up homes, but he may have a string of judgments against him that could bring him down in the middle of your project.

Once you have decided on a general location, now you are ready to pick your home. My suggestion is to shop it. Look at a lot of samples. You can look at drawings and see floor plans but it often takes the lay person a while before they can visualize a house from the drawings. Ask about special features. Ask how much more it would be to have the floors screwed down rather than just nailed. Screwing the floors can greatly reduce squeaks in years to come. The operative word is "reduce." Some squeaking is inevitable. Ask about a deeper basement. If they make the ceiling two feet higher it can be a lot nicer if you finish it off later. Finished basements require a secondary means of egress in an emergency. They can build that in on the front end and make it much easier to finish the basement later. If you plan on finishing the basement later, your heater may be undersized for the added space. Discuss this consideration with the Builder. Ask about a rough in for a basement bathroom. It's a lot easier to build it in now, even though you may not plan to finish the basement for several years. Ask about a passive radon system being installed during construction. This is the cheapest time to add it. If the house tests for a low radon count after you move in, the pipe through the house may come in handy as an electrical chase if you add circuits on the second floor. Upgrade items that will wear out. Heavier carpeting and better grade padding can be a good investment if you have a growing family. They have odor resistant carpet options if you have pets. Are they carrying you out of the home? Do you plan on spending the next 20 years or so in this house? If so, upgrade your roofing. A forty year roof should still look brand new at twenty years. A twenty five year roof will look pretty tired in twenty years. The highest quality is often your best investment. Considering tile flooring in the kitchen, but not yet? Builders can overbuild the floor supports to allow for extra dead weight in the building. A heavy tile floor on the wrong supports can end up bowing and all it takes is a little movement and your floor will crack at the joints. Single hung windows or double hung? I have seen very high quality homes built with single hung windows. The problem is you can't clean the top sash without hanging out the window. And don't forget the holiday lighting package. One switch and all the lights go on. It makes decorating in the winter a whole lot easier.

When buying a new home you get one chance to add a lot of quality of life items. Adding many of these items later is always possible. No matter what the question, the answer is money. It just can be a whole lot less money if you plan the details on the front end and work with the Builder. They are in the business of building homes and they may not present some of the options you may want a few years down the road.

ENERGY AUDITS

Energy use and its costs are not going away regardless of who gets elected. We can "Drill Baby Drill" but we will still have to "Pay Baby Pay." The problem with "Drill Baby Drill" as has become abundantly clear is it creates "Spill Baby Spill." We have a virtually unregulated industry that views safety and the environment as impediments to profit. At least one company, BP, appears to be devoid of moral restraint and basic human concern. With a corporate mission compassed by that basic tenant, it gives me pause to endorse future commitments to fossil fuel usage. If we don't make a serious transition to alternative energy sources, we, as a civilization, deserve what we get. Polluted oceans, filthy air, global warming, extinct life forms, and parched vegetation are just starters. Famine, pestilence, plagues, and wars over food and water will follow. So what can the average citizen do if they actually care about the planet? There are things we can do that involve getting outside help to lower your energy usage today. You may ask yourself, "Where do I begin if I want to significantly lower my energy usage?" One approach is to get some form of energy audit.

What is an energy audit? Years ago I had PECO[33] perform an energy audit on my home. PECO is the local gas and electricity provider in my area, southeastern Pennsylvania. They came out with a blower door and combined that test with a whole host of recommendations. We ended up insulating crawl spaces, changing shower heads, replacing windows, and other less costly adjustments such as more energy efficient lighting. I checked PECO's website recently and did not find a full energy audit mentioned. They did have kits you could buy that would address some of the items I just mentioned. Some utility companies are more aggressive in their promotion of better energy usage.

---

[33] Philadelphia Electric Company, local supplier of gas and electric.

In Florida, their electric companies have programs such as energy audits that are readily available.

There are some companies that still offer the blower door test. This type of energy audit and evaluation has its' benefits and limitations. The problem I have found with that type of analysis is the door creates extreme conditions. It is the equivalent of subjecting your home to winds of 40 to 50 MPH. In reality, these extreme conditions are not part of the regular weather pattern in Southeastern Pennsylvania. While it is a legitimate tool, it's not dealing with conditions we often encounter. If an energy door test is done, the most important part of the audit is an actual plan of attack with the data presented. Another problem I see with many of the energy audit programs offered is they are offered for "free." "Free" is a problem, you ask? Yes. The programs are primarily offered in our area by contractors who sell HVAC systems. Take a guess what their conclusion is after they give you a "free" audit. The solution is always within the limitations of abilities of the contractor to sell you services that they perform. In other words, "Here's your problem, buy my product to solve it." So what happened to "free?" Blower door tests are also not focused on HVAC systems efficiency and performance. They focus on air infiltration. If you have a house that's leaking energy, be it heat or cooling, and you install a more efficient unit for either need, you will lower your energy usage, all things being equal. That being said, the installation of caulk, attic insulation weather stripping, insulating the attic access, even film tints or awnings on windows may reduce energy usage more than a new five to seven thousand dollar central HVAC system. They may also cost a lot less. The sad reality is that after you just plunked down 7K, you still need all the other energy saving improvements. My feeling is the focus of the program should be on implementation of as many low tech, low cost DIY projects as possible before you take the 7K solution. Contractors giving "free" energy audits see it from a different paradigm.

Other energy audits include an infrared scan and what is called "thermography." This is a very sophisticated tool that looks like a video camera and it highlights temperature differentials in your home. This is pretty complex technology. It has many applications from finding roofing leaks to analyzing the efficiency of machinery in industrial applications. The television show "Mythbusters" also has a lot of fun with it. It is also used to check electrical lines and transformers. A trained thermographer will basically photograph the home and look for hot and cold spots on the walls and roofs. The person performing the test must be capable of analyzing the results. This type of inspection is best done in the morning when the sun hasn't heated the exterior. It's best done when the temperature difference between the inside and outside is greatest. This will show more detail in the winter and summer than spring or fall. Both this and a blower door test can yield considerable information. The problem is what do you do with it? Cold areas in walls can be an issue, but taking action in the way of adding insulation in areas with difficult access can be marginally effective in terms of cost. The best energy audits will take the data obtained and break it down with recommended action. This action should then be coupled with costs and a return on investment based on current prices. Both the blower door and the infrared camera are very useful tools as part of a complete evaluation of your energy loss. Just be sure that the motivation of the applicator is energy savings and not a boat payment. The most recognized professional training and classification program gives the energy auditor a RESNET certification. RESNET stands for Residential Energy Services Network. There are various levels of professional status within RESNET. My suggestion is you check out their website, www.resnet.us/professional for additional information. While what they are doing is valid, there are many steps a home owner can take to reduce energy use and make their home more efficient. Many of these DIY projects are discussed throughout this book.

There is a basic energy audit that looks at the home in terms of where it is most practical to make improvements so the return is quickest. The system we use takes into account the size of the home, the insulation present, the type of HVAC equipment present and the AFUE, (Annualized Fuel Utilization Efficiency), of the equipment. It will then show you where you can invest in changes and how long it will take you to realize a return on the investment based on current energy costs. The audit will make safety recommendations such as not installing insulation over knob and tube wiring. Often, we are looking at older homes. Older homes tend to be the most energy inefficient, and you can't improve them just by insulating everywhere. You need a systematic approach. More is not always better.

Some items, such as the furnace, we think of in terms of a large investment, and there is no question it is. Replacing an old furnace with an energy efficiency rating of 78% with an energy star furnace with a rating of 90% to 95% can result in a huge savings and relatively short payback time period. When you think of energy efficiency just imagine that with a 78% efficiency, for every dollar you pay in heat, you only get 78 cents worth of heat. Upgrading the unit can result in close to a 20% savings in your fuel usage. Heat is like beer. As Archie Bunker used to say, "We don't own beer, we only rent it." The same is true for heat. Our report will show you in real numbers how this investment will work for you.

A good energy audit will look at all of your appliances such as the water heater, refrigerator, and that 25 year old freezer in the garage. They are drain energy. You may save a lot on food by filling the freezer, but you may be spending it keeping the food frozen. The range and dishwasher gobble up energy as well. There are some ventilation devices that are often thought to lower costs that sometimes are not good investments. Attic fans are a good example. If there is inadequate attic ventilation, particularly soffit venting adding a fan can sometime increase cooling costs. The fan can pull conditioned air from the living area if the two areas, the attic and living area, are not properly sealed. When the conditioned air is pulled into the attic, outside air is pulled into the living area. This influx of warmer outside air now must be cooled. This can result in more energy usage to cool the home. Other items such as ceiling fans being used on mild days can be far more energy efficient than running the air conditioning. This is particularly true at night.

There are steps you can take as a Home Owner to reduce your costs. The approach you take can vary depending on your situation. If you have no plans to move, you can buy items with a longer payback time. If you see yourself moving other less costly renovations such as a programmable thermostat may make the most sense. Getting an energy audit will make more sense. Whether it involves an infrared scan or a blower door test, or just a complete analysis, getting an energy audit that gives you a plan of attack is a great place to start to reduce expenditures in the years to come.

Maintenance tip: If your home is over ten years old, get an energy audit.

ASBESTOS

"I missed out on asbestos, I'm not going to miss out on mold." This is a quote from a fine member of the legal profession present at a mold seminar I attended in Atlanta. The impetus for the national concern about asbestos has been fueled far more by the legal and financial consequences than by the health problems. Asbestos is a hot topic in Ambler Borough in suburban Philadelphia. It is the home of the Keasbey Mattison Plant, a principle manufacturer of asbestos for Johns Manville. Asbestos claims eventually bankrupted JM. Asbestos is a mineral that has high resistance to heat and fire. It was used extensively in the first half of the 20th century in building construction. It was also used in everything from automobiles to ships. There are five acres of asbestos waste and by products over 50' high just outside of Ambler. The white cliffs of Ambler are monuments to that era. Asbestos can become a health concern. If the material is in a friable or crumbling state it can be inhaled and damage the lungs. Asbestos, when damaged, breaks down into tiny microscopic particles. These particles become air born and if inhaled, settle into the lower cavities of the lungs. Once there, they don't leave. They remain there for years and become an irritant. The lungs then try and protect themselves from the irritant and develop a growth. This growth reduces the lung capacity of the lungs and eventually develops into asbestosis, a cancer like condition that can be fatal. Not everyone who is exposed develops asbestosis, but if you smoke and are exposed, you are far more likely to develop asbestosis or lung cancer.

The statistics on those exposed to small amounts of asbestos and contracting related health problems are extremely small. The workers who suffered serious health problems were generally exposed to large amounts of asbestos for extended periods of time. The combination of exposure and smoking tobacco products greatly increases the likelihood of serious medical issues from exposure to asbestos. If trace amounts of asbestos were found in your child's school, it is hardly a reason for panic.

If your home was built before World War II, the chance of you having asbestos in your home is very high. A common use of the product was wrapping heating pipes, particularly homes with steam heat. The pipes were wrapped with a white cardboard type material and had metal straps holding it together. If your pipes are wrapped with this type of material and you are not sure of its composition, call 1-301-975-NIST, (6478).This is a federal agency that will give you a list of accredited testing laboratories to test a sample. Their website is www.nist.gov. The asbestos used as pipe insulation can be a health concern, and should be addressed. Popular Mechanics wrote instructions for encapsulating it in 1986.The EPA does not endorse their recommendations. Their recommendations are:

1. Wear safety clothing and a respirator with a type H filter cartridge.
2. Spray soapy water over the material.
3. Wrap it in plastic kitchen wrap. (Home Centers has great plastic wrap that they use when you purchase materials you tie on the roof of your car.)
4. Wrap with good quality UL approved duct tape. Don't use the common grey material that Tim Allen pushed on Home Improvements. It dries out in about a year.
5. Paint the tape with acrylic latex paint and dispose of the clothing.

If you have 9 inch square floor tiles, the best approach is to leave them there, and cover them with another flooring material. Asbestos is often found in concrete siding and roofing materials developed in the 1920's but used extensively through the 1960's. It is often found in old roofing felt paper. Asbestos, if not air borne, is not a health concern. It is a good example of let sleeping dogs lie.

There are many other areas where asbestos may be found in older homes. There were solid cement-type boards that were concrete but contained asbestos reinforcing fibers in it. These boards were often called transite, but there are other asbestos containing products referred to as transite. I have seen transite boards used as wall material in some homes where drywall would be found in newer homes. The reason it was used in place of drywall is drywall wasn't invented yet. That makes using drywall rather difficult. It is a rigid board, relatively thin and rather brittle. I recently inspected a home where the kitchen walls appeared to made from this material. A common place it was used was to build a barrier around the heating system. Sometimes it is installed on the basement ceiling over the heater. I have also seen it used as wall material to sort of block off the heater area. This form of asbestos can be brittle and friable. Powder breaks off around the fasteners. Asbestos "mud", for lack of a better term, is also found in repairs to old furnaces and boilers. It was used to repair cracks in the fire box and I have seen it on the walls of the furnace around the opening to the fire box. Asbestos, in more of a transite form, was used to wrap the exterior of chimneys as they ran through the home. It was also used to wrap the duct work in heating systems. I have often seen it on the outside of the duct work. In extremely rare cases I have seen the duct work itself made of transite. There is also a baffle between the heater and the duct work that reduces vibration on the ducts from the heater's fan. This baffle is often asbestos in older systems. Most newer forced air heaters I have seen have removed this material and replaced it with a rubber like baffle. Pure asbestos was not used as a home insulation in walls or ceiling, but some vermiculite does contain asbestos. Vermiculite is a fine pebble like material that is sometimes used with house plants.

Asbestos roofing felts were very common in built up roofing. The asphalt is highly flammable so it made sense at the time to add a significant fire retardant to the felt paper. I have read studies on the removal of asbestos from older buildings where they used cutters to break through the roof and cut the old roof in squares that are then lifted off and thrown out. The studies put monitors on the roof to measure the air borne friable asbestos in the area and the amount of asbestos did not set off the alarms on the monitors. Asbestos dust in the exterior is very diluted and therefore has a much lower risk than in a confined area. I still would not recommend removal by an amateur. Wearing protective respiratory gear is a must. There are also asbestos roofing and siding tiles that were used residentially. The regulations on the removal of asbestos vary greatly from state to state. Once you have determined its presence, the next plan is removal, and my recommendation is to call in professionals. Keep in mind that in many instances, removal can increase the risk of exposure.

An additional source of information on asbestos is the Consumer Products Safety Commission who can be reached at 1-800-490-9198. The government website for information is www.epa.gov/asbestos/pubs/help. Additional information on the health concerns of asbestos can be found in articles compiled by the New York Times. The website for those articles is: http://topics.nytimes.com/topics/reference/timestopics/subj ects/a/asbestos/index.html. Many of those articles trace the litigation on the subject. I have had a business relationship with the *Journal of Light Construction* in the past and through that I discovered they had an article on the subject. Check the archives in their website. If we listen to every health official and follow their recommendations perfectly we would live in tunnels to protect us from the sun, wear respirators that protect us from polluted air, and not eat, since practically everything we eat has been known to be toxic in one form or another. In some cases it's from the food itself, others from the additives, and others from the handling or preparation process. Asbestos, like most health concerns, was on this planet when we arrived, and will be here when we leave. It makes sense to research it at the sites mentioned and remove it. It is not a reason to panic if you find it in your home. If you want a far more practical health tip, DON'T SMOKE! It doesn't matter what the health risk, whether it's radon, asbestos, or fatty foods, if you combine any of them with smoking cigarettes, the health risk increases logarithmically.

PRICE RANGES ON ITEMS

The first question I hear after I find a defective item in a home is, "How much is it to fix it?" The answer is, "I don't know." As a home inspector it is beyond the scope of my expertise to know how much it is to fix something. I don't give out repair prices and I can't be expected to know them. The heater is not working properly. It is not firing. It may be the flame sensor. This is an item that cost X amount for one model and Y amount for another. (It was $230.00 installed when I replaced it in my Carrier furnace in 2012). It also may not be the flame sensor. It may be something else. The valve that opens to allow gas into the fire chamber may be malfunctioning, or both items may be bad. As a home inspector, it is within my profession to inform the potential home owner that something is not working right. It is not within my professional services to give the cost of repairing it.

To compare it to baseball, I am like an umpire. I call balls and strikes. If the item is not performing according to industry standards, or is not installed according to industry standards, it is my job to observe that. It is not over the plate. I then inform you of my observations. I then explain to you what normal functions would be, what are taking place, and then provide you with written confirmation of what just transpired. To follow the umpire analogy further, it is not the umpire's job to tell the pitcher how to pitch. Specifying repairs is beyond the scope of a home inspection. If you have ever had work done on your car, you know that the mechanic doesn't just give you a price. The first thing he does is open up the suspected defective area. He then calls you with a price once he has had a chance to look at the broken item or items. Once we determine something is malfunctioning, we are not required to open it up and see what parts it needs to properly function again. One of the axioms of Murphy's Law is that "everything is more complicated to repair than it first appears".

Complicated = $$$. That being said, there are some price "ranges" I can provide. The prices are primarily the cost of completely replacing the item. The prices were secured from one or more of the following sources: The websites of several major home improvement and appliance companies such as Home Depot, Lowe's, and Sears. Other prices were secured from sources such as the RSMeans Building Construction Cost Data, CMC Energy Services, Dealtime.com, and Costhelper.com. This last one is great! It has lots of items on it. If you need help with pricing, try these sights yourself. Many other items are priced at these sights. The prices below are for the most common items discussed in an inspection. Some were secured from local contractors in Suburban Philadelphia. If you go to sites such as Carrier's, a major HVAC manufacturer, they do not list prices. If you go to the websites of local contractors, there are no prices on their sites. Why? They need to look at the conditions related to the installation. How much is a roof is like asking how much is a car.

The prices vary greatly depending upon conditions. That being said, as a service to you, the potential or actual Home Owner, listed below are replacement costs for various items based on the sources listed above. These are a price range only. If you use the prices, then go to buy the particular item, and it is a lot more money than listed here, don't call me and ask me to make up the difference. **ALWAYS GET EXACT QUOTES FOR REPAIRS/REPLACEMENT OF ANY ITEM FOUND DEFECTIVE DURING THE HOME INSPECTION BEFORE YOU PUT IN YOUR FINAL OFFER!** If that is not practical, you will have to depend on price ranges and hope the prices negotiated help defray the costs. After all, if you are buying or live in a used house, any item may break at any time. It may break the day after the inspection. A heater in a home I inspected did just that. The seller said I broke it when it ran for over 24 hours after I left. I have no idea how I could possibly make that happen. We will also make a deal with you the Home Owner, or you the buyer. If you take our prices, and negotiate with the seller, and you buy the home and it costs less than the price you negotiated, we don't want a kick back. That money is yours. So the deal is, I won't ask you for any money back if it's a lot cheaper, and you won't ask me for money if it's a lot more. Thank you. Listed below are prices for replacement of items based on the sources above. The labor rates are based on Blue Book pricing for various trades. The life expectancy list is based on various sources such as, but not limited to, information secured in reading related to the home inspection profession. Just as the life expectancy for humans is about 77, some die very young and some live much longer. The numbers are based on averages. This list is in the order that people ask me for prices. It is not in alphabetical order, or cost of items.

Roofing:
Slope Roofing:
Remove old roof: $2.00 to $3.50 per square foot depending on difficulty
Dumpster: $800 plus tonnage. This is base price.
Expect at least some plywood replacement with tear off: $2.5 0 per square foot.
New roof: $3.00 to $4.50 per square foot depending on difficulty or/and quality of shingle. Very high end shingles such as Carriage House cost considerably more.
Ridge vent: $15.00 a linear foot.
Gutters: $10.00 to $14.00 a linear foot depending on difficulty and size. Same for downspouts.
Slate roof: $30.00 square foot. Wood roof: Tear off and replace $12.00 a square foot, (Not recommended).
Flat Roofing:
Remove old roof: $2.00 to $3.50 per square foot depending on difficulty.

Dumpster: Same as above.
Modified Bitumen Roof: $4.50 per square foot.
EPDM roof: $7.00 per square foot.

HVAC:

Based on 1,500 to 2,000 square foot house.
New residential boiler, (gas): $7,000 to $9,000.
Residential furnace: $3,300 to $4,500.
Hydro Therm Oil fired boiler: $5,000 to $6,500.
Central A/C: $4,500 to $5,500.
Heat pump: $4,000 to $6,000.
Annual service for oil burner: $175 to $275.00
Please note: Many oil burner companies will provide FREE
annual service to its regular customers.

Replacement Windows:

Vinyl double hung 30" x 48" basic installation: $475.00
to $575.00 per window.
Price will increase significantly for windows over 60" tall.
Removal of metal windows in masonry walls get quotes.
Casement windows: $500.00 to $650.00.
Reglaze windows with failed seals if feasible, $160.00 to
$210 per pane.
Bay windows, bow windows, large picture windows, get
quotes. Some larger windows require float crystal glass.
Some locations, such as over bath tubs, require safety
glazing. Get quotes.
With windows, size matters. Larger windows can be priced
significantly higher.
The prices should also drop if you are getting a large
number of windows done. One to four windows expect to
pay these prices. The bigger the job, the more windows,
and the lower the unit cost should be.
Sliding glass door, basic 8' door: $1,800 to $2,300.

Labor Prices:

Electrician and helper: $125.00 to $150.00 per hour. W/O
helper: $75 to $95.00

Plumber: $85.00 to $1200.00 per hour. More on Holidays, Saturdays, Weekends, Plumber's daughter's birthday.

Carpenter: $110.00 to $170 per hour with helper. Carpenters very often need helper to hold wood while cutting, nailing, etc. Very often carpentry is a two person job.

Lawyer: $200 an hour and up. This rate is charged if he's thinking about your case while deep sea fishing on weekend in his 36' Boston Whaler 345 Conquest. (No offense intended for you lawyers out there. I joke).

Accountant: $150.00 to $200.00 per hr. depending on complexity of your accounting.

Fuel Costs:[34]
Prices based on Philadelphia area, 2016.

Natural gas:	$.80 per Ccf.
Propane gas:	$4.00 per gallon
Electric:	$.156 per kwt.
Oil:	$1.45 per gallon.

(Pre-paid for season, price may be lower).

Kerosene:	$2.75 per gallon
Coal:	$185.00 per ton
Wood:	$220 per cord
Wood pellets:	$1.24 per lb.

Please Note: Water heaters have increased significantly in cost in 2015/16 due to stricter regulations on efficiency. Get quotes. Some older units may still be available.

---

[34] 2016 prices. Please note. Utility prices have hidden charges. All are commodity prices subject to change

LIFE EXPECTANCY OF ITEMS

Life expectancy of many major items in home:
Basic strip shingle builder's grade roof: 12 to 16 years.
(May vary greatly depending on natural forces such as sun exposure, weather conditions, and slope of roof).
Dimensional shingle: 20 to 30 years depending on quality of shingle.
Wood Roof: 15 years.
Slate roof: 75 years plus. Metal work may fail requiring replacement. Individual slates will break requiring ongoing maintenance.
Gas fired furnace: 25 to 30 years.
Oil burner: 30 to 50 years if well maintained.
 Electric central heating: 25 to 30 years, heating elements, 10 to 15 years.
Heat pump: 15 to 20 years.
Central air conditioning: 15 to 20 years.
(Units made before 2010 run on R22 refrigerant. This material has skyrocketed in cost as it is phased out. This has made repairs much more costly. I have heard mixed reports on retrofitting older units with newer refrigerant. The simple answer is when the costs of repairs get too high, replace the unit. The newer unit will also be less costly to run. You will have to be the judge of that.)
Windows: Seal failure in insulated glazing: 10 to 20 years. This varies greatly depending upon sun and rain exposure.
 Prime windows: 20 to 50 years depending upon maintenance such as painting.
Water heater: 12 to 15 years. Oil fired 20 to 25 years.
Garbage disposal: 5 to 10 years.
Range: 12 to 15 years.
Dishwasher: 15 to 20 years.
GFCI electrical protection: 10 years.
Home wiring: 50 years.
Home plumbing: 50 to 70 years.
Stucco walls: May crack in first year if thin single coat. 10 to 15 years if well installed. Exposure to run off, rising

damp, or leaking behind stucco can cause complete system failure in <5 years.

Vinyl or aluminum siding: 30 to 50 years.

Brick or stone walls: 30 years plus. Some maintenance needed; may last hundreds of years under right conditions.

Frame homes: If maintained extremely well, they can last 200 years. (Colonial homes in historic districts). If made from T1-11, 30 to 50 years maximum.

Painting: 2 to 10 years depending upon preparation and exposure to elements.

HOUSEHOLD TIPS

Do you have that annoying friend that eats and drinks particular products and keeps reminding you that they are healthier because they are natural? Today's society seems to be built on the belief that whatever the condition, there is a drug or a chemical that was recently developed that will cure you of everything from cancer to the heartbreak of psoriasis. The truth is a lot of what that annoying friend is saying is right. Our homes and our lives are loaded with many chemical solutions for situations that can be solved with very unsophisticated nontoxic products that have been around for decades. In many cases, they are healthier products for us and our children, and they frequently cost less. Let's take a look at baking soda and vinegar. Vinegar makes an excellent weed killer on our block patio and it doesn't stain the bricks. Also pine trees love it. Pour a small bottle around the base of your pine tree each spring. Your pine tree will thank you. While on the subject of the pine tree, the condensate from newer high efficiency heaters is acidic and your pine trees will love that also. Run a plastic hose off the drain line over to tree that needs fertilizing. The other item, baking soda, we use in our pool. We use it to lower the ph. If the ph is too high, the chlorine won't be effective. Now, let's mix the two of them together. Take the box of baking soda out of your refrigerator and dump it in your garbage disposal. Now, add about a pint of white vinegar. Throw in a few ice cubes. When all the bubbling stops run the cold water and turn on your disposal. The combination of the vinegar and baking soda cleans the disposal, loosens fat in the drain, and the ice cubes sharpen the blades in the disposal. Always run cold water in your disposal. The cold water cools the motor and extends its' life. Heat creates wear on any motor.

About a half a cup of vinegar and a quarter cup of baking soda in a half gallon of water makes a good cleaner for shower stalls, chrome fixtures in the bathroom, and mirrors.

Air freshener? Add some lemon juice to the baking soda and vinegar and leave it around the house in small dishes rather than those chemical air fresheners that coat your nasal passages and diminish your sense of smell. Have problem with fruit flies? No, don't throw out the fruit. Put a couple table spoons of lemon juice in a saucer with liquid hand soap and set it next to the fruit. The scent attracts the flies, and once in the liquid, they can't get out.

Mold in the bathroom? A black mold often develops along the grout in the tub area. To clean it, mix one part of hydrogen peroxide, and two parts water together and apply with a spray bottle. Leave it on for about an hour before cleaning it off. If you have ever used any of those tile cleaners, you know how strong they smell and they are loaded with warnings about proper ventilation. For cleaning carpet stains, use the vinegar with equal parts of water. Allow the cleaner to sit on the carpet for a few minutes before cleaning off with a sponge and mild warm soapy water. No, this is not an advertisement for the vinegar makers of America. It's just that vinegar has a multitude of applications. Club soda is also very good on carpets.

Never using anything containing phosphates as a cleaner in your basement or other dark damp areas of the home. Also, never use them in any poorly ventilated area. Phosphates are like steroids for molds. They will stimulate their growth. Your house has mold spores. Every house does. Don't fertilize them with phosphates. Never mix bleach with any cleaner containing ammonia. The combination gives off a very toxic gas.

Does your roof have black or dark green streaks down it? If it doesn't, your roof is the exception. The streaks are caused by algae. You can treat them with tri-sodium phosphate, bleach and water, or you can reduce the streaking the natural way. Get Z-stop zinc strips and have them installed at the ridge area of the roof. Z-Stop can be contacted at 1-800-845-5863 or www.zstop.com. The rolls are 50' long, last 20 years and cost about $15.00 per roll. If you treat the roof with chemicals, count on going back up there in a few years and doing it again. Also, don't expect the lines from the streaks to completely go away.

Do you do windows? Cleaning windows can be a difficult job. I use rubbing alcohol. It seems to streak less than chemical cleaners. When cleaning windows use a horizontal motion on one side and a vertical motion on the other so if you get streaks, you know which side needs more work. Using old newspapers is good since it doesn't

leave any lint. Coffee filters are also excellent for cleaning windows and other surfaces. Are you having a problem with ants? Pour rubbing alcohol on their colony. It kills them quickly. By the way, the old adage of using moth balls to get rid of squirrels is a fallacy. A loud radio in the attic near their nest helps, but you really have to close off the openings if you want to keep them out. That often involves a professional. The picture above shows an attic fan that became a "tidy" little home for a family of squirrels. You look at that picture and think, "What if you turn on the fan?" Don't worry, the squirrels thought of that. They chewed away the wires from the floor below to the controls for the fan so no electricity got to the fan. The metal encased conduit to the fan itself was too tough for their little teeth. There are two things to remember in this picture. One, check your attic periodically to see if you have any tenants. The 2nd, KNOCK on the access hatch before you open it! If you open the hatch and a squirrel or raccoon is staring back at you, they get very upset and may not be cordial. While on the subject of moth balls, the vapors given off by moth balls can also coat the nostrils and reduce your sense of smell. Get a bag of cedar chips and leave them in the closet to keep moths away. It's the same idea as a cedar closet.

When you buy fruit at the store take it out of the plastic bags and wash it right away. The fruit will continue to ripen in the bags and it all may ripen at once and then rot. When you have a cluster of bananas, separate them. Leaving the cluster together accelerates the ripening process. Do you have a garden? I once grew very large tomatoes in my back yard. Fall came and I was depressed as I watched my green tomatoes rot away. If you want to still harvest some of them, bring them inside and wash them. Now wrap them individually in newspaper, (Remember newspapers?) Then slice up a few apples and put the tomatoes and apples in a brown paper bag and leave them in a cool dark place. The gas given off by the breakdown of the apples accelerates the ripening process. I mentioned carpet cleaning with natural products above. The best stain remover for carpets: In a medium spray bottle, mix together one teaspoon liquid dish soap, one tablespoon vinegar, one cup warm water and one teaspoon baking soda. Add baking soda last and hold bottle over sink. Put on lid fast! Shake gently. Spray on stain, let sit two minutes and wipe off. Substitute club soda? You are on your own. Too much carbonation. Another excellent spot remover for clothing is Lestoil. In my humble opinion it is far better than Mr. Clean. I can't stand the smell but my daughter loves it. (Same daughter gave me carpet cleaner recipe.)

Having a problem with humidity in your home? The chemical products I said may damage your lawn when you use them to melt snow, actually absorb moisture. Put them in trays and spread them out around the basement. They will absorb the moisture and lower the humidity. Once a week or so put them in the oven and bake them at a low heat, about 200 degrees for about twenty minutes. It will dry them out, and you can reuse them. If you still have a moisture problem, you may have to invest in a de-humidifier. Always remember, "DE-humidifier good, humidifier bad." This is a rule I follow. De-humidifiers can be good if properly maintained, but I have seen too much damage and problems from them to endorse them. If you want to add humidity to your home, add plants, get a pet, get an aquarium, a decorative water fountain or waterfall. The more life and living things in your house, the more moisture you will have. Living things give off moisture. Speaking of which, if you have a problem with mice, (everybody does now and then), I bought electronic mouse deterrents. I trapped a mouse in a mechanical trap directly under the electronic mouse deterrent. We found the trap to be easy to set and easy to dispose of your catch. They are also reusable. DON'T GET AN ELECTRONIC MOUSE DETERRENT. They give off a high pitched sound that is not audible to humans. On another subject, if you have living things with occasional problems with their bodily fluids, my daughter said Nature's Miracle is great for dog and cat urine problems. We live in our homes. We take twenty to twenty five thousand breaths in our home each day. Our houses are far tighter than they were twenty five or fifty years ago. It just makes sense not to add more and more chemicals to the air we breathe. One last piece of advice, make fall cleaning a habit rather than or in addition to spring cleaning. You will be closing up the house and making it tight for the winter. By cleaning it, you make it healthier all winter. I was not paid for any of the product endorsements in this book.

WILL IT FALL DOWN?

Houses move. They groan, they creak, and they "settle." People often think of "settlement" cracks as happening in the first year or two after a home is built. Houses actually suffer from settlement movement for the first ten years. There are some very simple logical explanations for this movement. I have talked extensively about moisture, water, and the effects it has on the living area. Moisture has a lot to do with some forms of settlement cracking. You may have heard the term kiln dried wood. The wood used to make houses is cut, shaved, measured, trimmed, and dried. It is run through a kiln to reduce the moisture levels in it. Years ago, the accepted moisture level in wood was 9%. That meant the wood was dried in the kiln for a significant amount of time. (I don't have the baking time handy). Then along came the 1980's. The biggest residential boom in housing was post World War II thanks to the GI Bill. This country experienced its greatest stretch of continuous prosperity from 1945 to about 1960. (Don't get me started on what the Government did to destroy our economy since then. This book is about houses, not politics, I'll spare you).

The 2nd biggest modern housing boom was the 1980's. But changing the requirements for drying wood was just one tiny change that took place during that time to accommodate money interests. (No matter what the question, the answer is money). The accepted moisture levels in wood were changed from 9% to 19% so the drying costs were reduced and the wood went from forest to home far more quickly. (Most wood is actually "farmed," today). The number 19% is rather important. Twenty percent is the level of moisture at which wood begins to rot and mold begins to grow. The theory is, the wood begins drying once it is cut down and loses its' moisture source, the ground. The wood will then be put in homes and the heat in the homes will dry it out. Wood is either expanding or contracting depending upon temperature and humidity. If you have a piece of wood at a constant humidity level and change the temperature from 100°F to 0°F, (not an easy task), the wood will change dimensions. It will move. The majority of the movement takes place in the width and thickness, the length stays pretty constant. This change in dimension can cause the wood to twist. Taking a look at the flip side of this, if you heat a piece of wood to 150°F, the wood will also move. It basically will release moisture, get lighter, get stronger, and work better in construction. There are a variety of ways wood is dried for construction, but every piece of wood on a construction site has been kiln dried in one way or another. A question I am often asked is why is there a rise in mold problems in homes today. I don't have a single answer. The tightening of our homes is a contributing factor. We add moisture to our homes with humidifiers, and other sources. They are also a factor. This increase in the moisture level of construction lumber can't help. This may or may not coincide with the rise of mold issues in modern homes. I have never seen any study addressing the issue from this perspective. Let's get back to the structure.

So what does this mean to the average Home Owner? Because of the movement of moisture from wood, and the related movement of the wood, cracks can appear in homes. When the wood moves, the wood wins. The drywall loses. When a home is being built, additional wood is added to open areas such as doorways and windows to support the lack of studs or framing members in these areas. This additional wood moves. It moves for two reasons. First, there is more wood there. They often double up studs on the sides of doorways. The 2nd reason is by bridging a gap such as a doorway, there is more stress on the wood. Therefore, it makes sense that doors and windows tend to get small cracks in the drywall periodically as the wood moves. (Remember, wood is always in motion). Wood will seek equilibrium with the atmosphere around it. The moisture levels and temperatures change in homes, so the wood moves accordingly. These cracks are generally not a problem. A good way to gauge the movement of the wood in a doorway or window is to open and close the door or window. If the movement of the wood is sufficient to effect the operation of the door or window, a problem may be developing. Put a level on the frame of the door or window. Check the top and sides. The bubble in the level should stay between the lines on the level. In very old houses, these may not be level. If the cracks appeared recently, or the door suddenly became very difficult to open or close, you should get a professional opinion. The only variation in this is old solid core wood doors tend to swell in the summer and shrink in the winter. This is due to the humidity levels increasing in the summer. Sanding the top of the door will usually get it work again. Any significant movement, >1/8" in a relatively short period of time requires inspection by a professional.

There are other forms of movement that surface in drywall. Nail pops are a common problem. As the wood moves, it squeezes the nail in the drywall. This pressure can force the nail back out resulting in a nail pop. Nail pops can also happen with screwed drywall as well. If there is not

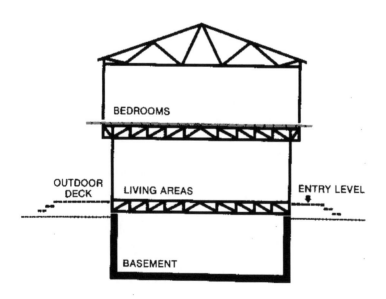

sufficient spackle covering the screw head, sometimes the spackle will break apart causing the nail pops. If the pop is due to a nail pushing back out, cut off the head and screw the drywall, then spackle. If it is caused by the screw head, you may have a periodic maintenance condition. Nail pops generally occur when the home is relatively new, (the first 10 years). Once the wood has dried and conditions are relatively stable, they are less likely to occur. Another form of cracking sometimes occurs where the walls on the second floor meet the ceiling. If you have a newer home, built after 1980, there is a good chance your roof framing is made of trusses. (See drawing above).[35] Trusses are engineered and manufactured framing members designed to support the roof or floor. They are made with smaller pieces of wood. They are basically a collection of triangles held together at the joints with metal plates called gusset plates. There may be some variation on this in a particular home, but this is a general description of them. When the home is built, the insulation is laid on the floor of the attic to keep the heat in the living area. Under the insulation is the bottom section of the truss. This piece of wood remains warm and cozy while the rest of the truss is sitting out in the open air of the attic freezing all winter and baking all summer. This difference in temperature and humidity can cause the truss to twist or move unevenly. This movement can cause cracks in the hall ceiling in particular. The wall studs should be secured to the trusses. If they are not adequately connected, you can get movement resulting in cracking. This is worst during a very harsh winter. The walls can be repaired and the house will stay up.

Your floors also move. Keep in mind that a floor starts with a floor joist. This is a large pieces of lumber, 2" x 8" to as large as 2" x 12".

---

[35] Truss-Framed System, US Department of Agriculture

They span a large area. The larger the piece of wood is, the greater the movement. The joists are then covered by plywood or some other hard sheet wood such as particle board. This wood is generally 1/2" to 5/8". That piece of wood is then topped with a smooth surfaced finished sheet of wood that is relatively thin, about a ¼". You now have a wood sandwich. You have three pieces of wood of different species, different density and grain, all working together to keep you from falling into the floor below. When you have that much wood you will get movement. This movement causes squeaks, and changes in the level of the floor. When a home is being built, the best way to build it is with the floor being both glued and screwed to the floor joists. You can still get movement. If you have hardwood floors, you have basically the same concept, a structural joist, a sub-floor and a smooth surface above. The only floors that don't squeak are cement floors on grade, or commercial buildings with pre-cast concrete floors. Live with the squeaks. As I mentioned, the floor joists are large pieces of wood with considerably movement. This movement can cause cracking right down the center of the ceiling on the floor below. Again, some spackle, sanding and paint should repair this but it will come back in time. This is fairly common on older homes. Buy older I mean, 40 years or more. It's a crack you get with time as opposed to settlement cracks that you get when the house is newer.

The floor joists can be trusses as shown in the illustration,[36] as well as engineered lumber. Engineered lumber are manmade beams and joists. The joists are basically wood I beams as shown in the picture on the left. One such system is SFS or Silent Floor System. They are designed to greatly reduce squeaking. They are very effective at it. If properly installed, they work extremely well. If you have them in your home, you don't want to see holes cut or hacked in them. They have templates in them where holes

---

[36] Boise Cascade, Southern Engineered Wood Products, Specifier Guide

can be made. You want to see all wires, ducts, plumbing lines, etc. run through pre-drawn holes in the joist. You don't want to see holes ripped through the lumber randomly. There are also laminated beams that are layers and layers of wood glued together. They look like very thick pieces of plywood. These are very hard. They are support members holding up the joists. If you walk on the floor above them, the floor is usually a little higher since they have virtually no shrinkage. They are very solid and really do not need any inspection for failure. I have never seen problems with them sagging or moving and I've been doing inspections since 1994.

For those of you brave enough, we will now look in the attic. I mentioned the truss system. Take a look at the truss. All the members should be nice and tight. The gusset plates should be snug to the framing members. If the plates have pulled off, or the truss members are bowed, this is a serious concern. By bowed, I mean a 4' length of wood has bowed >3/4". Put a 4' level next to it. A level has a nice straight edge. Have it touch the wood at each plate. Measure the distance between the wood and the level. If it's out by ¾" or more, call a structural engineer. If you have roof rafters, you have a completely different condition. The roof rafters are nailed to a ridge poll along the top of the home. Look at them. Have any of them split? Is the bottom half of the split separating from the top half? If so, look at the ridge poll. Is there a dirt line where the rafter used to be and it is now moved off of it? Are the nails securing the rafters to the ridge poll exposed between the rafters and ridge poll due to cracking of the rafters? Now look at the rafters themselves. Are there any cracks near the middle of the rafter going straight up from the bottom of the rafter towards the roof? (The bottom being the side facing down, not the edge all the way down where the roof meets the attic floor). This type of cracking is fairly common around knot holes in the wood. A crack on the bottom of the joists is caused by tension in the rafter. If you answered yes to any of these questions, you should then go outside and look at the roof line. Does it bow in the area of any of the conditions I just mentioned? If you have any of these conditions, a good framing carpenter can generally fix them. Ask the carpenter when you call them if they are familiar with repairing cracked or damaged roof rafters. This type of repair generally does not require an engineer. Movement in a truss system or failure of the gusset plates can be a far more complicated repair and an engineer should be consulted.

Now let's look at the basement walls. If you have a stone foundation you have a home built before World War II. There is a thin cement coat on it called a parge coat. This should be intact. If it is failing, you can get a mason to repair it. If you are handy, you may be able to repair it yourself. Cleaning the loose old coat off and removing any loose dirt is key to repairing it. Your new parge coat won't adhere to a crumbling surface. If you have a poured concrete foundation you have a nice wall. These foundations are prone to getting vertical cracking caused by the concrete curing. If there is no water coming through the crack and you can't get a dime in it, don't worry about it. It is a good idea to come back and check it every few months to see if it changes. There is a crack gauge mentioned in the Dry Basement section of this book that will help you monitor any cracking. Another common place for cracking in poured concrete is the corners. You will sometimes see a crack on each wall coming up diagonally from the corner. Again, measure the crack and monitor it. No movement is good. Inspecting a crack is a snap shot. You want a longer time span to determine if it's moving. If you find any cracks, rub your hand across them. The wall on each side of the crack should be level. If one side is different from the other side, there may be some external force that caused the crack. In new construction, a back hoe operator who was hurrying or not paying attention can back fill the foundation and cause this type of cracking. If it's an older home, check outside to see if a tree is nearby or water pushing against the home. Again, monitor it with a gauge.

If you have a cinder block foundation, you may have what are called stair step cracks. They run from one block, down, then across, then down like a stair step. This is

common below windows and in corners. It is rarely a structural concern. Put a four foot level on the wall and see if it's bowing. If there is bowing in the area of the crack, call an engineer. Any foundation wall that is bowing should be examined by a structural engineer. The biggest concern with cinder block foundation walls is a long horizontal crack about 3 feet below grade. This is cause by the ground freezing or becoming saturated with water. Clogged gutters or no gutters can cause this. A long horizontal crack, (by long I mean 20% of the length of the wall or longer), three feet down from the grade line outside should be inspected by an engineer. A gauge can be put on the crack to determine movement, but my advice is get it fixed. It is much easier to stabilize than to rebuild. The repair can vary. In some cases, they fill the blocks every 16" with concrete and rebar. They have to chop holes in the blocks to do this. It's a labor intensive job. Labor = money. Another method of repair is to drill holes in the block and drive rods through them. Large bolts are then attached and the other end of the rod goes off into the yard. The contractor digs a hole and finds the other end of the rod. They then set that end in concrete and the concrete creates what they call a "dead man". This keeps the wall in place and stabilizes it. Both of these jobs require professionals. Now let's take a look at the top of the wall where the floor joists sit on it. Get a long screw driver and try and ram it into the floor joists. Try right where the joists sit on the floor as well as the sides. Don't be timid. Use lots of force. The wood should not give as it did in the picture. If you can ram the screw driver into the joists, you have a problem.

In many cases this repair can be done by a carpenter familiar with repairing floor joists on foundation wall. In extreme cases I have seen an entire framed wall built below an entire row of floor joists. This is fairly common in homes over one hundred years old. If done right, this is a legitimate

repair. If you have one or two rotted joists, it is usually due to water entry in one location or termites. In many cases, they repair the joists by "sistering" to them. They attach framing members the same size as the original joist and bolt them to the old joist. Generally they are about 8' long. The bolts should be high and low about 1/3 the distance from the top and bottom and at least every 2'. They should sit firmly on the foundation wall. Often they are installed and then metal shims are hammered in to fill in the gap between the new wood and wall. Again, leave this to a pro. Your job as Home Owner is to check for these conditions, repairing them is a whole different matter. While you are looking at the joist, check the wood plate under them. In older homes the joist may sit on the wall, (see picture). In newer homes there is a piece of wood going horizontally holding the joists. This often rots and can be repaired. Again, this is a job for a pro. Check the entire joist while you are down there. You don't want any cracking in the joist perpendicular to the basement floor. You also don't want any horizontal cracking where the nails or fasteners are attached. If you can see the fasteners, they are supposed to be buried in the wood, the structure is weakened.

In some older homes the floor joist are fastened to the band joist that goes around the perimeter. The last 1½" or so of the floor joist is notched and the joist sits on a square piece of wood called a ledger board. (Picture on left). Take a look at the top outside corner of the ledger board where the joist sits on it. Is there a crack running out into the floor joist from this corner? In older homes, particularly at the basement stairs, the joist crack at this juncture. This weakens the home and needs professional repair. The joint in the picture is fine.

In summary, any movement, distortion, cracking, or loosening of the gusset plates in a floor or roof truss system should be inspected by an engineer. Any cracking or movement of the foundation walls should be monitored, repaired, or inspected by a structural engineer as mentioned above. In older homes, joist and rafter cracks or movement can often be repaired by a good framing carpenter familiar with that type of repair. Older homes lend themselves to repairs quite well. You reinforce, repair or replace each damaged member, then move onto the next one. If you live in an older neighborhood ask around and see if anyone else had similar work done. They may tell you who to use. They may tell you who to avoid. The information in either case is well worth having. Trusses are engineered systems that work in unison with the rest of the truss. Your basic framing carpenter is usually not trained to repair this condition. The purpose of this section is not to get you, the Home Owner, to practice engineering. It is to get you to go through the house and check these areas for any movement or evidence of cracking or failure. Gravity wins. It wants to pull the house down. Go through the house once a year, and see who is winning, gravity or the house.

I started this section by talking about noises your house makes. There are a few areas that will make noise regularly. Any plastic or vinyl material tends to move a lot with temperature change. Examples of this are Plexiglas windows in storm doors, skylights, and vinyl siding. Trusses and even framing members can creak or groan with temperature change. This happens frequently when the sun comes out from behind clouds or moves around to hit a new part of the home. If you have trees protecting your home, you may hear these noises in the winter but not the summer when the trees keep the sun off the house. As the house cools in the evening, you may also hear noises as the materials contort with the cooling process. Every house has its own noises. There is almost always a very simple explanation for them. It usually involves temperature or humidity. If you get noises, shadows, or strange events in the middle of the night, you may need more than a home inspector.

Thank you for purchasing this book. Let me remind you, it is not complete. There is no complete single book to cover all homes and all conditions. The intent of the book is to provide an easy to read, easy to use narrative to help the average Home Owner with many of the maintenance situations that arise in home ownership. I want to repeat my pledge to you. I stop answering questions when you stop asking them. If you have questions about anything with your home, call, e-mail me, send pictures and I will help in whatever way I can. I don't know everything, but hopefully, if I don't have the answer, I can point you towards it. Thanks again.

IS IT HAIL OR DID THE SHINGLES FAIL?

Asphalt shingle roofing is the most popular roofing material made. It comes in a variety of colors and styles. They can withstand a huge amount of abuse. The form of abuse that has proved to be the most costly and resulted in the need for replacement has been hail damage. Insurance companies are replacing shingle roofs damaged by hail with tremendous inconsistency. I do a considerable amount of roof consulting work and I am called in to examine hail damage on a regular basis. As a starter, there are services

that will contact roofing companies of zip codes where hail storms have occurred. I view this as a contractor's form of ambulance chasing. The contractors then start knocking on doors. They tell the home owners they will handle all the paperwork, file the claim, and essentially get the Home Owner a new roof at the expense of the insurance company.

You can't really blame the Home Owner. If someone knocked on your door and offered to help you get a new roof, you would probably take them up on it. One of the problems is the subjectivity of the replacement. I have seen obviously damaged roofs not replaced and I have seen some roofs with minimal damage torn off and a new roof installed. In most of the cases I have seen, the damage is marginal and the roof has many years of useful life in it. If you suspect your roof has had hail damage, you can begin by inspecting the air conditioner, your window trim, and the tops of the gutters. These often show damage as well as the roof. The picture above shows a roof with what I would describe as medium hail damage. There are a significant number of round indentations in the roof. I have seen roofs where the hail has latterly pulverized the shingles. Hail <½" will not cause this type of damage. This hail damage appears to be >1/2" to 1" in size. As a roofing consultant, I would recommend replacement of this roof. The damage is sufficient to significantly shorten the life expectancy of the roof. Generally when there is hail damage, the shingles on the ridge will experience the most damage. Hail comes down on an angle. If it hits a sloped surface, two things will happen. On one slope the hail will often bounce, deflecting the blow and causing very little if any damage. Conversely, on the opposite slope of the home, the hail will hit with full force. There is nowhere for the energy to go but into that poor roof. That causes the indentations and loosens the granules. The granules are a very important protective layer that reflects the ultra-violet rays, keeps the asphalt from drying out. Once the asphalt is exposed, the downhill spiral of the shingles is accelerated. Think about the tires on your car. Once you notice the tread is worn, the tires go downhill quickly. The same can be said of the asphalt.

If you experience a significant hail event, go outside and gather some of the hail stones in a zip lock bag and put them in the freezer. They will shrink some but that can provide you with a record of the size of the hail. That may be beneficial in you are involved in an insurance claim.

The other premature deterioration of roofing is caused by material failure. This is far less common but does happen. It can take on all forms but the photo on the left displays a fairly common pattern. If you look closely, some areas of the shingle are missing granules, while other areas of the same shingle are not. Hail hitting the roof would damage the entire shingle. Why are the granules washing out of one part of the shingle and not the other? Good question and I don't have the answer. I can speculate that there is a slightly different asphalt used on the raised area that is shedding granules but that would be speculation. My suggestion is that if your roof looks like this or like the preceding picture, have the roof inspected. If you still have documentation on who made the shingle, (this is rare), contact the shingle manufacturer and request a company representative inspect the roof.

There is another form of deterioration referred to as spider web cracking. This often appears in isolated areas of the roof. It is caused by excessive heat in one particular area such as near a dormer  or other large interruption in the roof. These interruptions do several things: They reflect heat and also block air flow that can cool the shingles. A third factor is they can block attic ventilation under these area of the roof. The roof therefore gets hotter in this area. The industry is less likely to pay a claim on this type of failure but in some cases they have. Just like the insurance companies being all over the place in claims for hail damage, the manufactures are equally unpredictable. One last thing, check your downspouts for granules washing off the roof. Roofs shed granules in the first year, and again when they are beginning to fail. If your roof is older and you see granules, call a roofer you can trust. See Contractor section of this book.

INDEX

Acid: 50, 54, 69, 94, 257, 289.

Amperage: 60.

Ants: 240-243, 268.

Asbestos: 27, 46-47, 110, 154, 277-281

Asphalt: 15, 27-29, 43, 135-136, 149, 27.

Caulk: 15, 30, 32, 33, 38, 43 49-51, 52, 54, 56, 59, 62, 100, 103, 118, 119, 123, 159, 219, 222, 224.

Carpets: 125, 146, 194, 290, 292.

Carbon monoxide: 79, 90-91, 125, 167-169, 178-180, 240, 246, 254, 256.

Concrete: 15, 19-21, 38, 50, 69, 71-73, 143, 145, 147, 149, 172, 194, 195, 253, 258, 266, 278, 279, 298, 300-302.

Condensation: 98, 120, 133, 160, 161, 198, 202, 203, 240.

Cracks: 15, 17, 19-22, 28, 38, 51, 53, 58, 103, 108, 149, 163, 164, 166, 177, 178, 190, 221, 279, 294-301.

Crawl space: 123, 124, 128-130, 135, 148, 149, 159, 161, 272.

Decks: 16-17, 58, 158, 204, 258.

Dishwasher: 92-94, 216, 217, 234, 239, 276, 287

Downspouts: 13, 40, 42-44, 51, 58, 144, 145, 150, 284.

Doors: 15, 27, 41, 42, 45, 49, 52, 57, 66, 75-78, 80, 84, 85, 90, 92, 93, 96, 111, 112, 118, 120, 124, 151, 152, 164, 166, 167, 174, 177, 190, 202, 204, 223, 224, 249, 251-256, 260, 268, 272, 276, 285, 295, 296, 304.

Driveway: 22, 136, 143, 252-259.

Electric: 8, 15, 23, 36, 60-65, 79, 81, 87, 88, 103, 104, 108, 126, 129, 134, 139, 144, 147, 170-172, 176, 178, 179, 184-188, 195-201, 205-207, 209-211, 231, 237, 238-242, 245, 246, 254, 270, 272-274, 285-287, 291.

Fiberglass: 9,23, 24, 28, 69, 73, 75, 108, 116, 121, 122, 128, 191.

Energy: 78, 93, 118, 120, 164, 173, 183, 186, 187, 194-196, 199, 246, 272-276, 283.

Fire: See Cooking Fires.

Fireplaces, 188 references.

Floors: 96, 127, 141-143, 170, 172, 253, 259, 267, 270, 297, 298.

Foundations: 13, 14, 38, 124, 146, 147, 159, 226, 300-303

Freezing: 37, 50, 67, 125, 127, 128, 140, 228, 297, 301.

GFCI (also GFI): 8, 11, 14, 15, 18, 64, 80-82, 129, 206, 207, 251, 254, 287.

Glass: 49, 57, 61, 77, 134, 164, 167, 187, 216, 219, 222, 224, 251, 255, 285.

Grading: 142, 150-156, 159, 275.

Gutters: 13, 33, 36-45, 49, 51, 57, 120, 138, 142, 144, 150, 159, 260, 284, 301.

Hail: 49, 135, 306-308

Heaters: 129, 170, 171, 178, 186, 192, 202, 237-240, 244-246, 279, 286, 289.

Humidity, humidifiers: 9, 38, 106, 108, 133, 134, 141-145, 148, 155, 161, 187, 190-192, 195, 200-204, 206, 216, 249, 292-297, 304.

Insulation: 9, 14, 15, 37, 55, 60, 62, 93, 99, 114, 116, 118-123, 128, 129, 131-133, 138, 149, 159, 161, 201, 204, 242, 252, 265, 273-275, 278, 279, 297.

Joists: 16, 48, 53, 57, 114, 120, 123, 124, 141, 159, 265, 297-299, 302, 303.

Kitchen: 15, 24, 79, 81-86, 92, 93, 125, 128, 158, 206, 213, 221, 224, 267, 270, 278, 279.

Ladder: 4, 13, 23-26, 39, 40, 61, 91, 104, 105, 120, 144, 145, 250.

Lawn: 17, 109, 216, 255, 258, 259, 292.

Lead: 104, 108, 110-113, 223-227, 229, 231, 234.

Leaks: 12, 31-35, 47, 48, 53, 55, 82, 92-94, 98, 100, 120, 159, 176, 180, 194, 221, 223, 234, 257, 274.

Masonry: 15, 19, 21, 22, 35, 37, 50, 99, 147, 285.

Mice: 14, 293.

Mold: 10, 37, 43, 56, 59, 88-90, 92, 100, 101, 125,

127, 129, 141, 142, 144, 157, 160, 161, 167, 169, 187, 189, 192, 201, 203, 221, 224, 277, 290, 294, 295.
Paint: 16, 23, 35, 38, 46, 52, 56, 59, 60, 69, 77, 99, 102-104, 106-112, 141, 142, 147, 160, 168, 175, 222, 278, 287, 288.
Pool: 66-70, 103, 106, 108, 233, 234, 236, 261, 289.
Putty: 102, 222.
Radiant: 104, 122, 136, 172, 194-196.
Radon: 11, 148, 151-156, 190, 270, 281.
Roof: Mentioned on 257 pages. See Asphalt Shingle -27, Finding Leaks-31. Is it hail or did the shingles fail? 306
Rodent (see Mice)
Siding: 37, 46-49, 55, 104, 278, 280, 288, 304.
Sink: 82, 92, 143, 213-216, 292.
Smoke detectors (see also carbon monoxide): 87-91, 114
Stains. Attic: 134, 175, 202, Exterior/roof: 54, Walls/ceiling: 35, 98, 100, 122, 221, Floor: 290, Stairs: 114-117, 119, 146, 255.

Stucco: 37, 55-59, 147, 159, 160, 175, 287.
Truss: 114, 115, 141, 297-301, 303, 304.
Termites: 6, 17, 87, 106, 146, 172, 262, 264-266, 302
Windows: 32, 33, 38, 47-49, 52, 56, 75, 77, 91, 102, 103, 106, 108, 111, 112, 123, 124, 134, 147, 160, 177, 187, 203, 240, 241, 249-251, 270, 272, 273, 285, 287, 291, 295, 301, 304.